Guide to

Professional

Programs

in

Canada

Admission, Application and
General Information for Canada's Top
Professional Programs

2nd Edition

SENTOR MEDIA INC.

Toronto, Ontario

Published By:
Sentor Media Inc.
388 Richmond St. W., Suite 1120
Toronto, Ontario
M5V3P1
Tel: 416-971-5090
Fax: 416-977-3782
E-mail: info@sentormedia.com
Internet: www.sentormedia.com
Bookstore: www.careerbookstore.ca

Kevin E. Makra, Publisher
Elizabeth Goncalves, Editor
Natalie Hosmer, Editor

Printed in Canada by Printcrafters

National Library of Canada Cataloguing in Publication

Guide to professional programs in Canada.

Biennial
2nd ed.-
Continues: Canadian professional schools admissions requirements.
ISSN 1713-5591
ISBN 978-1-896324-35-7(2nd edition)

1. Professional education--Canada--Directories.

L905.P87   378.1'55   C2004-905788-X

Table of Contents

I would like to extend a special thanks to
Jan Basso and the Canadian Career Information Association (CCIA),
initiators of this publication.

Part I

What You Need to Know Before Applying

INTRODUCTION

Guide to Professional Programs in Canada is designed to be an effective and easy-to-use resource for people considering further education in the professional fields. The basic admission requirements and application information is provided to assist the reader in deciding which options interest them enough to write the school for further information. This book is a continuation of the title *Canadian Professional School Admission Requirements*.

All 20 professional programs described admit applicants with a wide variety of backgrounds. For the purposes of this book, "professional" schools are defined as those offering programs that do not build directly on a candidate's academic background (although some course prerequisites may be necessary). For example, law schools admit candidates with backgrounds as different as chemistry and classics. Only programs at the bachelor's and master's level are included.

Guide to Professional Programs in Canada is published yearly and is distributed nationally. The information is updated by information supplied by the program's registrar or admissions officer.

Applying to professional programs can be an expensive and time-consuming process. It is our hope that this guide will reduce the time required by providing the reader with the basic information such as the prerequisites needed, deadline date to apply, etc., in one organized and easy-to-use source.

Guide to Professional Programs in Canada is an excellent planning tool which helps the reader identify what they have to do and when. It is also a cost saver as the reader can identify programs that are most relevant to their situation and apply only to them.

OPTIONS FOR FURTHER EDUCATION

The presidents and CEOs of organizations often preach about the value of a liberal arts education, but someone forgot to tell the recruiters that they are still looking for people with specific skill sets who they don't have to train and who can be productive quickly. Having completed your undergraduate degree or high school diploma, you may want to consider increasing your chances at career success by taking one of the following education paths:

- a college program
- a professional undergraduate or graduate-level program (e.g., journalism, speech pathology, pharmacy, law, etc.)
- an academic graduate program (master's or Ph.D.) to provide you with more depth in your subject area

- specialized workshops (e.g., The Banff Centre workshops in creative writing, publishing, acting, etc.), or professional development seminars in areas such as desktop publishing or presentation and time management skills

Each of these has its merits, depending on your objectives. Obtaining further education will provide you with more marketable skills and knowledge that will generally enhance your career opportunities (and your salary).

A community college diploma or certificate is particularly useful if the occupation you want requires very specific skills, for example, dental technologist, environmental technician, etc. Most community college programs admit candidates directly after high school, although some offer graduate diplomas that require an undergraduate degree as a prerequisite.

It is becoming more common for students with undergraduate degrees to combine their degree with a college program. This is a very useful combination of theory and practice. Colleges provide the practical skills you might not have learned in your undergraduate program. Also, some college diplomas include a practicum or internship which offers you valuable experience, making the transition into the workplace easier. For students who are particularly interested in research or want more depth of knowledge about a certain area in their subject, an academic graduate degree is the path to pursue. The basic difference between an academic graduate program and a professional program is that the former builds directly on the academic knowledge gained in an undergraduate degree. There's a direct link between the two levels. If you studied history at the undergraduate level, for example, you could then move on to an in-depth study of something as specific as "Anarchism and the Russian Revolution" or "The Political Economy of Housing Reform in Toronto, 1900-1921." A professional school, on the other hand, doesn't require a direct link between the undergraduate level and the professional program. You could, for example, be admitted to law school or to a professional program in journalism with a background in chemistry.

Think of your undergraduate degree or high school education as a building block on which you can add complementary college or professional programs. The following two scenarios are examples of this.

Scenario A
Journalism, for example, may not seem a logical choice if you have a degree in Art History. But a journalist who can write intelligently about the arts scene is a valuable asset to a specialty arts and entertainment magazine. Your degree in Art History has given you the knowledge base, and journalism provides a skill set that leverages that background.

Look for synergy, where the combination of dissimilar parts is greater than their sum.

Scenario B
A high school student who has a passion for working behind the scenes in the school's theatre productions might combine this interest with a college or university program in arts management. Here, their appreciation for the arts would be valued.

The key to any combination is your enthusiasm and how marketable your background is.

Whatever your choice, you can begin your research into further education options at your school's guidance or career centre, or use the addresses in this book to request detailed information from specific programs.

RESEARCHING YOUR OPTIONS

When applying to professional programs, it is important to do your homework. The more information you have about a particular program or school, the better quality decision you can make. Consider the following factors when choosing the right school for you.

Reputation of the Faculty

Although there may be many universities that offer the same professional program, each will have its own unique focus. The search for the best program becomes easier once you know what it is you are looking for. For example, one university's social work program may have a very good reputation, but if its excellence is in the area of geriatrics and you are interested in juveniles, it will not be the best program for you.

To determine the program's focus, obtain a copy of the research directory from the program's admissions chairperson. It will list the faculty and their areas of research. Remember, the faculty can only teach what they know.

Also, investigate the course selection in the calendar, remembering that due to sabbaticals and faculty course loads not all the courses are offered every year. You can also ask the admissions officer of the program to describe the program's strengths to you.

Two reliable indicators of how a program is received by the professional community are the program's placement records and a survey of what employers think of the program.

A word about rankings - use them cautiously. There is the possibility that top rankings reflect past glories rather than present realities. Also, the "best" program in a given field depends on how you define "best". Make sure you understand what criteria were used to rank, and determine if those factors are important to you.

Size, Facilities, Cost, Financial Aid

When considering the size of a program, one critical factor is the ratio of students to faculty. For professional programs that train you in specific skills (e.g., dentistry, physical therapy, etc.), low student-teacher ratios are necessary for effectively learning techniques.

Also, investigate the libraries, laboratories and research facilities available. Similarly, the breadth and depth of the library collection in your field of interest will be crucial to your success. The capabilities of the existing scientific equipment and computing facilities may also be critical factors in some graduate programs.

Further education is an expensive undertaking. To determine the full cost of study, take into consideration the cost of living in that particular city. Increasing tuition fees can be balanced by different sources of financial aid. Scholarships and bursaries are awarded by private corporations, institutions, and associations and are not always based on academic merit. Please note that aid for professional programs is usually more limited than financial assistance for academic graduate programs in history, for example.

When Should I Begin?

Begin early. Researching schools takes time. Some programs will require you to complete the appropriate admissions test (e.g., GMAT, LSAT, MCAT) which has to be planned for well in advance of the application deadline. Applying early can also increase your chances for financial aid, since deadline dates for scholarships are earlier than application deadlines. Financial aid is limited and if you apply late, you may obtain acceptance but not financial support.

Admission Requirements

The number one reason why people are refused admission is because they do not meet the minimum requirements (i.e. the necessary prerequisites and minimum average). Use the *Guide to Professional Programs in Canada* to plan your course selection to include all necessary prerequisites. Write the programs directly to request the current calendars and application forms and ensure yourself that you have the most up-to-date information.

Most students apply to about six schools. To maximize your chances of admission, it is advisable to apply to your first choice of schools (where your chances of being admitted may be tenuous) but also those you feel confident you are well qualified for. This strategy provides you with a safety net in case your first choice doesn't materialize. Do not waste your time and money applying to programs or schools you would not reasonably consider if you were accepted.

Where Can I Get Help?

Contact your guidance office or career centre. You can also call the admissions office of the program you are interested in and arrange a visit. Tours, as well as appointments, can be arranged with appropriate faculty.

Further education can be a stimulating and rewarding choice. Students are cautioned, however, not to make this choice because they fear they have no other options. Fully investigate all of your career opportunities.

WHAT TO DO WHEN:
A SAMPLE TIMELINE OF THE APPLICATION PROCESS

Some applicants have been successful by applying a few months before they plan to register. Please use this as a guide only! Planning 16 months in advance of when you would like to start your program can reduce the stress which often accompanies applying to professional programs.

May/June

(Of your second-to-last year of university if you are currently in an undergraduate program, or grade eleven if you are in high school)

- Send away for current calendars and application forms to all programs that you are interested in. Also, guidance centres, career centres and public libraries often have sets of calendars available. Many programs now have their calendars on their websites. Their Internet addresses are included in this book, where available.

- Check the admission requirements necessary for entry into the program. It is important to do this with the program's current calendar since it is the ultimate source. If you are lacking a course or two, you still have time to register in a summer course. Also check the calendar to see if you are required to write an admissions test.

- Apply to write admissions tests such as the GRE (Graduate Records Examination), the LSAT (Law School Admissions Test), GMAT (Graduate Management Admissions Test), etc. Application deadlines typically fall six weeks before the testing date. Please refer to the section on "Admissions Tests" for more information.

September/October

- If you are a university student, pick up application forms for scholarships such as the Natural Science and Engineering Research Council (NSERC) and Ontario Graduate Studies (OGS) Scholarships from the School of Graduate Studies. If you are in high school, check with your guidance counsellor regarding scholarships and awards. Many scholarships are offered by corporations, institutions, and associations that are independent of the university you are applying to. To find out more about these opportunities, ask your librarian for *The Grants Register*, published by St. Martin's Press. This book focuses more on scholarships for graduate-level education. For programs at the undergraduate level, refer to *Winning Scholarships*, by Michael Howell.

The section on "Key Resources" provides you with full bibliographic details.

- Identify programs that are of interest to you. Talking to professors/teachers can help you clarify your direction. Directories such as the *Canadian Directory of Universities*, *Guide to Professional Programs in Canada*, and *Spectrum* (for College programs) can also help.

September

- You will usually require references from two or three professors/teachers. Becoming involved in faculty/student committee work, departmental or class representative positions, and research projects will help professors/teachers get to know you better.

September-December

- Develop a short list of schools/programs you would most like to attend. If possible, visit their campuses and talk to current students over the Christmas holidays, reading week or summer vacation.

- Work on your portfolio if you are applying to programs such as architecture, art college, journalism, etc.

- Order official transcripts from the relevant educational institutions you have attended.

November/December

- Application deadlines for teacher's college, law school, medicine, and some social work programs precede deadline dates for many other programs. Apply to these programs in early to late November.

January-May

- Apply to programs of your choice. Most professional program application deadline dates fall between January and May. Deadline dates vary depending on the program and the university.

The waiting begins for the acceptance/rejection letters.

IMPROVE YOUR CHANCES OF BEING ADMITTED

Apply As Early As You Can

Applying early is especially important when programs such as law and business administration use rolling admissions (i.e., make decisions on applicants' files as soon as they are complete – the application form has been filled out and signed, the application fee paid, the admissions test score submitted, and official transcripts have been received). In addition, some schools require reference letters, personal statements, and medical documentation if illness has affected your performance.

For average or slightly below average applicants, applying early is especially advisable. At the beginning of the admissions cycle, the academic profile of the applicant pool is still unknown. The admissions committee has not had enough applications to be able to determine what the average grade point average (GPA) or admissions test score cut-off is for that year. Therefore, each file is assessed on a more individual basis. As the number of places become fewer, the admissions committee becomes progressively more selective.

Apply To As Many Schools As You Can

Initially, applying to a number of schools might seem too costly, and you may not want to move outside your home province. However, the fact is that if you want to be a doctor, teacher, speech pathologist, etc., you have to have that degree. Don't give up the chance to be admitted (the first step in your career) because you only wanted to live in Ontario, or you wanted to save $500 in application fees. Limiting the number of schools you apply to also limits your chance of acceptance. Think of the expense as a long-term investment in your future.

Fill Out Application Forms Carefully

Neatness counts when you are filling out application forms. It helps to photocopy the application form first and then make your first attempt on the copy. If you think of how many application forms the admissions committee has to read, you can imagine how frustrated they become when the form is illegible, not complete, or marred by spelling or grammatical errors. You are making a first impression. Having a neat, complete application form with perfect spelling and grammar counts as much as the content.

Also, pay attention to directions that specify how long your personal statement can be. Part of the assessment is often how succinct and precise you can be. For more information on personal statements, please refer to the section on "Pitfalls of Admission."

Apply Under As Many Admissions Categories As You Can

The most competitive category for admission is the Regular Category (i.e. you are applying directly after you have completed your university or high school program and have no extenuating circumstances). Other categories of admission such as Mature, Aboriginal, or Special Categories in which illness, culture, or language has been a barrier are also available at many professional programs.

Increase your chances of admission by investigating whether you are eligible to apply under more than one category. Find out how each school defines a mature student, since it often varies with the school. Perhaps your ancestry allows you to apply under a minority classification. A priority of some programs, such as law, is to promote the diversification of the student body to better reflect the people they serve.

Many students have a shaky beginning to their university careers due to illness or because they have selected a program for which they are not suited or are not interested in. Some programs take this into consideration. Some even allow these courses to be omitted from the calculation of the cumulative GPA.

Submit Your Application In Person

Not many programs grant interviews as part of their admissions process. However, delivering your application in person, taking a tour of the school, or briefly talking to someone who is on the admissions committee can help them put a face to the name on the application form. People make up the admissions committee, and although the admissions process can seem quite mechanical, whenever there are people involved it is a subjective process. When you fall in the grey zone - not a clear admit or reject - the objective criteria of grades and admissions test scores were not information enough to base a decision on. Other more subjective factors come into play. When it comes to deciding who will fill the last few places, admissions committees are usually choosing applicants whose qualifications are very similar. It is harder to say no to someone you have met than to just a piece of paper.

Remember This

Do not be intimidated by the high application-to-acceptance ratios that are quoted in the program descriptions. A more realistic overall ratio is 4:1. The ratios are inflated by people applying who do not meet the minimum requirements. Also, many applicants have applied to other professional schools to increase their options - but they can only accept one, leaving other spaces open.

If you are not accepted, but you really want to pursue that program, find out what the problem is and take steps to rectify it. Strong motivation and perseverance can overcome obstacles.

PITFALLS OF ADMISSION

The number one reason why applicants are refused admission is because they simply do not meet the minimum requirements (i.e. prerequisite courses). Check the prerequisites of the program carefully. Do not assume that good grades or extracurricular activities can compensate for the lack of a prerequisite; they can't. However, contact the admissions office and inquire if you can take the missing prerequisite the summer before the program starts. Some programs will grant offers of admission that are conditional upon the completion of a prerequisite prior to the commencement of classes. Be sure to send copies of your registration for the upcoming courses with your application material to prove you have made formal arrangements to enroll.

The number two reason why applicants are refused admission is because the program is not suited to the candidate's expectations. Be aware of what the program you are applying for is known for and what its strengths are so you can choose a school that meets your needs. Many programs require the applicant to write a personal statement describing their expectations of the program. Please see the section below on personal statements for more detail.

Persons directly involved with the admission process are looking for evidence that an applicant can succeed in the program. Some of the factors they use to assess a candidate's potential are grade point average, admissions test scores, statement of purpose, resumé presentation, reference letters, and an interview. The number of factors used in the admission process varies with the school. For specific information on how you will be assessed and what each school is looking for, please consult the chapter on that particular program and school.

Grade Point Average (GPA)

If your GPA in your last two years is 80% or better, admissions personnel will probably not subject it to closer inspection. However, if your average is in the "grey zone," a percentage or two below the average, it will be looked at more carefully. Please refer to the section "Improve Your Chances of Being Admitted" for advice in this area. If there is a medical reason for low grades, it is to your advantage to provide the admissions officer with an explanation and documented proof.

Remember that grades in the mid-70s with a lot of extracurricular activities are often better than grades in the 80s with no involvement. Also, GPAs that fall slightly below the average can be compensated for by a high admission test score.

For information on the average GPA score required by the various programs, please see the specific program chapters.

A Word About References

This is the one requirement that can probably hurt you more than help you. The admissions committee is expecting to see glowing reports since this is something you have control over. Therefore, nice letters are deadly. A poor reference letter looks even worse because it shows poor judgement on the part of the applicant for having chosen that person.

Do not assume everyone will give a good reference. Only choose people who you know will give you an excellent reference. After all, your references are supposed to be from people who are on your side. Help them to be as informed as possible about what your goals are and what the admissions committee is most interested in. Supply your references with a copy of your resumé so they are well informed about all aspects of your background.

Good reference letters are specific and measure results or achievements. The best references are people who know you in a work or school environment. Work references can attest to your ability to get along with colleagues, presentation skills, achievements, initiative, and potential to succeed in the profession. Academic references can comment on leadership ability, working with others, thinking logically, written and oral communication skills, as well as other abilities specific to your situation.

The most powerful effect occurs when all the references comment positively on the same characteristics, and there is a common theme. References from people with powerful titles who do not know you well are less impressive than references from those who have worked closely with you and can accurately evaluate you.

If your teachers/professors only know you as the student who sits in the second row of their class and got a B+ on the last test, here are some suggestions that can help you prepare them to write an excellent reference for you.

- Do not be intimidated. Teachers/professors want you to succeed and the fact that you want to continue studying indicates that they must have done their job well. Most teachers/professors are open to getting to know you well enough to write a recommendation.

- Before you approach a prospective referee, have some direction. Research your options and know what program(s) you want to apply to and why. You should be able to give them a "brief commercial message" that describes which programs you want to apply to and for what reasons.

- Provide them with information that will help them write you a good reference letter. If writing skills are a criterion for admission (as in journalism), supply them with the best story/assignment/essay that you have ever written. Similarly, if communication skills are important, point out your active participation in the debating club, or that terrific seminar you gave in their class. Also, supply them with a resumé that gives them a sense of who you are outside of school.

- Allot ample time to yourself and to your referee. You might want to meet with your referee initially in September of your final year to let them know about your plans. Approach them again about a month before the application is due to provide them with the specifics and the date it is due. Supplying them with stamped and addressed envelopes makes their job easier. Always check on the status of your application to ensure that your references have been received.

- When you have given them as much help as you can in getting a good picture of who you are and what you want, ask them if they feel comfortable writing you an excellent reference. Better to find out at this stage than having them send a mediocre letter. Remember that references go directly to the school you are applying to and you never see them. However, some programs will let you submit them as long as the referee has put them in the envelope provided, sealed it, and put their initials across the seal.

Interviews

An interview is the best method professional schools have of checking a candidate's interpersonal and communication skills. Group work and team building are very important parts of some programs and, as a result, more schools are making interviews an integral part of their admission process.

An interview can also be used to answer questions the admissions committee may have about your background, to give marginal applicants another opportunity to present a stronger case, or, in the case of international students, to evaluate their command of the school's working language. Be prepared. Interviews do not necessarily have to be conducted in person. A brief telephone call to ask a few questions is also an interview. You should be able to provide a concise explanation as to how the program fits into your career goal and how you will benefit.

The Presentation Of Your Resumé

Your resumé often gives the admissions officer his/her first impression of you and its presentation goes a long way in determining whether or not that impression is a favourable. Some practical suggestions are:

- It is easier for someone with five or 10 years of work experience to create a one-page resumé than it is for someone with little experience. The average length of a resumé for a recent high school or university graduate is two pages since your experience is drawn from extracurricular activities and interests, as well as work experience. The farther back in time you go, the more relevant the experience should be to the program you are applying to. For example, participating in an academic exchange in Malaysia during your third year of university is still relevant when you are 30 and pursuing an international MBA.

- It should be well organized, with no spelling or grammatical errors. Action verbs should be used to describe your transferable skills, such as "organized," "initiated," "supervised," "implemented," "surveyed needs," etc.

- For programs that stress group work, evidence of interpersonal skills and people-oriented activities is important. Remember to outline your achievements whether they are related to the program or not.

- Always try to make your resumé inviting to read by choosing a legible sized font and by leaving adequate margins and space in between sections.

- Group all your program-related experience together under one heading called "Related Experience." By using the word "experience" in the headline, you can include paid or volunteer examples. Then group all unrelated experience under another heading called "Other Experience." If possible, have your related experience section appear on the first page.

PERSONAL STATEMENTS

Some professional programs require applicants to write an essay or a detailed questionnaire on why they are applying to the program. The following advice will help you get started.

Your statement should:

- show you have direction and how a degree in Industrial Relations, for example, would help you achieve your goal. If you are not sure what you are looking for, take the time to talk to several people, or read books on careers in the area you might be interested in. This will give you more confidence about whether this is the right choice for you as well as help you write your personal statement.

- follow a logical argument and be well organized, with no spelling or grammatical errors. The statement of purpose is not only used for content, but as a check of writing skills.

- explain why you chose that particular program. The following is a sample introduction to a personal statement for the MBA program at the University of Calgary: "My plan is to start my own business. Therefore, I am particularly interested in being admitted to University of Calgary's program because of its strong Venture Capital department. I want to establish myself in Calgary and the project orientation of your program would help me to build a network in the Calgary area." This shows that you have researched their program and your expectations are ones that they can meet. demonstrate your unique qualities (i.e. speak three languages, raised in Johannesburg, Africa, or have lived in three different countries), or your background (i.e. worked for three years with CIDA in developing countries, or cycled across the Prairies to raise awareness of Multiple Sclerosis). Remember that professional programs encourage class participation and part of the learning process comes from sharing experiences with your fellow students. Think of what unique characteristics or experiences you have that might be an interesting addition to the mix.

Avoid:

- a generic letter. This shows little commitment to the program.

- using an arrogant or non-committal tone in the letter. How you say something can be just as important as what you say. Your level of maturity, confidence (or over-confidence), and commitment are aspects of your personality that can be revealed by the tone of your statement.

- leaving an impression that the program will be the solution to life's problems.

ABOUT PREPARATION COURSES
FOR ADMISSIONS TESTS

Many of the professional programs require admissions test scores as part of the assessment process. To prepare for these tests, many students take prep courses. Some say it helps and some say it doesn't. You might ask yourself the following questions when trying to decide whether or not you need to take one.

1. (a)   Do you prefer learning in a classroom setting, or
   (b)   Do you learn better on your own?

2. (a)   Is self-discipline a strength of yours and are you confident that you will take time to prepare, or
   (b)   Do you have so many demands on your time that the structure of knowing that a course is being offered on a certain date and time could increase your chances of taking the time to prepare?

3. (a)   From your past experience with multiple choice exams, have you found that this format is an advantage to you, or
   (b)   makes it more difficult for you?

4. (a)   Does writing under the pressure of time make you more effective, or
   (b)   less effective?

5. (a)   Do you feel quite confident about your ability to succeed on the test, or
   (b)   are you apprehensive and feel a prep course would make you more confident?

If you tend to answer "a" most of the time, taking a preparation course might not be an advantage for you. However, if you tend towards "b," maybe you should consider it. The decision is yours.

Preparing for Admissions Tests

Besides taking a prep course, there are several ways you can prepare. Find out how the professional schools you are applying to use the admissions test score. What weight do they assign it? Do not overemphasize a test they do not emphasize. How do they treat multiple scores if you retake the test? (Some schools take the highest score and some use an average.)

Read the test's information booklet carefully. If you are not confident you wrote to your ability, a score can be cancelled or a test retaken, but the regulations for that test must be followed precisely. Use the sample questions in the information booklet to familiarize yourself with the types of questions. Practice as much as you can. Aptitude tests can't be studied for, but you can be familiar with the type of questions and learn to pace yourself under the test's time constraints.

Anticipate the stress involved in preparing for and taking the test. Ensure you are taking the test at a time when you are less stressed than usual. Highly knowledgeable, highly prepared, burnt-out people do not write good tests.

The point of taking a test is not to achieve as close to a perfect score as possible. This attitude will increase your anxiety and keep you from achieving the best score you can. Accept that you are a human being and human beings get answers wrong. Then you can set the realistic goal of achieving a high enough score that your application will not be rejected based on that score.

ADMISSIONS TESTS

Some programs look at the results of specific admissions tests before accepting students. The following is a summary of various exams you may be required to take. Please note that when application fees are stated in U.S. currency, they must be paid as such.

The Law School Admissions Test (LSAT)

All Canadian common-law schools require the LSAT except the French common-law program at l'Université d'Ottawa and l'Université de Moncton. Civil-law schools do not require the LSAT. The LSAT is a half-day standardized test, consisting of five 35-minute sections of multiple-choice questions and a 30-minute writing test at the end. This written portion is not scored along with the others, but is sent to all law schools to which you apply. The LSAT provides law schools with a standard measure of skills that are essential for success in law school; the ability to read and comprehend complex texts, the ability to manage and organize information, and the ability to process this information to reach conclusions.

The Graduate Management Admission Test (GMAT)

The GMAT is designed to help graduate schools of business assess the qualifications of applicants for advanced study in management. Most graduate schools of management require you to take the GMAT, although many French-language universities in Canada do not. Traditionally, the test has been a multiple-choice measure of verbal and mathematical skills, with equal weight allotted to the two areas. Since October 1994, however, the GMAT has been expanded to include an analytical writing assessment (AWA), which requires written responses to two questions.

The Graduate Record Examinations (GRE)

Some Canadian and almost all American graduate schools require or recommend that their applicants submit scores on either the GRE General Test, a Subject Test (of which there are 16), or both. The GRE Tests are used by admissions personnel to supplement undergraduate records and other indicators of students' potential for graduate study. The scores provide a common measure for comparing the qualifications of applicants who come from a variety of universities with different standards. The GRE General test contains seven 30-minute sections designed to measure verbal, quantitative, and analytical abilities. The Subject Tests are designed to measure knowledge and understanding of subject matter basic to graduate study in specific fields. Each Subject Test lasts two hours and 50 minutes, except for the revised music test (it lasts about three hours). No Subject Tests are offered in June; most in December; only some in February; and all are offered in October.

The GRE is also offered on computer which allows applicants to write the test on any work day of the year. Five work days' notice is required and it must be done at a designated computer site.

The Medical College Admission Test (MCAT)

The goal of the MCAT is to help admission committees predict which of their applicants will be successful in medical school. The test assesses mastery of basic concepts in biology, chemistry (general and organic), and physics; facility with scientific problem solving and critical thinking; and writing skills. The verbal reasoning, physical sciences, and biological sciences portions of the exam are composed of multiple-choice items. The writing sample includes two 30-minute essays. Most medical schools in Canada and the United States require MCAT results.

The Dental Aptitude Test (DAT)

The DAT is a half-day-long test conducted by the Canadian Dental Association in conjunction with the American Dental Association and offers a standard measure of candidate admission potential to dental schools. While the English version of the test consists of four sections (measuring manual dexterity, knowledge of general sciences, perceptual ability, and reading comprehension), the French test has only three parts (no reading comprehension is required in this version).

The Pharmacy College Admission Test (PCAT)

The PCAT is a specialized test which helps identify qualified applicants to pharmacy colleges by measuring general academic and scientific knowledge necessary for the commencement of pharmaceutical education. It consists of approximately 300 multiple-choice questions, divided into five sections. These measure verbal ability, quantitative ability (mathematics), biology, chemistry, and reading comprehension respectively.

The Optometry Admission Test (OAT)

The OAT is designed to provide optometry schools with a standard measure of candidates' general knowledge of science (biology, inorganic and organic chemistry, and physics), and of their verbal and quantitative skills.

Test of English as a Foreign Language (TOEFL) and Test of Spoken English (TSE)

The purpose of the TOEFL is to evaluate the English proficiency of people whose native language is not English. Given in a single session of about three hours, the test consists of three sections: listening comprehension, structure and written expression, and vocabulary and reading comprehension. The TSE is an oral test that measures the candidate's proficiency in spoken English and is 30 minutes long. The TOEFL and TSE are offered once every month.

KEY RESOURCES

Use the following resources to help make a positive impression in your application.

Talk to People

- Professors/teachers - especially ones whose area of study is also your area of interest.

- People who work in the area you are interested in. For example, before you decide to apply to a pharmacy program, talk to a few pharmacists to get an understanding about what their job entails.

Using Book Smarts to Identify Programs

Directory of Canadian Universities, published by the Association of Universities and Colleges of Canada.

Admission to Faculties of Education in Canada, published by Canadian Education Association, Toronto, Ontario.

Funding Your Education

The Grants Register, published by St. Martin's Press, New York. Identifies scholarships for graduate education and is found in most career libraries.

Concordia University: The School of Graduate Studies Graduate Awards Directory. Identifies scholarships for all Canadian universities for graduate studies.

Winning Scholarships, by Michael Howell, published by University of Toronto Press, Toronto. Identifies scholarships for undergraduate education.

On Personal Statements

How to Write a Winning Personal Statement for Graduate and Professional School, by Richard J. Stelzer, published by Peterson's Guides, Inc., Princeton, New Jersey.

Graduate Admissions Essays - What Works, What Doesn't, and Why, by Donald Asher, published by 10 Speed Press, Berkeley, California.

Books on Careers In...

Canadian Writer's Guide, published by Fitzhenry & Whiteside, Markham, Ontario.

Careers for Writers & Others Who Have a Way with Words, by Robert Bly, published by McGraw-Hill Professional, Whitby, Ontario.

Careers in Architecture, by Blythe Camenson, published by McGraw-Hill Professional, Whitby, Ontario.

Careers in Business, by Lila Stair, published by McGraw-Hill Professional, Whitby, Ontario.

Careers in Engineering, by Geraldine Garner, published by McGraw-Hill Professional, Whitby, Ontario.

Careers in Journalism, by Jan Goldberg, published by McGraw-Hill Professional, Whitby, Ontario.

Careers in Law, by Gary Munneke, published by McGraw-Hill Professional, Whitby, Ontario.

Careers in Medicine, by Terence Sacks, published by McGraw-Hill Professional, Whitby, Ontario.

Careers in Nursing, by Terence Sacks, published by McGraw-Hill Professional, Whitby, Ontario.

Careers in Social and Rehabilitation Services, by Geraldine Garner, published by McGraw-Hill Professional, Whitby, Ontario.

Opportunities in Journalism Careers, by Donald Ferguson, published by McGraw-Hill Professional, Whitby, Ontario.

Opportunities in Occupational Therapy Careers, by Zona Weeks, published by McGraw-Hill Professional, Whitby, Ontario.

Opportunities in Pharmacy Careers, by Fred Gable, published by McGraw-Hill Professional, Whitby, Ontario.

Opportunities in Physical Therapy Careers, by Bernice Krumhans, published by McGraw-Hill Professional, Whitby, Ontario.

Opportunities in Social Work Careers, by Renee Wittenberg, published by McGraw-Hill Professional, Whitby, Ontario.

Opportunities in Veterinary Medicine Careers, by Robert Swope, published by McGraw-Hill Professional, Whitby, Ontario.

* This section has been written by Catherine Purcell for original publication in *Canadian Professional School Admission Requirements* with some minor updates to the text. We would like to thank Catherine for her permission to use this material.

Part II

Professional Programs

ARCHITECTURE

The following fact sheets outline general information including academic requirements and application procedures for Architecture Schools in Canada. The data have been compiled in a concise format to assist students interested in these professional schools. Information was obtained from updates completed by each school, or in some cases from the school's Internet website.

Architecture Schools in Canada

University of British Columbia*
University of Calgary
Carleton University*
Dalhousie University
Université Laval*
University of Manitoba*

McGill University
Université de Montréal*
Ryerson Polytechnic University*
University of Toronto*
University of Waterloo

Comments

1. These fact sheets act as a guide only. Students are advised to refer to the individual calendars or to write to the schools for more detailed information.

2. Application deadlines vary. Dates indicated refer to fall admission unless otherwise noted.

3. Tuition fees represent annual costs unless otherwise noted.

4. All of the schools listed above may not be represented.

* *This university has not updated its information. Please contact the university directly.*

University of British Columbia

School of Architecture
6333 Memorial Road
Vancouver, BC   V6T 1Z2
Tel: 604-822-2779
Fax: 604-822-3808
E-mail: soaadmit@interchange.ubc.ca
Internet: www.arch.ubc.ca

General Information:

Degree Offered: M.Arch.
Length: 7 semesters
Years: 3
Language: English

Admission Requirements:

Previous Education: Bachelor's degree, usually Arts or Science
Prerequisite Courses: As required for baccalaureate degree and following a broadly-based selection of courses in Arts, Social Sciences and Humanities and/or the Physical and Applied Sciences
Average GPA: 76% or 3.3
Range: 76% or 3.3 minimum on the last 2 years of first degree
Admission Test: Not required
Average Score: n/a
Score Report Deadline: n/a
Other Admission Criteria: Application form, portfolio, transcript, resume, statement of interest, reference letters, prior related instruction and experience preferred

Application Information:

Deadline: January 7 application and portfolio
Application Fee: $90
Applicant/Acceptance Ratio: 5:1
Size of Incoming Class: 45
Tuition: $4,200
Books/Materials: $1,000
$350 first-year workshop (mandatory)

University of Calgary

Faculty of Environmental Design
2500 University Drive N.W.
Calgary, AB   T2N 1N4
Tel: 403-220-6601
Fax: 403-284-4399
E-mail: evdsphd@ucalgary.ca or evdeinfo@ucalgary.ca
Internet: www.ucalgary.ca/evds/

General Information:

Degree Offered: M.E.Des. (thesis-based); M.Arch. (first professional degree, course-based)
Length: Semesters
Years: 2-4 (4 year maximum for B.Arch.; 6 year maximum for M.Arch.)
Language: English

Admission Requirements:

Previous Education: 4 year bachelor's degree (any area)
Prerequisite Courses: No specific undergraduate courses; computer knowledge is useful
Average GPA: 3.0/4.0 minimum; "Other Admission Criteria" heavily weighted in admission decision
Range: n/a
Admission Test: Applicants whose primary language is not English must provide proof of proficiency in the English language
Average Score: n/a
Score Report Deadline: n/a
Other Admission Criteria: Two letters of reference, personal statement of interest, portfolio of creative work for Architecture candidates, portfolio or writing sample for M.E.Des. applicants

Application Information:

Deadline: February 1 for September (Masters)
Application Fee: $100 Canadian citizens or permanent residents; $130 international applicants

Applicant/Acceptance Ratio: 5:1; competitive admission pool varies annually with number of applicants and available supervisory capacity
Size of Incoming Class: 22 – M.E.Des.; 24 M.Arch. first year; 16 – M.Arch. second year
Tuition: $M.Arch. (course-based) - $657.90 per half course + $928.63 annual general fees; M.E.Des. (thesis-based) – first year program fees are $5,148.39 + $923.63 annual general fees; subsequent years continuing fees - $1,497.87 + $923.63 annual general fees
Books/Materials: $1,000

Carleton University
Undergraduate Recruitment Office
(Admission Services)
Room 315 Robertson Hall
1125 Colonel By Drive
Ottawa, ON   K1S 5B6
Tel: 613-520-3663
Fax: 613-520-3847
Internet: www.admissions.carleton.ca

General Information:
Degree Offered: Bachelor of Architectural Studies
Length: 8 semesters
Years: 4
Language: English

Admission Requirements:
Previous Education: OSSD with six Grade 12 4U or 4M(U/C) courses
Prerequisite Courses: Grade 12 4U English, Physics and one of (Advanced Functions and Introductory Calculus) or (Geometry and Discrete Mathematics)
Average GPA: 72-75% on best six Grade 12 4U or 4M(U/C) courses; 60% for each prerequisite course
Range: n/a
Admission Test: Not required
Average Score: n/a
Score Report Deadline: n/a

Other Admission Criteria: Portfolio, graphic exercise, resume and covering letter

Application Information:
Deadline: February 1
Application Fee: $100 (Ontario University Application Centre OUAC fee)
Applicant/Acceptance Ratio: 14:1
Size of Incoming Class: 74
Tuition: $4,669 to $6,144 (depending on program)
Books/Materials: $800 to $1,700 (depending on program)

Comments: All supporting documentation must be received by April 30

Dalhousie University
School of Architecture
P.O. Box 1000
Halifax, NS   B3J 2X4
Tel: 902-494-3973
Fax: 902-423-6672
E-mail: arch.office@dal.ca
Internet: www.archplan.dal.ca

General Information:
Degree Offered: Bachelor of Environmental Design Studies; Master of Architecture
Length: 11 terms (including 3 work terms)
Years: 2 years (BEDS) + 2 years (MArch)
Language: English

Admission Requirements:
Previous Education: Two years in any university degree program
Prerequisite Courses: A full-year course (or two half-courses) in mathematics or natural sciences, for which Grade 12 math is a prerequisite (i.e. algebra, calculus, trigonometry, astonomy, biology, botany, chemistry, engineering, geology, geography, physics, zoology); 1 half-year university course in written composition (other courses listed in the calendar as "writing intensive" are also acceptable);

two half-year university-level courses in humanities or social sciences
Average GPA: 3.3 (varies in relation to quality of design portfolio)
Range: Minimum 2.5 GPA
Admission Test: TOEFL for non-Canadian applicants whose native language is not English
Average Score: Minimum TOEFL scores – 580 Written; 237 Computer; 90 Internet
Score Report Deadline: Same as application deadline
Other Admission Criteria: Submission of a design portfolio that demonstrates creativity and/or artistic skill; letter of intent; two letters of recommendation

Application Information:
Deadline: March 1 for BEDS; February 1 for March; November 1 for transfer students
Application Fee: $70
Applicant/Acceptance Ratio: 4:1
Size of Incoming Class: 65
Tuition: Approx. $3,000 per term
Books/Materials: $800 per term

Comments: The central activity of the BEDS/MArch program is architectural design - the creative study of buildings and cities. The undergraduate program consists mainly of classes in design, representation, humanities, technology and professional practice. It provides a base of academic knowledge and skill from which a student may proceed to the graduate program in architecture. The Architecture program also includes co-op workterms in which students acquire professional experience in an architectural office in Canada or abroad. The program is fully accredited by the Canadian Architectural Certification Board (CACB).

Université Laval
Denise Piché
École d'Architecture
Québec, QC   G1K 7P4
Tel: 418-656-2131, poste 3103

General Information:
Degree Offered: B.Arch.
Length: 8 semesters
Years: 4
Language: français

Admission Requirements:
Previous Education: CEGEP (DEC)
Prerequisite Courses: Math 103; Physique 101; Chimie; Biologie
Average GPA: 75% approx.
Range: n/a
Admission Test: Examen de français obligatoire
Average Score: 82%
Score Report Deadline: 15 April
Other Admission Criteria: n/a

Application Information:
Deadline: March 1
Application Fee: $55
Applicant/Acceptance Ratio: 6:1
Size of Incoming Class: 80
Tuition: $732 full-time Québec students (12 cr.)
Books/Materials: $400 - 500 (for 2 semesters)

Comments: A 2-year Master of Architecture program is also available. Application address:
Service d'admission
Bureau de registraire
Pavillon Bonenfant
Université Laval
Ste-Foy, Québec G1K 7P4

University of Manitoba

Environmental Design Program
216 Architecture II Building
Winnipeg, MB   R3T 2N2
Tel: 204-474-7488
Fax: 204-474-7533
E-mail: shakhan@cc.umanitoba.ca
Internet: www.umanitoba.ca/architecture

General Information:

Degree Offered: B.Env.Design
Length: n/a
Years: 3
Language: English

Admission Requirements:

Previous Education: Qualifying year (one year, 30 credit hours)
Prerequisite Courses: Should have English 40 and Math 40S or their equivalent. * See Comments
Average GPA: n/a
Range: C minimum
Admission Test: Not required
Average Score: n/a
Score Report Deadline: n/a
Other Admission Criteria: n/a

Application Information:

Deadline: March 1
Application Fee: $75
Applicant/Acceptance Ratio: 2:1
Size of Incoming Class: 110
Tuition: $4,500
Books/Materials: $4,000

Comments: Check the website for more information. *To be considered for admission an applicant must have completed 30 credit hours of university-level course work with a grade of not less than C in each course. All applicants must meet the criteria for option 1 or option 2. Please see the website for updated information. Students are required to complete within the 30 credit hour Qualifying Year, 3 credit hours of Written English or its equivalent and 3 credit hours of Mathematics. Program 1 of 2.

University of Manitoba

Admissions Office
Department of Interior Design
Winnipeg, MB   R3T 2N2
Tel: 204-474-9558
www.umanitoba.
ca/faculties/architecture/id

General Information:

Degree Offered: B.I.D.
Length: n/a
Years: 4
Language: English

Admission Requirements:

Previous Education: Qualifying year (one year, 30 credit hours).
Prerequi site Courses: * See Comments
Average GPA: n/a
Range: C minimum
Admission Test: Not required
Average Score: n/a
Score Report Deadline: n/a
Other Admission Criteria: n/a

Application Information:

Deadline: March 1
Application Fee: $50
Applicant/Acceptance Ratio: 2:1
Size of Incoming Class: 65
Tuition: $4,174
Books/Materials: $4,000

Comments: A Master's Program in Architecture is also offered. Contact the Chairman, Admissions Committee, Faculty of Architecture at the above address. *To be considered for admission an applicant must have completed 30 credit hours of university-level course work with a grade of not less than C in each course. Course work in the 30 credit hour Qualifying Year must consist of 6 credit hours from courses offered by the Faculty of Arts; 6 credit hours of courses offered by the Faculty of Science; 6 credit hours of courses offered by either Arts or Science; and 12 credit hours of open electives.

Students are required to complete within the 30 credit hour Qualifying Year, 3 credit hours of Written English or its equivalent and 3 credit hours of Mathematics. Program 2 of 2.

McGill University

School of Architecture
815 Sherbrooke Street West, Room 201
Montreal, QC   H3A 2K6
Tel: 514-398-6700
Fax: 514-398-7372
E-mail: profdegree.architecture@mcgill.ca
Internet: http://www.mcgill.ca/architecture

General Information:
Degree Offered: M.Arch.I (Professional)
Length: Semesters
Years: 1½ for holders of the McGill B.Sc.(Arch.)
Language: English

Admission Requirements:
Previous Education: McGill B.Sc.(Arch.) or equivalent
Prerequisite Courses: Completion of the McGill B.Sc.(Arch.) program or equivalent degree
Average GPA: 3.0
Range: n/a
Admission Test: TOEFL
Average Score: 550 (paper); 213 (computer)
Score Report Deadline: n/a
Other Admission Criteria: High academic standing and strong portfolio; previous university studies are considered; two letters of recommendation required; minimum six months work experience, curriculum vitae. Please note that this is a limited enrolment program and, therefore, admission is competitive.

Application Information:
Deadline: February 1
Application Fee: $80
Applicant/Acceptance Ratio: n/a

Size of Incoming Class: 30-35
Tuition: $1,801.24 for residents of Quebec; $3,487.54 for residents in all other provinces; fees subject to change
Books/Materials: $1,500 approx.

Comments: Candidates whose backgrounds include a non-professional degree in architecture equivalent to the McGill B.Sc.(Arch.) may be eligible for admission directly to the M.Arch. (Professional) program. Candidates whose backgrounds include a university degree in a non-related area should apply to the B.Sc.(Arch) program. Other programs include: M.Arch.II (post-professional) programs (Affordable Homes, Minimum Cost Housing, Cultural Landscapes, Architectural History/Theory, and Urban Design), Graduate Diploma in Housing, and Doctor of Philosophy in Architecture.

Université de Montréal

École d'architecture
Att: Georges Adamczyk, Director
C.P. 6128, Succ. Centre-ville
Montréal, QC   H3C 3J7
Tel: 514-343-6007
Fax: 514-343-2455

General Information:
Degree Offered: Baccalauréat en architecture
Length: 8 trimestres
Years: 4
Language: français

Admission Requirements:
Previous Education: Diplôme d'études collégiales (DEC)
Prerequisite Courses: Sciences de la nature, sciences humaines, technique d'architecture, lettres, arts, sciences
Average GPA: 80% approx.
Range: n/a
Admission Test: French test
Average Score: minimum 70% on French test

Score Report Deadline: July
Other Admission Criteria: Other university profiles as "special cases" by Board of Admissions

Application Information:
Deadline: March 1
Application Fee: $30
Applicant/Acceptance Ratio: 5:1
Size of Incoming Class: 88
Tuition: $932 per trimestre for Canadian Student - Quebec Resident
$1532 per trimestre for Canadian Student - non-Quebec Resident
Books/Materials: $500 per trimestre

Comments: Options "Conservation de l'environnement bati" "Conception/Modélisation/Fabrication Assistées de l'Ordinateur" (CMFAO) of the Master Program (M.Sc.A.) are offered - 3 trimestres.

Ryerson Polytechnic University

Admissions/Liaison/Curriculum Advising
350 Victoria Street
Toronto, ON   M5B 2K3
Tel: 416-979-5036
E-mail: inquire@ryerson.ca
Internet: www.ryerson.ca/prospective

General Information:
Degree Offered: B.Arch.Sc.
Length: 8 semesters
Years: 4
Language: English

Admission Requirements:
Previous Education: O.S.S.D. with six Grade 12 U/M courses
Prerequisite Courses: Grade 12 U courses in: English, Physics (SPH4U) and Mathematics (one of Geometry and Discrete Mathematics (MGA4U) or Advanced Functions and Introductory Calculus (MCB4U)) with a minimum of 60 percent or higher in each of these courses
Average GPA: n/a

Range: 60%
Admission Test: n/a
Average Score: n/a
Score Report Deadline: n/a
Other Admission Criteria: Applicants may be required to attend an on-campus information session, to submit a collection of their work, to complete an Admissions Questionnaire and to forward other relevant documentation in support of their application. Further information regarding the above will be sent by the Office of Undergraduate Admissions as part of the admissions process. These criteria will be used in the selection process.

Application Information:
Deadline: March 1
Application Fee: $85 subject to change
Applicant/Acceptance Ratio: 4.5:1
Size of Incoming Class: 151
Tuition: $3,589.78
Books/Materials: $2,500

University of Toronto

Faculty of Architecture
Landscape and Design
230 College Street
Toronto, ON   M5T 1R2
Tel: 416-978-5038
Fax: 416-971-2094
E-mail: enquiry.ald@utoronto.ca
Internet: www.ald.utoronto.ca

General Information:
Degree Offered: M.Arch.
Length: 7 Terms (17.5 credits)
Years: 3-1/2
Language: English

Admission Requirements:
Previous Education: 4 Year B.A. (in any discipline – B.A., B.Sc., B.A.Sc., B.Es., B.F.A., B.Comm., etc.) from a recognized university
Prerequisite Courses: Grade 12 Calculus; Grade 12 Physics; University Architectural History (half credit)

Average GPA: n/a
Range: mid-B minimum
Admission Test: Not required
Average Score: n/a
Score Report Deadline: n/a
Other Admission Criteria: Preparation in the visual arts, such as drawing, sculpture, graphics, photography, film, or new media is desirable, as well as computing and advanced writing skills.

Application Information:
Deadline: February 1
Application Fee: $85 plus $35 assessment fee
Applicant/Acceptance Ratio: n/a
Size of Incoming Class: 36
Tuition: $6,431 + $819 incidental fees
Books/Materials: Approximately $2,400

Comments: Preference of admission is given to individuals who have completed a balances undergraduate education that includes study in the arts, sciences, and humanities, and who demonstrates leadership potential in the field.

University of Toronto
Faculty of Architecture
Landscape and Design
230 College Street
Toronto, ON   M5T 1R2
Tel: 416-978-5038
Fax: 416-971-2094
E-mail: enquiry.ald@utoronto.ca
Internet: www.ald.utoronto.ca

General Information:
Degree Offered: M.L.A.
Length: Semesters
Years: 3 (15.5 credits)
Language: English

Admission Requirements:
Previous Education: 4 Year B.A. (in any discipline – B.A., B.Sc., B.A.Sc., B.Es., B.F.A., B.Comm., etc.) from a recognized university

Prerequisite Courses: University level Biology/Ecology; Geography; English; History
Average GPA: n/a
Range: mid-B minimum
Admission Test: Not required
Average Score: n/a
Score Report Deadline: n/a
Other Admission Criteria: Preparation in the visual arts, such as drawing, sculpture, graphics, photography, film, or new media is desirable, as well as computing and advanced writing skills.

Application Information:
Deadline: February 1
Application Fee: $85 plus $35 assessment fee
Applicant/Acceptance Ratio: n/a
Size of Incoming Class: 12
Tuition: $6,431 + $819 incidental fees
Books/Materials: n/a

Comments: For students applying with a professional Bachelor of Architecture or Landscape Architecture degree, advanced standing may be granted; this decision will be made on a case-by-case basis upon admission.

University of Waterloo
Office of the Registrar
Architecture Admissions
200 University Avenue West
Waterloo, ON   N2L 3G1
Tel: 519-888-4567
Fax: n/a
E-mail: n/a
Internet: www.architecture.uwaterloo.ca

General Information:
Degree Offered: B.A.S.
Length: Trimesters
Years: 4
Language: English

Admission Requirements:
Previous Education: Secondary School

Diploma, including six Grade 12 U or M courses; one must be ENG4U
Prerequisite Courses: *Advance Functions; Calculus and Vectors; English; Physics
Average GPA: n/a
Range: Low 80s
Admission Test: Not required
Average Score: n/a
Score Report Deadline: n/a
Other Admission Criteria: English précis-writing exercise, portfolio, Admissions Information Form; interview

Application Information:
Deadline: February 15
Application Fee: $110
Applicant/Acceptance Ratio: 10:1
Size of Incoming Class: 70
Tuition: $2,655
Books/Materials: $1050-$1400 books & supplies/4-month term; $125-$4,300 field trips/4-month term

Comments: *Although not required, the following courses are recommended: Grade 11 or 12 M Art courses; Independent art studies; Creative and cultural studies such as visual arts and history

BUSINESS ADMINISTRATION

The following fact sheets outline general information including academic requirements and application procedures for Business Administration Schools in Canada. The data have been compiled in a concise format to assist students interested in these professional schools. Information was obtained from updates completed by each school, or in some cases from the school's Internet website.

Please see section on Admissions Tests for information on the Graduate Management Admissions Test (GMAT) which is a prerequisite for most M.B.A. programs.

Business Administration Schools in Canada

University of Alberta
Athabasca University
University of British Columbia
University of Calgary*
Concordia University*
Dalhousie University
HEC Montréal
Laurentian University*
Université Laval*
University of Manitoba
McGill University
McMaster University
Memorial University of Newfoundland*

Université de Moncton
University of Ottawa
University of New Brunswick
Queen's University*
Saint Mary's University*
University of Saskatchewan*
Simon Fraser University
University of Toronto*
University of Victoria
University of Western Ontario*
Wilfrid Laurier University
University of Windsor*
York University

Comments

1. These fact sheets act as a guide only. Students are advised to refer to the individual calendars or to write to the schools for more detailed information.

2. Application deadlines vary. Dates indicated refer to fall admission unless otherwise noted.

3. Tuition fees represent annual costs unless otherwise noted.

4. All of the schools listed above may not be represented.

* This university has not updated its information. Please contact the university directly.

University of Alberta
Alberta MBA Programs
2-30 Business Building
Edmonton, AB   T6G 2R6
Tel: 780-492-3946
Fax: 780-492-7825
E-mail: mba@ualberta.ca
Internet: www.mba.net

General Information:
Degree Offered: MBA
Length: 16 months
Years: 2 full-time
Language: English

Admission Requirements:
Previous Education: Undergraduate
Degree
Prerequisite Courses: None
Average GPA: 3.4/4.0 or B+
Range: 3.0-4.0
Admission Test: GMAT
Average Score: 600
Score Report Deadline: May 31
Other Admission Criteria: Three letters of
reference, statement of intent, minimum
of two years work experience, TOEFL
(international students)

Application Information:
Deadline: April 30
Application Fee: $100
Applicant/Acceptance Ratio: 4:1
Size of Incoming Class: 55
Tuition: $24,000 (entire program)
Books/Materials: $2,000 (entire program)

Comments: The Alberta MBA offers
world-class training to a diverse group of
students from a variety of disciplines and
countries. The program is unquestionably
challenging, inspiring, focused, effective
and real world. Small classes, an applied
hands-on learning style, work internships,
and a multi-disciplinary education with
a global perspective provide grads with
strong analytical, problem solving and
communication skills. Alberta MBA grads
compete successfully in the marketplace
with a 94+% placement rate.
In addition to a well rounded business
education, the Alberta MBA Program
offers unique specializations, including
Natural Resources & Energy, Technology
Commercialization, International Business,
Leisure and Sport Management, and
Public Management. Students are also
able to complete joint degrees in law,
engineering, agriculture, and forestry.

Athabasca University
Centre for Innovative Management
301 Grandin Park Plaza, 22 Sir Winston
Churchill Avenue
St. Albert, AB   T8N 1B4
Tel: 1-800-561-4650 or 780-459-1144
Fax: 1-800-561-4660 or 780-459-2093
E-mail: cimoffice@athabascau.ca
Internet: www.mba.athabasca.ca

General Information:
Degree Offered: M.B.A.
Length: Distance education (online)
Years: Minimum 2 years, maximum 5
years
Language: English

Admission Requirements:
Previous Education: A first degree at
an accredited university or college or
equivalent
Prerequisite Courses: None
Average GPA: n/a
Range: n/a
Admission Test: n/a
Average Score: 570
Score Report Deadline: n/a
Other Admission Criteria: At least
3 years of acceptable professional
or management experience with
undergraduate degree; or at least 5 years
of acceptable professional or management
experience. Special circumstances can lead
to admission to the Advanced Graduate
Diploma in Management program
(GDM) if 8-10 years of substantive

experience in operating a business or in managing within an organization can be demonstrated to the admission committee.

Application Information:
Deadline: February 15 for program starting in May; June 15 for program starting in September; and October 15 for program starting in January
Application Fee: $175 (CDN)
Applicant/Acceptance Ratio: 3:1
Size of Incoming Class: 100-130 divided into smaller cohorts
Tuition: $42,000 for the program
Books/Materials: Students without computer equipment will need to purchase or lease equipment for use during their studies. Lotus Notes software and course materials are included in tuition.

Comments: The MBA and diploma programs are offered only through a dynamic, interactive, electronic environment allowing students the flexibility of choosing when and where to study. Programs offered include: Executive MBA and Graduate Diploma in Management.

University of British Columbia
MBA Office
Sauder School of Business
160 - 2053 Main Mall
Vancouver, BC   V6T 1Z2
Tel: 604-822-8422
Fax: 604-822-9030
E-mail: mba@sauder.ubc.ca
Internet: www.sauder.ubc.ca/mba

General Information:
Degree Offered: MBA (Full Time Program); MBA (Part-time Program)
Length: n/a
Years: 15 months (Full Time Program)
Language: English

Admission Requirements:
Previous Education: Four-year undergraduate degree
Prerequisite Courses: None*
Average GPA: 76% in senior level course work (300 and 400 level courses)
Range: n/a
Admission Test: GMAT; TOEFL (if degree was not completed in an English speaking institution)
Average Score: 640
Score Report Deadline: February 28 (Full Time International) and April 30 (Full Time Domestic)
Other Admission Criteria: Three references and official transcripts; 2-3 years of full time work experience required

Application Information:
Deadline: April 30 - Canada and U.S.; February 28 - International
Application Fee: $125
Applicant/Acceptance Ratio: n/a
Size of Incoming Class: 120
Tuition: $38,203 plus student fees over 15 months
Books/Materials: $2,000

Comments: UBC also offers two joint programs: MBA/LL.B. with the Faculty of Law and MBA/MAPPS with the Institute of Asian Research. *None, however, it is recommended that students complete basic-level courses in Economics, Financial Accounting, Statistics, and Computers prior to commencement of the program.

University of Calgary
Haskayne School of Business
M.B.A. Program
2500 University Drive N.W.
Calgary, AB   T2N 1N4
Tel: 403-220-3808
Toll Free: 1-877-220-3808
E-mail: mbarequest@haskayne.ucalgary.ca
Internet: www.haskayne.ucalgary.ca/students/programs/graduate/mba/

General Information:
Degree Offered: M.B.A.
Length: Semesters
Years: 2 full-time
Language: English
Admission Requirements:
Previous Education: Undergraduate degree from a recognized institution
Prerequisite Courses: None
Average GPA: 3.20/4.00
Range: 3.00/4.00
Admission Test: GMAT (Recommended Score: 550)
Average Score: 606 (last year)
Score Report Deadline: March for Fall admission
Other Admission Criteria: Three years working experience

Application Information:
Deadline: May 1
Application Fee: $60
Applicant/Acceptance Ratio: 4:3
Size of Incoming Class: 75
Tuition: $1,109 per course (20 courses)
Books/Materials: $1,500-2,000 per year

Concordia University
M.B.A. Program
GM 201, 1455 de Maisonneuve Blvd. West
Montreal, QC   H3G 1M8
Tel: 514-848-2424 ext. 2717
Fax: 514-848-2816
E-mail: mba@jmsb.concordia.ca
Internet: www.johnmolson.concordia.ca/mba

General Information:
Degree Offered: M.B.A.
Length: 4 semesters (minimum)
Years: 16 months; 2 years full time or 3-5 years part-time
Language: English

Admission Requirements:
Previous Education: Bachelor's degree (any discipline) with high standing or qualifications accepted as equivalent
Prerequisite Courses: In certain cases, an undergraduate mathematics course is required
Average GPA: 3.6
Range: 3.0 - 4.3
Admission Test: GMAT
Average Score: 670
Score Report Deadline: GMAT written before deadline
Other Admission Criteria: 2 letters of reference, competence in mathematics and computer skills, and 2 years full-time work experience

Application Information:
Deadline: June 1st - Fall admission
October 1st - Winter admission
February 28 - Summer admission
Application Fee: $50
Applicant/Acceptance Ratio: 5:1
Size of Incoming Class: Capped at 100 students
Tuition: Canadian: $10,000; Quebec residents: $5200; International: $26,000
Books/Materials: $1200

Comments: Students may attend on a full-time or part-time basis and may change status during the program.

Dalhousie University
M.B.A. Program Manager
School of Business
6100 University Avenue
Halifax, NS   B3H 3J5
Tel: 902-494-1814
Toll Free: 1-800-432-5622
Fax: 902-494-7154
E-mail: mba.admissions@dal.ca
Internet: www.dal.ca/MBA

General Information:
Degree Offered: M.B.A.
Length: 4 semesters
Years: 2
Language: English

Admission Requirements:
Previous Education: Bachelor's degree
Prerequisite Courses: None
Average GPA: 3.6
Range: B (or 3.0/4.3 minimum)
Admission Test: GMAT
Average Score: 580 (550 minimum)
Score Report Deadline: June 1
Other Admission Criteria: 2 letters of
references (1 academic required)
and work experience (2 years of full-time
or better preferred, but not required)

Application Information:
Deadline: June 1
Application Fee: $70
Applicant/Acceptance Ratio: 5:1
Size of Incoming Class: 50
Tuition: $6,750 per year
Books/Materials: $1.200 per year

Comments: Detailed program information
can be found on their website.

HEC Montréal
Office of the Registrar
3000, chemin de la Côte-Sainte-Catherine
Montreal, QC   H3T 2A7
Tel: 514-340-6151
Fax: 514-340-5640
E-mail: mba@hec.ca
Internet: www.hec.ca
General Information:
Degree Offered: M.B.A.
Length: 1 year
Years: 1 full year**
Language: English or French

Admission Requirements:
Previous Education: Bachelor's degree
with satisfactory average
Prerequisite Courses: n/a
Average GPA: n/a
Range: n/a
Admission Test: GMAT, TOEFL
Average Score: TOEFL: minimum score
600 or IELTs Test or HECTOPE business
English Test administered by HEC Montréal

Score Report Deadline: Application
deadline
Other Admission Criteria: Must have
minimum three years of relevant full-time
work experience; a detailed resume; two
letters of recommendation

Application Information:
Deadline: Rolling admission process**
Ultimate deadlines: March 15 (Fall),
October 1 (Winter); International students:
February 1
Application Fee: $75
Applicant/Acceptance Ratio: 2:1
Size of Incoming Class: 250 per year
Tuition: Quebec residents: $5,800 per
year; Non Quebec residents: $12,200 per
year; International students: $23,300
Books/Materials: $2,500; Portable
Computer: $2,300

Comments: * Full-time program is 1 year
in duration, part-time program is 3 years
in duration.
** In the Fall: part-time and full-time
admissions; in Winter: part-time admission
only.

Laurentian University
Office of Admissions
Ramsey Lake Road
Sudbury, ON   P3C 2C6
Tel: 705-675-1151, ext. 3204
E-mail: lweber@laurentian.ca
Internet: www.laurentian.ca/graduate
calendar/BusAdministration.pdf

General Information:
Degree Offered: M.B.A.
Length: 20 courses (3 credits each)
Years: 18 months (full-time); 4 years
part-time
Language: English

Admission Requirements:
Previous Education: Undergraduate
degree (4 years)
Prerequisite Courses: None

Average GPA: 70%
Range: B or 2nd-class honours minimum
Admission Test: GMAT
Average Score: 500 is the required score
Score Report Deadline: May 31
Other Admission Criteria: Proficiency in spoken and written English and at least 2 years of relevant full-time work experience

Application Information:
Deadline: May 31
Application Fee: $55
Applicant/Acceptance Ratio: n/a
Size of Incoming Class: 35
Tuition: $995 per full course
Books/Materials: n/a

Comments: Limited enrolment program, designed to be taken on a part-time basis. However, students can pursue studies on a full-time basis with most of the courses being offered in the evening.

Université Laval
Directeur des programmes M.B.A. et D.A.
Faculté des sciences de l'administration
Ste-Foy, QC   G1K 7P4
Tel: 418-656-7325
Fax: 418-656-2624
E-mail: ddtc@fsa.ulaval.ca
Internet: www.fsa.ulaval.ca

General Information:
Degree Offered: M.B.A.
Length: n/a
Years: 2 years
Language: français

Admission Requirements:
Previous Education: Undergraduate degree in any discipline
Prerequisite Courses: University-level course in both mathematics and statistics; fluency in French and mastery of written English
Average GPA: 3.2/4.3
Range: n/a
Admission Test: GMAT not required

Average Score: n/a
Score Report Deadline: n/a
Other Admission Criteria: n/a

Application Information:
Deadline: February 1
Application Fee: $30
Applicant/Acceptance Ratio: 3:1
Size of Incoming Class: 40
Tuition: About $950 for 15 credits
Books/Materials: n/a

University of Manitoba
Asper MBA
Graduate Program Office
I.H. Asper School of Business
324 Drake Centre
Winnipeg, MB   R3T 5V4
Tel: 204-474-8448
Fax: 204-474-7544
E-mail: asper_grad@umanitoba.ca
Internet: www.umanitoba.ca/asper

General Information:
Degree Offered: M.B.A.
Length: 11 months to 6 years
Years: n/a
Language: English

Admission Requirements:
Previous Education: Bachelor's degree or equivalent
Prerequisite Courses: None
Average GPA: 3.4
Range: 3.0 - 4.5
Admission Test: GMAT
Average Score: 580
Score Report Deadline: May 1 for Canadians/permanent residents, Jan 15 for international applicants
Other Admission Criteria: Three years work experience normally required, management experience desirable, and 3 references

Application Information:
Deadline: May 1 for Canadians/permanent residents, Jan 15 for

international applicants
Application Fee: $75 (Canadian students); $90 (International students)
Applicant/Acceptance Ratio: 4:1
Size of Incoming Class: Maximum 30
Tuition: $19,600
Books/Materials: $3,000

Comments: Students may complete our MBA program on a part-time basis taking up to a maximum of 6 years to complete the program. The School also offer Ph.D and M.Sc programs in Management.

McGill University
Admissions Office
M.B.A. Program
Faculty of Management
1001 Sherbrooke Street West
Montreal, QC   H3A 1G5
Tel: 514-398-4066
E-mail: mba.mgmt@mcgill.ca
Internet: www.management.mcgill.ca

General Information:
Degree Offered: M.B.A.
Length: First year: 3 semesters; Second year: 2 semesters
Years: 20 months
Language: English

Admission Requirements:
Previous Education: Undergraduate degree from an accredited university
Prerequisite Courses: Candidates who hold a Bachelor of Commerce degree from a North American university with three or more years of full time work experience following graduation may be eligible for advanced standing for the first year of the program. Advanced standing candidates can complete the program in 15 months on a full time basis or 36 months on a part-time basis. Also offered is a 4½ year M.B.A./Law program.
Average GPA: 3.34 or B+ or 75%
Range: 3.0 - 3.99 or 70% or B minimum

Admission Test: GMAT; no minimum
Average Score: 650
Score Report Deadline: February 15
Other Admission Criteria: Two year of full-time work experience following graduation is required; recommendations, extra-curricular activities, and leadership skills. Application is online at www.management.mcgill.ca/mba

Application Information:
Deadline: March 15 International; June 1 domestic. Decisions are made on a rolling admissions basis, six weeks after the file is complete
Application Fee: $100 plus $500 deposit fee
Applicant/Acceptance Ratio: 6:1
Size of Incoming Class: 80
Tuition: Quebec residents: $3,351.48/year; Non-Quebec residents: $6,724/year (these fees include student services, society fee, administrative and academic service fees)
International Students: approx. $20,000/year (excluding student services ($1,251), society fees and health insurance ($765 single coverage)
Books/Materials: $2,500 over 2 years

Comments: The refreshed McGill MBA curriculum focuses on maximizing student preparation for future careers through a stream-lined, modular Core and an updated selection of concentrations. Emphasizing the significant research and teaching strengths of McGill's international faculty while responding to current business imperatives, the curriculum offers an integrated multi-disciplinary, problem-solving approach grounded in practice. Advanced management concepts are integrated with case studies and examples to ground theory in the real world. Within our basic academic framework, students find diverse opportunities to explore management subjects of personal interest and apply their learning to real life business situations. They are given the opportunity to develop their unique profiles as the next generation of leaders and entrepreneurs.

The program also provides tomorrow's managers with immediate professional and social contact, networking opportunities and career development assistance. The first semester is dedicated to the Core curriculum which is comprised of five modules – Global Leadership, Business Tools, Managing Resources, Value Creation, Markets and Globalization – and a final case competition. It offers an integrated, multi-disciplinary approach that will allow you to work across managerial boundaries and to fully understand how managers and their enterprises function in an international context. For those students entering the program without the required technical background, you must attend a compulsory Base Camp prior to the beginning of the academic year.

Concentrations: Focused Knowledge
After completing the Core, students will select one or two concentrations to tailor their studies toward their specific career goals and interests. Choosing from over 50 elective courses, students pursue in-depth study in one of four areas of concentration: Finance, Marketing, Global Leadership or Technology and Innovation Management.

Experiential Component
MBA students have several opportunities to develop practical experience over the summer or in their second year. Students are required to apply, and participate in a selection process for both the internship and international exchange.

Internships
Graduate internships are typically undertaken near the completion of the MBA program. For a minimum of three months, interns work full time on one or more projects, under the supervision of a faculty member or administrator in the host organization. Students receive guidance from Career Centre staff and faculty selecting the field and organization that best suits their interests, skills, and career goals.

Practicum
Students may opt to analyze a specific facet of their professional experience through a practicum. McGill MBA students work under the guidance of a faculty member to generate a thorough report exploring an area of graduate-level management theory using their own work experience as the subject.

International Opportunities
McGill is part of the Program in International Management (PIM), a consortium of 20 leading business schools in North America, South America, Europe, and Asia. Through this association and with other independent agreements, McGill students have the opportunity to take part in a range of exchange programs in 29 countries in Africa, Europe, North America, Latin America and the Far East. The Summer Abroad Program further offers courses in international locations including Brazil, China, Mexico and Spain.

McMaster University
MBA Program
DeGroote School of Business
1280 Main Street West
Hamilton, ON   L8S 4M4
Tel: 905-525-9140, ext. 27024
Fax: 905-521-0907
E-mail: mbainfo@mcmaster.ca
Internet: www.degroote.mcmaster.ca

General Information:
Degree Offered: MBA
Length: 20 months
Years: n/a
Language: English

Admission Requirements:
Previous Education: Canadian bachelor's degree or equivalent
Prerequisite Courses: University level Calculus and Linear Algebra are recommended
Average GPA: B+
Range: B or 75% minimum in last two years of undergraduate degree
Admission Test: GMAT (TOEFL for students whose primary language is not English)
Average Score: 600 (Minimum 28 in both verbal and quantitative scores are required)
Score Report Deadline: May 1
Other Admission Criteria: Work experience, extra-curricular and community involvement, two references

Application Information:
Deadline: June 15
Application Fee: $150
Applicant/Acceptance Ratio: 4:1
Size of Incoming Class: 60 full-time, 120 co-op, 20 part-time
Tuition: $24,000 for full-time; $31,000 for co-op; $1,400 per course for part-time
Books/Materials: $1,000 per year

Comments: Full-time, co-op, and part-time options available. Areas of concentration offered: Accounting & Financial Management Solutions, Finance, General, Health Services Management (Co-op & P/T only), Human Resources & Management, Operations Management, Strategic Marketing, Management of Innovation, Management & New Technology, eBusiness

Memorial University of Newfoundland
Associate Dean, Academic Programs
Faculty of Business Administration
St. John's, NL   A1B 3X5
Tel: 709-737-8522
Fax: 709-737-2467
E-mail: mba@mun.ca
Internet: www.business.mun.ca

General Information:
Degree Offered: M.B.A.
Length: 4 Semesters*
Years: 1 - 2 **
Language: English

Admission Requirements:
Previous Education: Four-year bachelor's degree in any field
Prerequisite Courses: None
Average GPA: 3.5
Range: B minimum, no exceptions
Admission Test: GMAT
Average Score: 580
Score Report Deadline: March 15
Other Admission Criteria: Three references

Application Information:
Deadline: March 15
Application Fee: $40
Applicant/Acceptance Ratio: 2:1
Size of Incoming Class: 53 (full and part-time)
Tuition: $6,000 program fee payable in six or nine installments
Books/Materials: $500 per semester

Comments: Admission is limited and competitive. Part-time study available with admission possible at the beginning of any semester. *Two semesters for students with strong undergraduate business degrees. **Year 1 consists of 11 required courses which cover the functional areas of management (i.e. Marketing, Finance, Accounting) as well as the support disciplines of Statistics, Economics, and

Information Systems. Some exemptions/ advanced standing possible depending on type/content/quality of undergraduate degree. Year 2 is comprised of 9 courses, allowing for advanced study and research. Students given advanced standing to term 3 must do three specified courses and seven elective courses.

Université de Moncton
Doyen
Faculté d'administration
Moncton, NB   E1A 3E9
Tel: 506-858-4205
Fax: 506-858-4093
E-mail: leblanga@moncton.ca
Internet: www.umoncton.ca/mba

General Information:
Degree Offered: MBA-COOP
Length: 45 crédits
Years: 2
Language: français

Admission Requirements:
Previous Education: Any Bachelor's degree
Prerequisite Courses: Statistics
Average GPA: 3.0/4.0 or B
Range: 3.0/4.2
Admission Test: Not required
Average Score: n/a
Score Report Deadline: n/a
Other Admission Criteria: Knowledge of French and English, possible interview

Application Information:
Deadline: March 31
Application Fee: $50
Applicant/Acceptance Ratio: 2:1
Size of Incoming Class: 30
Tuition: $170/credit = $7,650, $500 internship session
Books/Materials: $1,500

Comments: The coop program alternates three study sessions with two internship sessions. A distance education MBA is also offered in different locations throughout New Brunswick through video conferencing and the Internet.
Note: The MBA Director is Tania Morris, Faculté d'administrative, Tel: 506-858-4218; Fax: 506-858-4093; E-mail: tania. morris@umoncton.ca

University of New Brunswick
Director of Graduate Studies
Faculty of Business Administration
P.O. Box 4400
Fredericton, NB   E3B 5A3
Tel: 506-451-6817
Fax: 506-453-3561
E-mail: MBAContact@unb.ca
Internet: www.unbf.ca

General Information:
Degree Offered: M.B.A., or the M.B.A. in Sport and Recreation Management; *M.B.A. in Engineering Management; **M.B.A. and L.L.B. joint program
Length: 4 semesters; *3 semesters; **8 semesters
Years: 2; *1; **4
Language: English

Admission Requirements:
Previous Education: An undergraduate degree in any discipline (B.A., B.Sc., B.Ed., etc.); *requires an undergraduate degree in Engineering
Prerequisite Courses: n/a
Average GPA: 3.0 or B or 70%
Range: 3.0 minimum
Admission Test: GMAT (may be waived in certain circumstances)
Average Score: 550
Score Report Deadline: April 30
Other Admission Criteria: Resume of work history and 3 letters of reference

Application Information:
Deadline: March 31 for September (January 31 for International applicants); good late applications are accepted as space permits

Application Fee: $50
Applicant/Acceptance Ratio: 3:1
Size of Incoming Class: 40
Tuition: $750 per 3-credit hour course
Books/Materials: $1,000 (approximately)

Comments: Part-time M.B.A. is also offered. Specializations in finance and entrepreneurshp is also offered. Internships are offered on an optional basis in the summer between first and second year. Top ranked in Canada for student/faculty ratio.

Queen's University
M.B.A. Program
Kingston, ON   K7L 3N6
Tel: 613-533-2302
Internet: http://business.queensu.ca

General Information:
Degree Offered: M.B.A.
Length: n/a
Years: 12 months
Language: English

Admission Requirements:
Previous Education: Undergraduate degree in Science or Engineering. Other degrees will be considered along with work experience in the areas of science and technology
Prerequisite Courses: Statistics, Calculus
Average GPA: 3.3
Range: 2.7 - 4.0
Admission Test: GMAT
Average Score: 680
Score Report Deadline: n/a
Other Admission Criteria: Minimum 2 years full-time work experience required, 2 letters of recommendation required, personal interview

Application Information:
Deadline: December 1 (for May starting date)
Application Fee: $100

Applicant/Acceptance Ratio: 4:1
Size of Incoming Class: 60
Tuition: $51,000
Books/Materials: All books and cases are included in the price of tuition. Students are required to purchase or lease a notebook computer.

Comments: In order to maintain the broadest possible level of accessibility, the M.B.A. Program for Science and Technology has entered into an agreement with the Royal Bank of Canada to provide an attractive financing package for individuals who are Canadian citizens or landed immigrants. This Income Contingent Loan Plan allows students to borrow their full tuition fee and an extra $10,000 to cover personal living expenses. Queen's University covers the interest costs on the entire loan while the student is in the Program, and the interest on the tuition portion for 6 months or until the individual is back in the workforce and earning at least $50,000 per year. Program begins first week of May; duration is 52 weeks. A personal interview will be required as part of the admission process.

Saint Mary's University
Greg Ferguson
Director of Admissions
923 Robie Street
Halifax, NS   B3H 3C3
Tel: 902-420-5414
Fax: 902-496-8100
E-mail: mba@stmarys.ca
Internet: www.smu.ca/mba/html/admissions.html

General Information:
Degree Offered: M.B.A.
Length: 4 semesters (standard program)
Years: 2 (standard program)
Language: English

Admission Requirements:
Previous Education: Bachelor's degree
Prerequisite Courses: None
Average GPA: 3.0
Range: 3.0 - 4.0
Admission Test: GMAT
Average Score: 550
Score Report Deadline: May 31 of the year prior
Other Admission Criteria: Interview (certain candidates may be asked)

Application Information:
Deadline: May 31 of the year prior
Application Fee: $40
Applicant/Acceptance Ratio: 2:1
Size of Incoming Class: 85
Tuition: $4,500
Books/Materials: $800 - $1,000

Comments: Students with work experience contribute more to the program and benefit more from the program. We expect full-time applicants to normally have at least 2 years of work experience. Part-time applicants should have four or more years of experience. Initiative and leadership roles demonstrated through extra-curricular activities will also be considered.

University of Saskatchewan
Director, MBA Program
College of Commerce
25 Campus Drive
Saskatoon, SK   S7N 5A7
Tel: 306-966-8678
Fax: 306-966-2515
E-mail: mba@commerce.usask.ca
Internet: www.commerce.usask.ca/programs/mba

General Information:
Degree Offered: M.B.A.
Length: 3 semesters
Years: 12 months
Language: English

Admission Requirements:
Previous Education: Four-year bachelor's degree
Prerequisite Courses: Introductory courses in Economics, Statistics, Math and Computers
Average GPA: 75% or B+ or 3.2/4.0
Range: 70% minimum in last 2 years of undergraduate degree
Admission Test: GMAT
Average Score: 565
Score Report Deadline: June 30
Other Admission Criteria: Three letters of recommendation

Application Information:
Deadline: June 30th; March 31st is recommended
Application Fee: $50 CAD
Applicant/Acceptance Ratio: 3:1
Size of Incoming Class: 25
Tuition: $17,000 for 2004/05, includes use of laptop computer
Books/Materials: approximately $2,000

Comments: Under special circumstances, applications will be processed after the deadlines.

Simon Fraser University
500 Granville Street
Vancouver, BC   V6C 1W6
Tel: 778-782-5013
Fax: 778-782-5122
E-mail: mba@sfu.ca
Internet: www.business.sfu.mba

General Information:
Degree Offered: M.B.A.
Length: 12 months
Years: 1
Language: English

Admission Requirements:
Previous Education: Non-business undergrad degree
Prerequisite Courses: n/a
Average GPA: 3.0

Range: 75% or B minimum
Admission Test: GMAT; minimum score 550
Average Score: 615
Score Report Deadline: April 1
Other Admission Criteria: Less than five years of work experience; official transcripts; passport-style photo; three letters of reference; resume; self evaluation; English proficiency

Application Information:
Deadline: April 1
Application Fee: $75
Applicant/Acceptance Ratio: 3:1
Size of Incoming Class: 40
Tuition: $27,000
Books/Materials: $2,000

Comments: At the end of their program, students participant in a three to eight month paid internship. Students also have the option of an international field study trip which is estaimated at approximately $2,000.

Simon Fraser University
Executive Director, EMBA
Faculty of Business Administration
500 Granville Street
Vancouver, BC   V6C 1W6
Tel: 778-782-5013
Fax: 778-782-5122
E-mail: emba_program@sfu.ca
Internet: www.business.sfu.ca/emba

General Information:
Degree Offered: Executive M.B.A.
Length: 5 semesters
Years: 18 months; weekend program
Language: English

Admission Requirements:
Previous Education: Bachelor's degree (any discipline) or professional designation such as CGA, CMA, CFI, P.Eng. Candidates with a two-year technology diploma and outstanding grades may be admitted.

Prerequisite Courses: None
Average GPA: 3.55
Range: 3.0 minimum
Admission Test: GMAT; minimum 550
Average Score: 620
Score Report Deadline: March 1
Other Admission Criteria: Six to 10 years work experience and four to five years management experience; three letters of reference; official transcripts from each post-secondary institution attended; resume; personal statement.

Application Information:
Deadline: March 1
Application Fee: $75
Applicant/Acceptance Ratio: 2:1
Size of Incoming Class: 35
Tuition: $47,500
Books/Materials: Included in tuition.

Comments: The SFU Executive MBA program is designed for experienced, mid-career managers and professionals seeking to improve their capacity to lead, strategize and manage change. Our team-based environment permits stimulating and thoughtul discussion which results in values-oriented decision making. Classes, held all day Friday and Saturday, every other weekend at our downtown Vancouver campus, balance learning with your career and personal demands.

Simon Fraser University
Master of Financial Risk Management (FRM)
500 Granville Street
Vancouver, BC   V6C 1W6
Tel: 778-782-7962
Fax: 778-782-5122
E-mail: mfrm@sfu.ca
Internet: www.business.sfu.ca/mfrm

General Information:
Degree Offered: Master of Financial Risk Management (FRM)
Length: 12 months full time

Years: 1 year
Language: English

Admission Requirements:
Previous Education: Undergraduate degree in business, commerce, economics, mathematics, physics, or other suitable programs
Prerequisite Courses:
Average GPA: 3.0
Range: 75% or B minimum
Admission Test: GMAT; minimum score 550
Average Score: 640
Score Report Deadline: April 1
Other Admission Criteria: Strong verbal and written communication skills; preference will be given to students with two or more years of related work experience; official transcripts; official GMAT score, passport-style photo; three letters of reference; resume; self evaluation; English proficiency

Application Information:
Deadline: April 1
Application Fee: $75
Applicant/Acceptance Ratio: n/a
Size of Incoming Class: n/a
Tuition: $23,000
Books/Materials: approximately $1,500

Years: 1-2 years
Language: English

Admission Requirements:
Previous Education: Undergraduate degree in a discipline other than business or commerce
Prerequisite Courses: Candidates should have previously completed a university course in mathematics or statistics
Average GPA: 2.5 (3.0 preferred)
Range: approximately 65%
Admission Test: n/a
Average Score: n/a
Score Report Deadline: Varies, as there are three intakes a year
Other Admission Criteria: Official transcripts; passport-style photo; three letters of reference; resume; self evalutation; English proficiency

Application Information:
Deadline: Fall semester (September) – June 1; Spring semester (January) – October 31; Summer semester (May) – March 1
Application Fee: $75
Applicant/Acceptance Ratio: n/a
Size of Incoming Class: n/a
Tuition: $13,750
Books/Materials: Included in tuition fee.

Simon Fraser University
Graduate Diploma in Business Administration (GDBA)
500 Granville Street
Vancouver, BC   V6C 1W6
Tel: 778-782-5256
Fax: 778-782-5122
E-mail: gdba@sfu.ca
Internet: www.business.sfu.ca/gdba

General Information:
Degree Offered: Graduate Diploma in Business Administration (GDBA)
Length: 12 months full time, 24 months part-time (program is offered online)

Simon Fraser University
Global Asset and Wealth Management MBA (GAWM)
500 Granville Street
Vancouver, BC   V6C 1W6
Tel: 778-782-7962
Fax: 778-782-5122
E-mail: gawm@sfu.ca
Internet: www.business.sfu.ca/gawm

General Information:
Degree Offered: Global Asset and Wealth Management MBA
Length: 16 months full time, 28 months part-time (no summer classes)

Years: 1½
Language: English

Admission Requirements:
Previous Education: Undergraduate degree in business, commerce, economics, engineering, or a professional designation such as CFA
Prerequisite Courses: n/a
Average GPA: 3.0
Range: 75% or B minimum
Admission Test: GMAT; minimum score 550
Average Score: 620
Score Report Deadline: April 1
Other Admission Criteria: At least two years of experience relevant to the financial services industry; strong verbal and written communication skills; official transcripts; official GMAT score; passport-style photo; three letters of reference; resume; self evalutation; English proficiency

Application Information:
Deadline: April 1
Application Fee: $75
Applicant/Acceptance Ratio: n/a
Size of Incoming Class: n/a
Tuition: $32,500 (includes career management and professional development workshops, guest speaker series, and Toronto business trip)
Books/Materials: approximately $2,000

Comments: For the full time option, qualified students complete paid internships in the summer term (May-August).

Simon Fraser University
Management of Technology/
Biotechnology MBA
500 Granville Street
Vancouver, BC   V6C 1W6
Tel: 778-782-5259
Fax: 778-782-5153
E-mail: motmba@sfu.ca
Internet: www.business.sfu.ca/mot (www.business.sfu.ca/biotech)

General Information:
Degree Offered: Management of Technology/Biotechnology MBA
Length: 24 months months part-time
Years: 2
Language: English

Admission Requirements:
Previous Education: Undergraduate degree in any discipline
Prerequisite Courses: n/a
Average GPA: 3.0
Range: 75% or B minimum
Admission Test: GMAT; minimum score 550
Average Score: 620
Score Report Deadline: April 1
Other Admission Criteria: At least two years of related work experience; official transcripts; official GMAT score; passport-style photo; three letters of reference; resume; self evalutation; English proficiency

Application Information:
Deadline: April 1
Application Fee: $75
Applicant/Acceptance Ratio: n/a
Size of Incoming Class: n/a
Tuition: $31,000
Books/Materials: $1,500 ($2,000 for Biotech)

University of Toronto

Master of Management and Professional
Accounting Program Office
Kaneff Centre, Room 108
3359 Mississauga Road
Mississauga, ON   L5L 1C6
Tel: 905-828-3985
Fax: 905-569-4306
Internet: www.mgmt.utoronto.ca/mmpa

General Information:
Degree Offered: M.M.P.A.
Length: Sessional
Years: Full-time - 27 months, including
two work terms; 24 or 16 months with
advanced standing
Language: English

Admission Requirements:
Previous Education: Bachelor's degree or
equivalent
Prerequisite Courses: None
Average GPA: 3.0
Range: 75% or mid-B minimum
Admission Test: GMAT
Average Score: 570
Score Report Deadline: January 31
Other Admission Criteria: Transcripts;
three professional and/or academic
reference letters; personal interview may
be requested

Application Information:
Deadline: January 31; admission is in June
Application Fee: $300
Applicant/Acceptance Ratio: 3:2
Size of Incoming Class: 45
Tuition: $19,000
Books/Materials: $1,200

University of Victoria

Uvic Business
P.O. Box 1700, Station CSC
Victoria, BC   V8W 2Y2
Tel: 250-721-6058
Fax: 250-721-7066
E-mail: mba@business.uvic.ca
Internet: www.business.uvic.ca/mba

General Information:
Degree Offered: Full and Part-time M.B.A.
Length: n/a
Years: 17 months (full time); 29-33
months (part-time)
Language: English

Admission Requirements:
Previous Education: Baccalaureate degree
from a recognized Canadian university or
foreign equivalent
Prerequisite Courses: None
Average GPA: B
Range: B average minimum in last half of
degree (A 5.0 average on 9.0 scale)
Admission Test: GMAT
Average Score: Approx. 600
Score Report Deadline: April 30
Other Admission Criteria: At least 2 years
of work experience preferred

Application Information:
Deadline: April 30
Application Fee: $75 for domestic
applicants; $100 for international
applicants
Applicant/Acceptance Ratio: 6:1
Size of Incoming Class: 45 full-time, 10
part-time
Tuition: Approximately $25,000
Books/Materials: $1,500 - $2,000

University of Western Ontario

Richard Ivey School of Business
Admissions Office
London, ON   N6A 3K7
Tel: 519-661-3212

General Information:
Degree Offered: M.B.A.
Length: 4 semesters
Years: 2
Language: English
Admission Requirements:
Previous Education: Undergraduate
degree
Prerequisite Courses: None
Average GPA: 79% or B+ or 3.3
Range: 70% or B- or 2.7 minimum to A

Admission Test: GMAT
Average Score: 650
Score Report Deadline: Take test by February
Other Admission Criteria: Average full-time work experience of 5 years; minimum 2 years of full-time work experience, extracurricular activities, achievements, and leadership skills

Application Information:
Deadline: April 1 for all applicants (rolling admission - best to apply early)
Application Fee: $100
Applicant/Acceptance Ratio: 4:1
Size of Incoming Class: 280
Tuition: $18,000
Books/Materials: $2,000

Comments: The Ivey Business School is recognized as one of the world's leading business schools by the Economist Intelligence Unit, Business Week, Asia Inc., Asian Business and as Canada's premier business school by Canadian Business magazine. Cases, role playing, simulations and negotiation exercises are used in a 2-year general management program with a global perspective. An extensive exchange program worldwide is offered. M.B.A./ LL.B., E.M.B.A., Ph.D. programs available.

Wilfrid Laurier University
M.B.A. Program
75 University Avenue West
Waterloo, ON   N2L 3C5
Tel: 514-884-0710, ext. 6220
E-mail: wlumba@wlu.ca
Internet: www.wlu.ca/mba

General Information:
Degree Offered: M.B.A.
Length: 3 semesters
Years: 1
Language: English

Admission Requirements:
Previous Education: Bachelor's degree or equivalent from a university or college of recognized standing
Prerequisite Courses: None
Average GPA: B+ or 77 - 79% approx.
Range: B or 73% minimum in final year
Admission Test: GMAT
Average Score: 600, minimum 550
Score Report Deadline: n/a
Other Admission Criteria: Minimum 2 years' work experience (average 7 years)

Application Information:
Deadline: First deadline: March 15; Final deadline: May 1; August admission only
Application Fee: $100
Applicant/Acceptance Ratio: 4:1
Size of Incoming Class: 2 sections of 50
Tuition: $6,666 per term plus incidental fees
Books/Materials: $150 average per course, plus incindental fees

Comments: Wilfrid Laurier offers several MBA format options. In Waterloo, students can pursue the one-year full time MBA or the 20 month full time MBA with co-op (for those students with no work experience), or the part-time week day evening MBA program. In Toronto, we offer the same full graduate MBA degree in our part-time alternate weekend format where students attend classes on alternate weekends at our MBA campus in the heart of downtown Toronto. Full time and full time co-op begins every August. Part-time evenings begin every September, and part-time weekends in Toronto begins every April.

University of Windsor
MBA Office
Odette School of Business
Windsor, ON   N9B 3P4
Tel: 519-253-3000, ext. 3097
Fax: 519-973-7073
E-mail: mba@uwindsor.ca
Internet: www.mba.uwindsor.ca

General Information:
Degree Offered: MBA Fast Track*, MBA Co-op**, MBA Traditional**, MBA/LLB *
Length: *= 11 months, **= 23 months, ***= maximum
Years: 6 years
Language: English

Admission Requirements:
Previous Education: *Graduation from a recognized university with a B.Comm.
**Graduation from a recognized university with a non-business degree
Prerequisite Courses: Introductory micro and macro economics and 1st year math
Average GPA: 77%; Minimum is 70% overall or 75% in last 2 years of study
Range: 70-96%
Admission Test: GMAT
Average Score: 575, minimum total=500 verbal = 26 quantitative = 30
Score Report Deadline: Must write GMAT by first week of July
Other Admission Criteria: Personal interview and 500-word essay required for co-op program

Application Information:
Deadline: See Note in "Comments"
June 1st of year applying for Fall admission
Application Fee: $100
Applicant/Acceptance Ratio: 6:1
Size of Incoming Class: * 25, ** 55
Tuition: $2,492 CDN per semester
Books/Materials: $500 - $700 per semester

Comments: The Co-op program combines the academic component of the traditional MBA with 2 career-related paid work placements.
The Fast-Track MBA is a one year, co-op program, which is geared towards students who have already completed a 4-year honours degree in Business Administration.
NOTE: Online application and request for information is available at www.mba.uwindsor.ca

York University
Schulich School of Business
4700 Keele Street
Toronto, ON   M3J 1P3
Tel: 416-736-5060
Fax: 416-650-8174
E-mail: admissions@schulich.yorku.ca
Internet: www.schulich.yorku.ca

General Information:
Degree Offered: M.B.A., I.M.B.A., MBA/LLB, MBA/MFA/MA
Length: 60 credit hours
Years: 2 (full-time); 6 (part-time - maximum)
Language: English

Admission Requirements:
Previous Education: Bachelor's degree in any discipline. GMAT with a score of 600 (75th percentile) required for all degrees. Two years relevant experience following graduation is preferred.
Prerequisite Courses: None
Average GPA: B+
Range: B- to A-
Admission Test: GMAT
Average Score: 640
Score Report Deadline: Five months prior to entry
Other Admission Criteria: Experience, recommendations, and extra-curricular activities

Application Information:
Deadline: Canadian full-time applicants - April 1; Canadian part-time applicants - May 1, February 15, October 15; International applicants - March 1
Application Fee: $125
Applicant/Acceptance Ratio: n/a
Size of Incoming Class: n/a
Tuition: $10,750 full-time; $4,250 part-time (per term)
Books/Materials: $1,000 to $2,000 depending on program

Comments: The I.M.B.A. is a 20 month, full-time program beginning in September only.

DENTISTRY

The following fact sheets outline general information including academic requirements and application procedures for Dentistry Schools in Canada. The data have been compiled in a concise format to assist students interested in these professional schools. Information was obtained from updates completed by each school, or in some cases from the school's Internet website.

Dental Schools in Canada

University of Alberta*
University of British Columbia
Dalhousie University
Université Laval*
University of Manitoba*

McGill University*
Université de Montréal
University of Saskatchewan
University of Toronto*
University of Western Ontario

Comments

1. These fact sheets act as a guide only. Students are advised to refer to the individual calendars or to write to the schools for more detailed information.

2. Application deadlines vary. Dates indicated refer to fall admission unless otherwise noted.

3. Tuition fees represent annual costs unless otherwise noted.

4. All of the schools listed above may not be represented.

* This university has not updated its information. Please contact the university directly.

University of Alberta

Office of Admissions
Faculty of Medicine and Dentistry
3028 Dentistry-Pharmacy Centre
Edmonton, AB   T6G 2N8
Tel: 780-492-1319
Fax: 780-492-7536
E-mail: admissions@dent.ualberta.ca
Internet: www.dent.ualberta.ca

General Information:
Degree Offered: D.D.S.
Length: The first three years contain three terms:
15 weeks; 15 weeks; 10 weeks
Years: 4
Language: English

Admission Requirements:
Previous Education: Minimum of 2 years university approved by the Faculty of Medicine and Dentistry
Prerequisite Courses: Full courses in the following: Organic Chemistry, Inorganic Chemistry, Physics, Biology (Zoology if Biology is not available), and English. Half year courses in Biochemistry and Statistics
Average GPA: Determined by Admission's Committee
Range: n/a
Admission Test: Canadian Dental Aptitude Test
Average Score: Determined by Admission's Committee
Score Report Deadline: January 15 of application year
Other Admission Criteria: Personal interview

Application Information:
Deadline: November 1 of year prior to the year admission is sought
Application Fee: $60
Applicant/Acceptance Ratio: 9:1
Size of Incoming Class: 30
Tuition: $16,802
Books/Materials: $11,470 for first year

University of British Columbia

Undergraduate Admissions
Office of the Dean, Faculty of Dentistry
278 - 2199 Wesbrook Mall
Vancouver, BC   V6T 1Z3
Tel: 604-822-3416
Fax: 604-822-8279
E-mail: fodadms@interchange.ubc.ca
Internet: www.dentistry.ubc.ca

General Information:
Degree Offered: D.M.D.
Length: Semesters
Years: 4
Language: English

Admission Requirements:
Previous Education: Three academic years in the Faculty of Arts or Science at UBC or equivalent (90 post-secondary credits)
Prerequisite Courses: Please consult www.dentistry.ubc.ca for current required pre-requisites
Average GPA: 3.80 or 80% approximately
Range: 77 - 90%; minimum to apply 70%
Admission Test: (Canadian) Dental Aptitude Test
Average Score: 21
Score Report Deadline: Nov 2 (changes annually - check website for current deadlines)
Other Admission Criteria: Personal qualities as evidenced by pre-dental scholastic records, aptitude test, letters of recommendation, and personal interview

Application Information:
Deadline: November 12 (changes annually - check website for current deadlines)
Application Fee: $200
Applicant/Acceptance Ratio: 7:1
Size of Incoming Class: 40
Tuition: $14,000 for first year
Books/Materials: $27,064 for first year

Comments: Ontario Grade 13 subjects are not equivalent to UBC first-year courses. Quebec first-year CEGEP subjects are not equivalent to UBC first-year courses.

Dalhousie University

Faculty of Dentistry
Halifax, NS B3H 3J5
Tel: 902-494-2274 or 902-494-1400
Fax: 902-494-2527
E-mail: denadmis@dal.ca
Internet: www.dentistry.dal.ca

General Information:
Degree Offered: D.D.S.
Length: Semesters
Years: 4
Language: English

Admission Requirements:
Previous Education: Minimum 2 years of university study
Prerequisite Courses: A minimum of 10, full-year academic classes which include classes in Biology; General Chemistry; Organic Chemistry; Physics; and three full-year academic classes chosen from the humanities and/or social sciences, one of which must involve a significant written component. Courses must also include Introductory Biochemistry; Introductory Microbiology; Vertebrate Physiology.
Average GPA: 3.7
Range: A- minimum
Admission Test: Dental Aptitude Test (D.A.T.)
Average Score: 15 or better on each of the components
Score Report Deadline: When available
Other Admission Criteria: Interview; references; Personality Trait Questionnaire

Application Information:
Deadline: December 1 of the year prior
Application Fee: $70
Applicant/Acceptance Ratio: 5:1
Size of Incoming Class: 36
Tuition: $14,074
Books/Materials: $21,710 over 4 years, including instruments

Université Laval

René Guy Landry
Médecine dentaire
Québec, QC G1K 7P4
Tel: 418-656-5293

General Information:
Degree Offered: D.M.D.
Length: 8 Semesters
Years: 4
Language: French

Admission Requirements:
Previous Education: Two years of College (CEGEP)
Prerequisite Courses: Option in Health Sciences, Math, Physics, Biology, Chemistry
Average GPA: 80% approx. in science subjects
Range: n/a
Admission Test: Dental Aptitude Test
Average Score: Carving dexterity - 15/30, PAT - 17/30
Score Report Deadline: March 1
Other Admission Criteria: Knowledge of French and positive medical evaluation

Application Information:
Deadline: March 1
Application Fee: $55
Applicant/Acceptance Ratio: 9:1
Size of Incoming Class: 46
Tuition: $3,300
Books/Materials: $5,200/year

Comments: Priority is given to Quebec, Ontario and New Brunswick residents. Must have Canadian citizenship or landed immigrant status and speak French.

University of Manitoba

Office of the Dean
Faculty of Dentistry
D113 - 780 Bannnatyne
Winnipeg, MB   R3E 0W2
Tel: 204-789-3631
Fax: 204-789-3912
E-mail: dean_dent@umanitoba.ca
Internet: www.umanitoba.ca/faculties/
dentistry

General Information:
Degree Offered: D.D.S.
Length: Semesters
Years: 4
Language: English

Admission Requirements:
Previous Education: Two years university
Prerequisite Courses: See "Comments"
Average GPA: 2.5
Range: n/a
Admission Test: Dental Aptitude Test
Average Score: n/a
Score Report Deadline: n/a
Other Admission Criteria: Personal
interview, must be C.P.R. certified

Application Information:
Deadline: n/a
Application Fee: $60
Applicant/Acceptance Ratio: 9:1
Size of Incoming Class: 30
Tuition: $13,854
Books/Materials: $3,300 (entire program)
+ $21,778 for instruments (entire
program)

Comments: Required Courses: Two
years university must include one full
course in each of the following: General
Biology or Zoology (half-year of Botany
and a half-year Zoology will be accepted
but not one year of Botany alone) with
laboratory, Inorganic or General Chemistry
with laboratory, Mathematics, Physics
with laboratory, Organic Chemistry with
laboratory, Cell and Molecular Biology or
one complete year of Biochemistry

McGill University

Strathcona Anatomy & Dentistry Building
3640 University Street
Montreal, QC   H3A 2B2
Tel: 514-398-7203
Fax: 514-398-8900
E-mail: undergrad.dentistry@mcgill.ca
Internet: www.mcgill.ca/dentistry

General Information:
Degree Offered: D.M.D., D.D.S.
Length: 8 Semesters
Years: 4
Language: English

Admission Requirements:
Previous Education: Undergraduate
degree
Prerequisite Courses: Introductory
Chemistry, Biochemistry, Organic
Chemistry, Physics, Biology, English; of the
remaining 4 full courses, one must be in
the Social Sciences
Average GPA: 3.5
Range: n/a
Admission Test: Canadian Dental Aptitude
Test (DAT)
Average Score: 20.41
Score Report Deadline: n/a
Other Admission Criteria: Reference
letter, autobiographical letter, and
interview

Application Information:
Deadline: January 15
Application Fee: $60
Applicant/Acceptance Ratio: 8:1
Size of Incoming Class: 25
Tuition: $3,559.04 for residents of Quebec
(1st year); $9,389.44 for residents of all
other provinces (1st year)
Books/Materials: $9,022 for first year

Comments: The Applicant Information
Bulletin is the official statement on
requirements. Request most recent edition
for specific information such as deadline
for DAT scores.

Université de Montréal

Faculté de médecine dentaire
Pavillon Roger Gaudry
C.P. 6128, Succursale Centre-ville
Montréal, QC   H3C 3J7
Tel: 514-343-7076
Fax: 514-343-2233

General Information:
Degree Offered: D.M.D.
Length: 10 Semesters
Years: 5
Language: français

Admission Requirements:
Previous Education: DEC with health science profile
Prerequisite Courses: Two years college
Average GPA: n/a
Range: n/a
Admission Test: Dental aptitude test; Percep. Sculpture
Average Score: DAT - 10; Percep. Sculpture - 5
Score Report Deadline: Three to five months before academic year
Other Admission Criteria: Knowledge of French language, Canadian citizenship or permanent residency, motivation letter, possible interview or any other tests may be required

Application Information:
Deadline: March 1 for college students; January 15 for others
Application Fee: n/a
Applicant/Acceptance Ratio: 6:1
Size of Incoming Class: 85
Tuition: Pre-dental $2,800; Year 1: $2,900; Year 2: $3,250;
Year 3: $3,000; Year 4: $2,400; n.b. This can change without notice
Books/Materials: Year 1: $8,000; Year 2: $7,900
Year 3: $3,700; Year 4: $400; n.b. This can change without notice.

Comments: Any other information is available on the university website – www.futursetudiants.umontreal.ca.

University of Saskatchewan

College of Dentistry, Admissions
B526 Health Sciences Building
Saskatoon, SK   S7N 5E5
Tel: 306-966-5117
Fax: 306-966-5126
E-mail: dentistry.admissions@usask.ca
Internet: www.usask.ca/dentistry

General Information:
Degree Offered: D.M.D.
Length: Terms/Sessions
Years: 4
Language: English

Admission Requirements:
Previous Education: Two 30 credit unit pre-dentistry years in College of Arts & Science
Prerequisite Courses: Biology – one full year (two terms) of introductory level biology; General Chemistry – one half year (one term) of introductory general chemistry; Organic Chemistry – one half year (one term) of introductory organic chemistry; Physics – one full year (two terms) introductory level university physics (acceptable topics include mechanics, wave motion and sound, heat, electricity and magnetism, light and modern physics); Social science/Humanities – one full year (two terms) of social science/humanities courses; Biochemistry, molecular – one half year course that covers molecular biology; Biochemistry, metabolism – one half year course that covers metabolism
Average GPA: 75% for two best 30 credit unit years and 70% in required pre-dentistry courses
Range: n/a
Admission Test: Dental Aptitude Test (CDA DAT) is required

Average Score: n/a
Score Report Deadline: March
Other Admission Criteria: Interview and 3 letters of reference

Application Information:
Deadline: January 15
Application Fee: $125 (CDN)
Applicant/Acceptance Ratio: 3:1
Size of Incoming Class: 28
Tuition: $32,000 per year
Books/Materials: $1,830 (books/manuals); $7,206 (equipment/instruments/other)

Comments: All applications and supporting documentation (except for completed references) should be forwarded directly to: Admissions, Student & Enrolment Services, University of Saskatchewan, 105 Administration Place, Saskatoon, SK, S7N 5A2.
References are to be forwarded to: Admissions, College of Dentistry, University of Saskatchewan, 105 Wiggins Road, Saskatoon, SK, S7N 5E4.

University of Toronto
Admissions Office
Faculty of Dentistry
124 Edward Street
Toronto, ON   M5G 1G6
Tel: 416-979-4901, ext. 4373
Fax: 416-979-4944
E-mail: admissions.dental@utoronto.ca
Internet: www.utoronto.ca/dentistry

General Information:
Degree Offered: D.D.S.
Length: Semesters
Years: 4
Language: English

Admission Requirements:
Previous Education: Three years of university (i.e. 15 full courses or equivalent)

Prerequisite Courses: Two full courses (or equivalent) in the Life Sciences and one full course (or equivalent) in Social Sciences or Humanities. Effective 2006-2007 four full courses (or equivalent) in Life Sciences with at least one full course in biochemistry and one full course in Human Physiology and one full course (or equivalent) in Social Sciences or Humanities.
Average GPA: 3.3 (B+) to 3.7 (A-)
Range: 2.7 (B-) minimum
Admission Test: Canadian Dental Aptitude Test (or equivalent): components used in the selection process are the Academic Average (AA) and Perceptual Ability Test (PAT)
Average Score: 19 (AA), 18 (PAT)
Score Report Deadline: Test must have been taken within the last two years and may be taken no later than November of proposed year of entry. The latest DAT scores will be used in the selection process.
Other Admission Criteria: n/a

Application Information:
Deadline: December 1
Application Fee: $200 non-refundable
Applicant/Acceptance Ratio: 7:1
Size of Incoming Class: 64
Tuition: $24,671 (including instruments)

Comments: A limited number of places are also available for international students. Please consult the Admissions Office for further information.

University of Western Ontario
Admissions Coordinator
Dentistry, Schulich School of Medicine & Dentistry
London, ON   N6A 5C1
Tel: 519-661-3744
Fax: 519-850-2958
E-mail: dental.admissions@schulich.uwo.ca
Internet: www.schulich.uwo.ca/dentistry

General Information:
Degree Offered: D.D.S.
Length: 2 semesters
Years: 4
Language: English

Admission Requirements:
Previous Education: Minimum 2 years of university which will include a minimum of 4 honours courses (senior 2nd year) or equivalent level within the first 10 courses completed
Prerequisite Courses: One full-laboratory course in each of Biology, General Chemistry, and Physics. At least a half course in Organic Chemistry and at least a half course in Biochemistry. A full course in human or mammalian physiology will also be required.
Average GPA: 84.75% (2007-08)
Range: 80% minimum
Admission Test: Canadian Dental Aptitude Test
Average Score: 98/150 (2007-08)
Score Report Deadline: December of year of application
Other Admission Criteria: Applicants are advised that it is to their advantage to take a program which includes at least five full courses or equivalent in each academic year, taken concurrently (excluding summer sessions). Primary consideration will be given to the best two academic years and the DAT scores. However, overall academic performance (consistency, trend), honors degree (if applicable) and graduate education will also be used as selection criteria. The School reserves the right to require an interview as part of the admission process.

Application Information:
Deadline: December 1
Application Fee: $250
Applicant/Acceptance Ratio: 11:1
Size of Incoming Class: 52 Canadian; up to 4 international

Tuition: $19,945 (CDN) (2007-08) Canadian; $40,000 (CDN) international
Books/Materials: Year 1: $1,500. Dental Instruments: (2007-08) Year 1: $10,510

Comments: A limited number of positions are available for international students, who must satisfy similar requirements, as well as English language proficiency. Please contact the Admissions Coordinator for details. One position is available for applicants supported by the Canadian International Development Agency or similar agency.

ENGINEERING

The following fact sheets outline general information including academic requirements and application procedures for Engineering Schools in Canada. The data have been compiled in a concise format to assist students interested in these professional schools. Information was obtained from updates completed by each school, or in some cases from the school's Internet website.

Engineering Schools in Canada

University of Alberta*
University of British Columbia
University of Calgary*
Carleton University
Concordia University
École Polytechnique de Montréal
University of Guelph
Lakehead University
Laurentian University*
Université Laval
University of Manitoba
McGill University
McMaster University
Memorial University of Newfoundland*
Université de Moncton

University of New Brunswick*
University of Ottawa*
Université du Québec à Trois-Rivières
Queen's University
University of Regina*
Royal Military College of Canada
Ryerson Polytechnic University*
University of Saskatchewan
Université de Sherbrooke
Simon Fraser University
University of Toronto
University of Victoria
University of Waterloo*
University of Western Ontario*
University of Windsor

Comments

1. These fact sheets act as a guide only. Students are advised to refer to the individual calendars or to write to the schools for more detailed information.

2. Application deadlines vary. Dates indicated refer to fall admission unless otherwise noted.

3. Tuition fees represent annual costs unless otherwise noted.

4. All of the schools listed above may not be represented.

* This university has not updated its information. Please contact the university directly.

University of Alberta

Office of the Registrar
201, Administration Building
Edmonton, AB   T6G 2M7
Tel: 780-492-3113
Fax: 780-492-7172
Internet: www.registrar.ualberta.ca

General Information:
Degree Offered: B.Sc.(Eng.)*
Length: Semesters
Years: 4 years (traditional program); 5 years (co-op education program)
Language: English

Admission Requirements:
Previous Education: High School Matriculation
Prerequisite Courses: Chemistry 30, English 30, Math 30, Math 31, Physics 30
Average GPA: Minimum Application Average for 2003 - 80% (Competitive Average in 2003 - 80%)
Range: n/a
Admission Test: n/a
Average Score: n/a
Score Report Deadline: n/a
Other Admission Criteria: English Language Proficiency: May be met with a minimum score in one of the following: ELA30-1, 18 Higher Level English, AP English, TOEFL, IELTS, MELAB. For more information on ELP Requirements, go to www.registrar.ualberta.ca

Application Information:
Deadline: May 1
Application Fee: $100
Applicant/Acceptance Ratio: 2:1
Size of Incoming Class: n/a
Tuition: $5,393.36
Books/Materials: $1,100.00

Comments: *Specialization in Chemical; Chemical (Computer Process Control Oil Sands); Civil; (Construction, Environmental, Geotechnical, Structural, Surveying, Transportation, Water Resources); Computer, Electrical (Biomedical, Communications, Control Systems, Digital Systems, Electronic Material & Nanotechnology, Electronics, Electromagnetic & Photonics, Power); Engineering Physics (not available in Co-operative Program); Materials; Mechanical (Solid Mechanic & Dynamics, Fluid Mechanics, Thermodynamics, Design, Engineering Management); Mining, Petroleum, Biomedical.

University of British Columbia

Faculty of Applied Sciences
1100-2332 Main Mall
Vancouver, BC   V6T 1Z4
Tel: 604-822-6556
Fax: 604-822-2021

General Information:
Degree Offered: B.A.Sc.
Length: Semesters
Years: 4 (5 years for Engineering Physics)
Language: English

Admission Requirements:
Previous Education: OSSD
Prerequisite Courses: English 12, Chemistry 12, Principles of Mathematics 12 and Physics 12
Average GPA: n/a
Range: 80%
Admission Test: None
Average Score: n/a
Score Report Deadline: n/a
Other Admission Criteria: English Lanuage Proficiency

Application Information:
Deadline: February 28
Application Fee: $60 domestic; $100 (international)
Applicant/Acceptance Ratio: varies
Size of Incoming Class: varies
Tuition: $141.91/credit, $5,108/year approx.
Books/Materials: $1,000 approx.

Comments: Specializations in Chemical and Petroleum, Civil, Computer and Software, Electrical, Geomatics, Mechanical, and Manufacturing Engineering

University of Calgary
Faculty of Engineering
2500 University Drive N.W.
Calgary, AB   T2N 1N4
Tel: 403-220-5732
Fax: 403-284-3697
E-mail: graduate@ucalgary.ca
Internet: www.eng.ucalgary.ca

General Information:
Degree Offered: M.Sc. (Eng); M. Eng, Ph.D.
Length: Semesters
Years: 2 - 4 years
Language: English

Admission Requirements:
Previous Education: B.Sc. degree or equivalent
Prerequisite Courses: Varies with programs
Average GPA: 3.0 / 4.0
Range: n/a
Admission Test: Not required
Average Score: n/a
Score Report Deadline: n/a
Other Admission Criteria: Varies with programs

Application Information:
Deadline: Varies with programs
Application Fee: $60
Applicant/Acceptance Ratio: varies
Size of Incoming Class: varies
Tuition: $4,750 per year
Books/Materials: $1,000 approx.

Comments: *Specializations in Chemical and Petroleum, Civil, Computer and Software, Electrical, Geomatics, Mechanical Engineering, and Manufacturing Engineering.

Carleton University
Undergraduate Recruitment Office
(Admission Services)
315 Robertson Hall
1125 Colonel By Drive
Ottawa, ON   K1S 5B6
Tel: 613-520-3663
Fax: 613-520-3847
Internet: www.admissions.carleton.ca

General Information:
Degree Offered: B.Eng.*
Length: 8 semesters
Years: 4 (also co-op)
Language: English

Admission Requirements:
Previous Education: OSSD with six Grade 12 4U or 4M(U/C) courses
Prerequisite Courses: Grade 12 4U Advanced Functions, Chemistry, Physics, 1 credit from Calculus*, Biology, or Earth and Space Science, 2 additional credits (Calculus* recommended). English or French recommended.
Average GPA: 70% to 85%
Range: n/a
Admission Test: None
Average Score: n/a
Score Report Deadline: n/a
Other Admission Criteria: None

Application Information:
Deadline: June 1
Application Fee: $110 (Ontario University Application Centre (OUAC) fee)
Applicant/Acceptance Ratio: 4:1
Size of Incoming Class: 700
Tuition: $5,081 to $6,891 (depending on program)
Books/Materials: $1,300 (depending on program)

Comments: *Specializations:Aerospace; Biomedical & Electrical; Biomedical & Mechanical; Civil; Communications; Computer Systems; Electrical; Engineering Physics; Environmental; Mechanical; Software; Sustainable & Renewable Energy

Concordia University

Faculty of Engineering & Computer Science
1455 de Maisonneuve Blvd. West
Montreal, QC   H3G 1M8
Tel: 514-848-2424 ext. 3055
Fax: 514-848-8646
E-mail: mona@encs.concordia.ca
Internet: www.encs.concordia.ca

General Information:
Degree Offered: B.Eng.
Length: 120.00 credits
Years: 4-5
Language: English

Admission Requirements:
Previous Education: Diploma of Collegial Studies (Quebec) or equivalent, students lacking the necessary background may be admitted to the Extended Credits Program (ECP)
Prerequisite Courses: Math, Physics, Chemistry, Humanities/Social Science, Computer Literacy
Average GPA: Minimum 2.5 - 3.0, depending on program
Range: n/a
Admission Test: No
Average Score: n/a
Score Report Deadline: n/a
Other Admission Criteria: English language proficiency for foreign students (TOEFL, IELTS or MELAB)

Application Information:
Deadline: February 1 (International) March 1 (Regular deadline). Applications received after the deadlines will be reviewed subject to time/space limitations.
Application Fee: $75
Applicant/Acceptance Ratio: n/a
Size of Incoming Class: n/a
Tuition: See below
Books/Materials: $1,500 per year approx.

Comments: A Bachelor of Computer Science (B.Comp.Sc.) is also offered; contact the school at the address above for additional information.
Tuition: Quebec residents: $55.61 per credit
Non-Quebec residents: $155.03 per credit
International (Visa): $387.61 per credit
Plus: Academic & Service fees

École Polytechnique de Montréal

Bureau du registraire
C.P. 6079, Succursale Centre-ville
Montreal, QC   H3C 3A7
Tel: 514-340-4724
Fax: 514-340-5836
E-mail: Registraire@polymtl.ca
Internet: www.polymtl.ca
General Information:
Degree Offered: Baccalauréat en ingénierie
Length: 8 trimestres
Years: 4
Language: français

Admission Requirements:
Previous Education: Diplôme d'études collégiales (13 ans)
Prerequisite Courses: Profil sciences pures et appliquées
Average GPA: 75%
Range: n/a
Admission Test: n/a
Average Score: n/a
Score Report Deadline: n/a
Other Admission Criteria: n/a

Application Information:
Deadline: 1er mars (automne) / 1 novembre (hiver) for Canadian students; 15 janvier (automne) / 15 septembre (hiver) for International students
Application Fee: $50
Applicant/Acceptance Ratio: 70%
Size of Incoming Class: 900
Tuition: $1,200/trimestre (Quebec students); $2,900/ trimestre (Canadian students); $6,900/ trimestre (International students)
Books/Materials: $600/année approx.

University of Guelph
Liaison Officer
School of Engineering
Guelph, ON   N1G 2W1
Tel: 519-824-4120 ext. 52436
Fax: 519-836-0227
E-mail: enginfo@uoguelph.ca
Internet: www.soe.uoguelph.ca

General Information:
Degree Offered: B.Eng. Regular or Co-op
Length: 8 semesters
Years: 4
Language: English

Admission Requirements:
Previous Education: Secondary School
Diploma, including Six Grade 12 U and/or
M courses
Prerequisite Courses: Calculus; Advanced
Functions; English; two credits from
Biology, Chemistry, Physics; and one
additional credit
Average GPA: n/a
Range: 75 - 78% minimum
Admission Test: Not required
Average Score: n/a
Score Report Deadline: n/a
Other Admission Criteria: n/a

Application Information:
Deadline: January 12
Application Fee: $75
Applicant/Acceptance Ratio: n/a
Size of Incoming Class: 135
Tuition: $4,544.00
Books/Materials: $400 per semester

Comments: Degrees offered in Biological
Engineering, Environmental Engineering,
Water Resources Engineering, and
Engineering Systems and Computing. An
M.Sc., Ph.D. and M.Eng. are also offered
in particular disciplines.

Lakehead University
Faculty of Engineering
955 Oliver Road
Thunder Bay, ON   P7B 5E1
Tel: 807-343-8321
Fax: 807-343-8928
Internet: www.lakeheadu.ca

General Information:
Degree Offered: B.Eng. (Chemical, Civil,
Electrical, Mechanical, Software)
Length: Semesters
Years: 4 (2 years post-diploma)
Language: English

Admission Requirements:
Previous Education: OSSD, sic Grade 12U
or M courses (or equivalent), including
program prerequisites, 70% average
Prerequisite Courses: Advanced
Functions, Physics, Chemistry, three
additional credits (English, Calculus and
Vectors is strongly recommended), one
credit in Math, Science or Tech. Ed. is also
recommended.
Average GPA: From high school requires
70% average and 60% minimum in
Advanced Functions; admission to
the post-diploma program requires a
minimum of 70% average in the final year
of technology.
Range: n/a
Admission Test: n/a
Average Score: n/a
Score Report Deadline: n/a
Other Admission Criteria: There are two
admission points: one for high school
graduates, the second for Engineering
Technology graduates

Application Information:
Deadline: No published deadline
Application Fee: $105 for high school
applicants; $110 + $40 supplementary
document evaluation fee for post-diploma
applicants
Applicant/Acceptance Ratio: n/a

Size of Incoming Class: n/a
Tuition: 2007-2008 Full Year (fall/winter) $5,300; Summer Transition (July-August) $2,500
Books/Materials: $750 - $2,400 per year

Comments: Lakehead's unique engineering program enables students to earn an Engineering Technology diploma by the end of year two of the B.Eng. program.
Transfer students must take a Summer School transition program between Diploma and Degree studies.

Laurentian University
Office of Admissions
Ramsey Lake Road
Sudbury, ON   P3H 2C6
Tel: 705-675-4843
E-mail: admissions@laurentian.ca
Internet: http://laurentian.ca/calendar/admissions.pdf
General Information:
Degree Offered: B.Eng. (Regular and Co-op)
Length: 8 terms
Years: 4
Language: English

Admission Requirements:
Previous Education: Ontario School Diploma (OSSD) or equivalent or diploma from colleges of Applied Arts & Technology
Prerequisite Courses: OAC or U level Chemistry, Physics, Calculus, Algebra, and Geometry; two other OAC's or U or M level courses
Average GPA: 60%
Range: n/a
Admission Test: n/a
Average Score: n/a
Score Report Deadline: n/a
Other Admission Criteria: n/a

Application Information:
Deadline: n/a
Application Fee: None
Applicant/Acceptance Ratio: n/a
Size of Incoming Class: 40 - 55
Tuition: $4,879.95 (plus $300/academic term for co-op fee)
Books/Materials: $400 - 600 per year

Comments: A Master's of Science and Master's of Engineering are also available. Mining Engineering and Extractive Metalurgical Engineering are offered at the Bachelor's level. The first two years of Mechanical, Chemical and Civil are also offered. To complete these degrees, students transfer to another university.

University of Manitoba
Faculty of Engineering
350 Engineering Building
Winnipeg, MB   R3T 5T6
Tel: 204-474-9807
E-mail: eng_info@umanitoba.ca
Internet: www.umanitoba.ca/faculties/engineering

General Information:
Degree Offered: B.Sc.(Eng.)*
Length: 8 or 10 terms
Years: 4 or 5
Language: English

Admission Requirements:
Previous Education: Secondary Scool Diploma
Prerequisite Courses: Chemistry 40S, Mathematics 40S (pre-calculus), and Physics 40S
Average GPA: 85%
Range: n/a
Admission Test: Not required
Average Score: n/a
Score Report Deadline: n/a
Other Admission Criteria: Students may also enter Engineering after a

preliminary year of university-level studies including courses in Math, Chemistry, Computer Science, Physics, English and/or Philosophy. A minimum C average is required, a higher average may be necessary to be competitive.

Application Information:
Deadline: February 2
Application Fee: $35
Applicant/Acceptance Ratio: 2:1
Size of Incoming Class: n/a
Tuition: $4,500
Books/Materials: $1,400

Comments: *The engineering programs available are: Biosystems (BE), Civil (CE), Computer (TE), Electrical (EE) and Mechanical (ME) Engineering (including Manufacturing Engineering).

McMaster University

Admissions Office
1280 Main Street West
Hamilton, ON   L8S 4L8
Tel: 905-525-9140, ext. 24646

General Information:
Degree Offered: B.Eng.*; B.Eng.Biosci.**;
B.Eng.Mgmt**; B.Eng.Society***
Length: Semesters
Years: *4; **5
Language: English

Admission Requirements:
Previous Education: OSSD or equivalent
Prerequisite Courses: Chemistry, Physics, Calculus and English
Average GPA: 83%
Range: 79-81% by selection
Admission Test: None
Average Score: n/a
Score Report Deadline: n/a
Other Admission Criteria: n/a

Application Information:
Deadline: July 15
Application Fee: $85

Applicant/Acceptance Ratio: 5:1
Size of Incoming Class: 800
Tuition: $6,265
Books/Materials: $800 approx.

Comments: Within the Bachelor of Engineering, the following concentrations exist: Chemical, Civil, Computer, Electrical, Mechanical, Engineering Physics, Materials, and Software.

Memorial University of Newfoundland

Faculty of Engineering and Applied Science
St. John's, NL   A1B 3X5
Tel: 709-737-8813
Fax: 709-737-8011
E-mail: adeanugs@engr.mun.ca
Internet: www.engr.mun.ca

General Information:
Degree Offered: B.Eng. (Co-op)
Length: 10 academic and 6 work terms
Years: 6
Language: English

Admission Requirements:
Previous Education: Grade 12
Prerequisite Courses: English, Mathematics, Physics, Chemistry, Arts
Average GPA: 70% minimum
Range: n/a
Admission Test: n/a
Average Score: n/a
Score Report Deadline: n/a
Other Admission Criteria: n/a

Application Information:
Deadline: March 1
Application Fee: $40 (applicants from Memorial); $80 (applicants outside Newfoundland & Labrador)
Applicant/Acceptance Ratio: 3:1
Size of Incoming Class: 200
Tuition: $1,275 per academic semester (Canadian and Permanent Residents); $4,400 per academic semester

(International Students); $340 per work term
Books/Materials: $500 per semester

Comments: Five programs are available: Civil, Computer, Electrical, Mechanical, Ocean and Naval Architectural Engineering with Offshore Oil and Gas options in all programs

Université de Moncton
Faculté d'ingénierie
Moncton, NB   E1A 3E9
Tel: 506-858-4300
Fax: 506-858-4082
Internet: www.umoncton.ca/genie
page1.htm

General Information:
Degree Offered: B.1ng
Length: 10 semestres
Years: 5 années
Language: français

Admission Requirements:
Previous Education: Titulaire d'un diplôme de fin d'études secondaires
Prerequisite Courses: Réussite des cours terminaux de français mathématique et deux cours parmis la biologie, la chimie ou la physique
Average GPA: n/a
Range: Est admissible, candidat(e) qui a maintenu une moyenne de 65% de français terminal et 60% dans chacun des autres cours (N.B., N.E., I.P.E., T.N., QUÉ., ONT.)
Admission Test: n/a
Average Score: n/a
Score Report Deadline: n/a
Other Admission Criteria: Aucune

Application Information:
Deadline: 15 juin pour la session d'automne et 15 novembre pour la session d'hiver. Pour un(e) non-résident(e), 1 février pour la session d'automne et le 15 septembre pour la session d'hiver

Application Fee: $39
Applicant/Acceptance Ratio: 60%
Size of Incoming Class: n/a
Tuition: $4,920/année (Canadien); $8,149/année (Étranger) par année

Books/Materials: $1,000 (environ) + achat ordinateur portable selon une liste suggérée

Comments: *Génie civil, électrique, mécanique.

University of New Brunswick
Admissions Office
P.O. Box 4400
Fredericton, NB   E3B 5A3
Tel: 506-453-4865
Fax: 506-453-5016
E-mail: admissions@unb.ca

General Information:
Degree Offered: B.Sc.(Eng.)
Length: 8 terms
Years: 4
Language: English

Admission Requirements:
Previous Education: High school - 6 appropriate courses including senior-year English
Prerequisite Courses: Senior-year Mathematics, Chemistry, and Physics
Average GPA: 80% approx.
Range: Average of 6 courses used for admission (75% for all provinces)
Admission Test: n/a
Average Score: n/a
Score Report Deadline: n/a
Other Admission Criteria: None

Application Information:
Deadline: March 31
Application Fee: $35
Applicant/Acceptance Ratio: 2:1
Size of Incoming Class: 200
Tuition: $4,770
Books/Materials: $800 - $1,000

Comments: Engineering degrees in the following areas are available – Chemical, Civil, Computer, Electrical, Geological, Geomatics, Mechanical, and Software Surveying. A separate engineering degree in Forest Engineering is also offered.

University of Ottawa
Office of the Registrar, Admissions
550 Cumberland Street
Ottawa, ON   K1N 6N5
Tel: 613-562-5700
Fax: 613-562-5290
E-mail: liaison@uottawa.ca
Internet: www.engineering.uottawa.ca

General Information:
Degree Offered: B.A.Sc. (Engineering)
Length: 8 Semesters
Years: 4
Language: French or English

Admission Requirements:
Previous Education: OSSD + 6 eligible courses (4 University or 4 Masters) or equivalent
Prerequisite Courses: Geometry, Calculus, Chemistry, Physics, English or français
Average GPA: 70% minimum
Range: 70 - 78%
Admission Test: n/a
Average Score: n/a
Score Report Deadline: n/a
Other Admission Criteria:

Application Information:
Deadline: June 30 - high school students; April 30 - all other applicants
Application Fee: $85
Applicant/Acceptance Ratio: n/a
Size of Incoming Class: 592
Tuition: $5,200
Books/Materials: $400 - $800

Comments: Co-operative education is offered in all disciplines (Chemical, Civil, Computer, Electrical (with 4 technical options), Mechanical Software, and Computer Science). Computer Science no longer requires chemistry. All may be combined with Computing Technology for a B.Sc + B.A.Sc. All have options in Engineering Management and Entrepreneurship.

Queen's University
Admission Services
Richardson Hall
Kingston, ON   K7L 3N6
Tel: 613-533-2218
E-mail: admissn@post.queensu.ca
Internet: www.queensu.ca/admission

General Information:
Degree Offered: B.Sc.
Length: 2 terms/year
Years: 4
Language: English

Admission Requirements:
Previous Education: Successful completion of the Secondary School graduation diploma including 4 Grade 12U courses or equivalent
Prerequisite Courses: Four of: English, Geometry and Discrete Mathematics, Advanced Functions and Introductory Calculus, Chemistry, and Physics; and one U or M course from any discipline (check admissions criteria website for details)
Average GPA: n/a
Range: 78% minimum
Admission Test: None
Average Score: n/a
Score Report Deadline: n/a
Other Admission Criteria: Personal statement of experience

Application Information:
Deadline: February 20
Application Fee: $75
Applicant/Acceptance Ratio: 5:1
Size of Incoming Class: 630
Tuition: $3,874 plus $553 student interest fees
Books/Materials: $665

University of Regina
Admissions, Registrar's Office
Regina, SK   S4S 0A2
Tel: 306-585-4591
Fax: 306-585-5203

General Information:
Degree Offered: B.A.Sc.
Length: Semesters
Years: 4 without Co-op, 5 with Co-op
Language: English

Admission Requirements:
Previous Education: Saskatchewan
Secondary level standing or equivalent
Prerequisite Courses: English A30, English
B30, Math B30, Math C30, Chemistry 30,
Physics 30
Average GPA: 70%
Range: n/a
Admission Test: n/a
Average Score: n/a
Score Report Deadline: n/a
Other Admission Criteria: International
students must submit evidence of English
proficiency

Application Information:
Deadline: Fall: Canadian and U.S.
applicants - July 1; Applicants from other
countries - April 1; Winter: Canadian and
U.S. applicants - November 1; Applicants
from other countries - August 1
Application Fee: $60 (subject to change)
Applicant/Acceptance Ratio: n/a
Size of Incoming Class: n/a
Tuition: $3,890 (subject to change) plus
compulsory fees per year (VISA student
tuition differs)
Books/Materials: $1,200 - $1,500

Comments: Faculty of Engineering's
BASc can include the Co-op Work/Study
program. Program Majors: Electronics
Systems Engineering, Industrial
Systems Engineering, Environmental
Systems Engineering, Petroleum
Systems Engineering, Software Systems

Engineering. A Masters of Applied Science
& Doctorate degree in Engineering
are also offered. For more details on all
programs visit www.uregina.ca.

Royal Military College of Canada
Faculty of Engineering
P.O. Box 17000, Station Forces
Kingston, ON   K7K 7B4
Tel: 613-541-6000, ext. 6361
Fax: 613-542-8612
Internet: www.rmc.ca

General Information:
Degree Offered: B.Eng.
Length: 1st year - General Program, 2nd
year - Specific Program (second term)
Years: 4 (total)
Language: English/French (Graduates are
bilingual)

Admission Requirements:
Previous Education: Grade 12 at a pre-
university level
Prerequisite Courses: Grade 12 English,
Algebra/Geometry, Calculus, Chemistry,
Physics
Average GPA: Although high academic
achievement is desirable (<80%), equal
weight is given to personal suitability, i.e.,
community involvement, athletics, and
leadership qualities
Range: n/a
Admission Test: Basic Officer Training
Course (passing stan- dard); Pre-
enrolment Test (passing standard)
Average Score: n/a
Score Report Deadline: n/a
Other Admission Criteria: Canadian
citizen, minimum medical standards,
preferably 16 years of age by January 1 of
year of admission

Application Information:
Deadline: Selection takes place in spring
based on medical examinations (Canadian
Forces standards), some testing, and

a personal interview which normally begins in the autumn of the final year of secondary school

Application Fee: None (applications are made at any Canadian Forces Recruiting CFNIRE)

Applicant/Acceptance Ratio: n/a

Size of Incoming Class: n/a

Tuition: Tuition is provided by the Department of National Defence and graduates are obliged to serve 5 years in the Canadian Forces

Books/Materials: Provided by the Department of National Defence

Comments: The role of the Royal Military College is to educate and train officer cadets and commissioned officers for careers of effective service in the Canadian Forces. Engineering degrees in Chemical Engineering, Civil Engineering, Electrical Engineering, Computer Engineering, Mechanical Engineering and Aerospace Engineering are available.

Ryerson Polytechnic University

Admissions/Liaison & Curriculum Advising
350 Victoria Street
Toronto, ON   M5B 2K3
Tel: 416-979-5036
E-mail: inquire@ryerson.ca
Internet: www.ryerson.ca/prospective

General Information:
Degree Offered: B.Eng., Chemical Engineering*; Civil Engineering**
Length: 8 semesters
Years: 4
Language: English

Admission Requirements:
Previous Education: O.S.S.D. with six Grade 12 U/M courses
Prerequisite Courses: Grade 12 U courses in: English, Advanced Functions and Introductory Calculus (MCB4U), Geometry and Discrete Mathematics (MGA4U),

Physics (SPH4U) and Chemistry (SCH4U)
Average GPA: 60%
Range: n/a
Admission Test: n/a
Average Score: n/a
Score Report Deadline: n/a
Other Admission Criteria: n/a

Application Information:
Deadline: March 1
Application Fee: $80 (subject to change)
Applicant/Acceptance Ratio: *5:1; **3:1
Size of Incoming Class: Chemical - 55; Civil - 84
Tuition: $4,151.33
Books/Materials: $2,500

Comments: These programs are accredited by the Canadian Engineering Accreditation Board. Program 1 of 3

Ryerson Polytechnic University

Admissions/Liaison & Curriculum Advising
350 Victoria Street
Toronto, ON   M5B 2K3
Tel: 416-979-5036
E-mail: inquire@ryerson.ca
Internet: www.ryerson.ca/prospective

General Information:
Degree Offered: B.Eng. Aerospace Engineering*; Industrial Engineering**; Mechanical Engineering***
Length: 8 semesters
Years: 4
Language: English

Admission Requirements:
Previous Education: O.S.S.D. with six Grade 12 U/M courses
Prerequisite Courses: Grade 12 U courses in: English, Advanced Functions and Introductory Calculus (MCB4U), Geometry and Discrete Mathematics (MGA4U), Physics (SPH4U) and Chemistry (SCH4U)
Average GPA: 60%
Range: n/a

Admission Test: n/a
Average Score: n/a
Score Report Deadline: n/a
Other Admission Criteria: n/a

Application Information:
Deadline: March 1
Application Fee: $80 (subject to change)
Applicant/Acceptance Ratio: *5:1; **4:1;
***5:1
Size of Incoming Class: Aero - 115;
Industrial - 50; Mechanical - 120
Tuition: $4,151.33
Books/Materials: $2,500

Comments: All programs are accredited
by the Canadian Engineering Accreditation
Board. Program 2 of 3

Ryerson Polytechnic University
Admissions/Liaison & Curriculum Advising
350 Victoria Street
Toronto, ON   M5B 2K3
Tel: 416-979-5036
E-mail: inquire@ryerson.ca
Internet: www.ryerson.ca/prospective

General Information:
Degree Offered: B.Eng., Electrical &
Computer Engineering
Length: 8 semesters
Years: 4
Language: English

Admission Requirements:
Previous Education: O.S.S.D. with six
Grade 12 U/M courses
Prerequisite Courses: Grade 12 U courses
in: English, Advanced Functions and
Introductory Calculus (MCB4U), Geometry
and Discrete Mathematics (MGA4U),
Physics (SPH4U) and Chemistry (SCH4U)
Average GPA: 60%
Range: n/a
Admission Test: n/a
Average Score: n/a
Score Report Deadline: n/a
Other Admission Criteria: n/a

Application Information:
Deadline: March 1
Application Fee: $80 (subject to change)
Applicant/Acceptance Ratio: 4:1
Size of Incoming Class: 262 (Fall 1999)
Tuition: $4,151.33
Books/Materials: $2,500

Comments: This program is accredited by
the Canadian Engineering Accreditation
Board. Program 3 of 3

University of Saskatchewan
College of Engineering
Saskatoon, SK   S7N 5A9
Tel: 306-966-5274
Fax: 306-966-5205
E-mail: Cathy.McKenna@engr.usask.ca
Internet: www.engr.usask.ca

General Information:
Degree Offered: B.E. (Agriculture and
Bioresource, Chemical, Civil, Computer,
Electrical, Geological, Mechanical and
Engineering Physics)
Length: 8 Terms
Years: 4
Language: English

Admission Requirements:
Previous Education: Saskatchewan High
School (or equivalent)
Prerequisite Courses: English A30, English
B30, Algebra 30*, Geo-Trigonometry 30*,
Chemistry 30, Physics 30, and Calculus 30
Average GPA: 78% approx.
Range: n/a
Admission Test: n/a
Average Score: n/a
Score Report Deadline: n/a
Other Admission Criteria: n/a

Application Information:
Deadline: May 1
Application Fee: $90
Applicant/Acceptance Ratio: n/a
Size of Incoming Class: 410

Tuition: $5,000 plus student fees
Books/Materials: $2,000 maximum

Comments: Enrolment is limited for entry into the College of Engineering. The minimum average is approximately 78% from Saskatchewan high schools. There are also enrolment limits for all programs in engineering in second year.

Simon Fraser University
School of Engineering Science
9851 Applied Sciences Building
8888 University Drive
Burnaby, BC   V5A 1S6
Tel: 604-291-4371
Fax: 604-291-4951
E-mail: ensc-adm@sfu.ca
Internet: www.ensc.sfu.ca

General Information:
Degree Offered: B.A.Sc.
Length: 156-157 sem. hr. of credit
Years: 4-2/3 minimum (8 semesters)
Language: English

Admission Requirements:
Previous Education: B.C. Grade 12 or equivalent
Prerequisite Courses: Physics, Mathematics, Chemistry, English
Average GPA: 75%
Range: n/a
Admission Test: n/a
Average Score: n/a
Score Report Deadline: n/a
Other Admission Criteria: Once admitted, students must maintain a cumulative GPA of 2.4 to remain in the program

Application Information:
Deadline: April 30 for Fall semester, September 30 for Spring, January 31 for Summer
Application Fee: $25
Applicant/Acceptance Ratio: 6:1
Size of Incoming Class: 160

Tuition: $151.10 per semester hour
Books/Materials: $800

Comments: Students intending to enter Simon Fraser University to study in the Engineering Science program must be eligible for general admission to the university.

University of Victoria
Faculty of Engineering
P.O. Box 3055, Stn CSC
Victoria, BC   V8W 3P6
Tel: 250-721-8678
Fax: 250-721-8676
E-mail: info@engr.uvic.ca
Internet: www.engr.uvic.ca

General Information:
Degrees Offered: B.Eng, B.SEng, B.Sc., M.A.Sc., M.Eng., Ph.D., M.A., M.Sc.
Length: 8 academic terms & 4 work terms
Years: 5-7
Language: English

Admission Requirements:
Previous Education: B.C. Grade 12 or equivalent
Prerequisite Courses: Math 12, Physics 12, and Chemistry 11 or 12
Average GPA: 3.25
Range: 2.5 - 4.0
Admission Test: None
Average Score: n/a
Score Report Deadline: n/a
Other Admission Criteria: Entry after one year of college (university transfer) or through Bridge Program (technology program graduates) is also possible

Application Information:
Deadline: April 30
Application Fee: $60-100
Applicant/Acceptance Ratio: 4:1
Size of Incoming Class: 220
Tuition: $4,500 - $4,900 per academic year
Books/Materials: $300 - $600 per term

Comments: B.Eng. Programs in Computer, Electrical, Mechanical Engineering and Bachelor of Software Engineering. B.Sc. programs in Computer Science. Masters and Ph.D. programs offered by all departments. All academic and terms are 4 months in length. Students receive regular salaries while on co-op terms.

University of Waterloo
Associate Director of Admissions
Undergraduate Office
Faculty of Engineering
200 University Avenue West
Waterloo, ON   N2L 3G1
Tel: 519-888-4894
E-mail: admissions@mail.eng.uwaterloo.ca
Internet: www.eng.uwaterloo.ca

General Information:
Degree Offered: B.A.Sc.
Length: 4-month terms
Years: 4-2/3 including 6 co-op work terms
Language: English

Admission Requirements:
Previous Education: Secondary School Diploma, including five Grade 12 U courses and one Grade 12 U or M course
Prerequisite Courses: Advanced Functions and Introductory Calculus; Chemistry; English (ENG4U); Geometry and Discrete Mathematics; Physica; one other U or M course
Average GPA: n/a
Range: Low to mid 80's
Admission Test: Not required
Average Score: n/a
Score Report Deadline: n/a
Other Admission Criteria: Admission Information Form, letter of reference

Application Information:
Deadline: March 1: applications due April 1: all supporting documents due at the University of Waterloo
Application Fee: $85 (Ontario University Application Centre (OUAC) fee)

Applicant/Acceptance Ratio: Varies
Size of Incoming Class: 979 (all applicable areas of Engineering)
Tuition: $3,916
Books/Materials: $450 approx.

University of Western Ontario
Faculty of Engineering
Spencer Engineering Building
London, ON   N6A 5B9
Tel: 519-661-2128
E-mail: contactWE@eng.uwo.ca
Internet: www.eng.uwo.ca

General Information:
Degree Offered: M.E.Sc.
Length: 8 semesters
Years: 4
Language: English

Admission Requirements:
Previous Education: Honours Bachelor's degree in Engineering from an accredited university
Prerequisite Courses: n/a
Average GPA: n/a
Range: 70% or B minimum
Admission Test: None
Average Score: n/a
Score Report Deadline: n/a
Other Admission Criteria: n/a
Application Information:
Deadline: July 2 of the year prior
Application Fee: $75
Applicant/Acceptance Ratio: OAC info only: applicants: 1,023; offers: 957; acceptances: 406
Size of Incoming Class: 350
Tuition: $4,647.36
Books/Materials: $800 approx.

University of Windsor
Faculty of Engineering
401 Sunset Avenue
Windsor, ON   N9B 3P4
Tel: 519-253-3000, ext. 2566
http://cronus.uwindsor.ca/engineering

General Information:
Degree Offered: B.A.Sc.
Length: Semesters & co-op work terms
Years: 4
Language: English

Admission Requirements:
Previous Education: Secondary School Diploma
Prerequisite Courses: New Grade 12 U level: English, Advanced Functions, Chemistry, Physics. Calculus and Vectors is strongly recommended.
Average GPA: n/a
Range: 76%
Admission Test: Not required
Average Score: n/a
Score Report Deadline: n/a
Other Admission Criteria: n/a

Application Information:
Deadline: March 1 (from outside North America); August 1 (from within North America) for fall term; December 1 (from within North America) for winter term
Application Fee: $105
Applicant/Acceptance Ratio: 3:1
Size of Incoming Class: 350
Tuition: $5,772.00
Books/Materials: $500-$1,000/semester

Comments: Civil Engineering, Environmental Engineering, Electrical Engineering, Industrial Engineering, Mechanical Engineering, Mechanical Engineering (Materials option) and Mechanical Engineering (Automotive option)

Mechanical Engineering (Environmental option)

HEALTH SERVICES ADMINISTRATION

The following fact sheets outline general information including academic requirements and application procedures for Health Services Administration Schools in Canada. The data have been compiled in a concise format to assist students interested in these professional schools. Information was obtained from updates completed by each school, or in some cases from the school's Internet website.

Health Services Administration Schools in Canada

University of Alberta
University of British Columbia
Dalhousie University

University of Ottawa
University of Toronto

Comments

1. These fact sheets act as a guide only. Students are advised to refer to the individual calendars or to write to the schools for more detailed information.

2. Application deadlines vary. Dates indicated refer to fall admission unless otherwise noted.

3. Tuition fees represent annual costs unless otherwise noted.

4. All of the schools listed above may not be represented.

Dalhousie University

School of Administration
5599 Fenwick Street
Halifax, NS   B3H 1R2
Tel: 902-494-7097
Fax: 902-494-6849
E-mail: health.services.administration@dal.ca
Internet: www.dal.ca/shsa

General Information:
Degree Offered: M.H.A.
Length: Semesters
Years: 2
Language: English

Admission Requirements:
Previous Education: Bachelor's degree in
any subject area
Prerequisite Courses: None
Average GPA: B+
Range: n/a
Admission Test: GMAT
Average Score: 550
Score Report Deadline: n/a
Other Admission Criteria: 2 letters of
academic reference, resume, statement
of career interests, TOEFL for foreign
applicants

Application Information:
Deadline: April 1 for automatic scholarship
consideration; June 1 is final deadline
Application Fee: $75
Applicant/Acceptance Ratio: n/a
Size of Incoming Class: 20 - 25
Tuition: $7,000 approx.
Books/Materials: $500 - $800 approx. per
2 years

Comments: A one-year diploma program
in Health Administration is also offered.
Deadline date is June 1. A one-year
Diploma in Emergency Health Services
Management is also available. Both
diploma programs are conducted through
the Internet via BLS. Deadlines are: for
September admission is July 1; for January
admission is November 15; and for May
admission is March 15. Other graduate
programs: MN/MHA and LLB/MHA.

University of Ottawa

M.H.A. Program
Telfer School of Management
55 Laurier Avenue East
Ottawa, ON   K1N 6N5
Tel: 613-562-5884
Fax: 613-562-5164
E-mail: mha@telfer.uottawa.ca
Internet: www.mha.uottawa.ca

General Information:
Degree Offered: M.H.A.
Length: 16 months (full-time)
Years: 16 months (full-time) to 6 years
(part-time)
Language: English/French

Admission Requirements:
Previous Education: Baccalaureate degree
Prerequisite Courses: n/a
Average GPA: 70% minimum
Range: n/a
Admission Test: GMAT
Average Score: 50th percentile
Score Report Deadline: April 1
Other Admission Criteria: 2 year full-time
work experience

Application Information:
Deadline: April 1
Application Fee: $75
Applicant/Acceptance Ratio: 3:1
Size of Incoming Class: 20 full-time, 5
part-time
Tuition: $16,650
Books/Materials: $1,500

INDUSTRIAL RELATIONS

The following fact sheets outline general information including academic requirements and application procedures for Industrial Relations Schools in Canada. The data have been compiled in a concise format to assist students interested in these professional schools. Information was obtained from updates completed by each school, or in some cases from the school's Internet website.

Industrial Relations Schools in Canada

Queen's University*
University of Toronto

Comments

1. These fact sheets act as a guide only. Students are advised to refer to the individual calendars or to write to the schools for more detailed information.

2. Application deadlines vary. Dates indicated refer to fall admission unless otherwise noted.

3. Tuition fees represent annual costs unless otherwise noted.

4. All of the schools listed above may not be represented.

* This university has not updated its information. Please contact the university directly.

Queen's University

School of Industrial Relations
Policy Study Building
138 Union Street
Kingston, ON   K7L 3N6
Tel: 613-533-2972
Fax: 613-533-2560
E-mail: irschool@post.queensu.ca
Internet: http://qsilver.queensu.ca/irl

General Information:
Degree Offered: M.I.R.
Length: 3 semesters
Years: 1 (12 months)
Language: English

Admission Requirements:
Previous Education: 4-year bachelor's degree
Prerequisite Courses: Full credit in Micro and Macro Economics and Statistics at the university level
Average GPA: n/a
Range: 75% minimum over 4 years of study
Admission Test: None
Average Score: n/a
Score Report Deadline: n/a
Other Admission Criteria: Transcripts, two recommendations (typically from professors under whom the applicant has studied), background information sheet, resume

Application Information:
Deadline: March 1
Application Fee: $60
Applicant/Acceptance Ratio: 8:1
Size of Incoming Class: 35
Tuition: $1,669.67 per term (3 semesters)
Books/Materials: $900

Comments: The School encourages applications from mature students with work experience in human resources, labour relations and other related fields.

University of Toronto

Admissions
Centre for Industrial Relations
121 St. George Street
Toronto, ON   M5S 2E8
Tel: 416-978-2927
Fax: 416-978-5696
E-mail: cir.info@utoronto.ca
Internet: www.chass.utoronto.ca/cir

General Information:
Degree Offered: MIRHR
Length: Sessional
Years: 12 month advanced standing MIRHR option or 2-year MIRHR program
Language: English

Admission Requirements:
Previous Education: 4-year Bachelor's degree or equivalent
Prerequisite Courses: None; however, advanced standing option based on related academic degree
Average GPA: A-
Range: B+ (77%) standing, minimum, in each of the final two years of bachelor's degree
Admission Test: GRE or GMAT required from applicants who completed their degrees outside of Canada. English language proficiency required for students where english is not their primary language.
Average Score: n/a
Score Report Deadline: April 15
Other Admission Criteria: Two letters of reference, preferably academic

Application Information:
Deadline: April 15
Application Fee: $100 (CDN)
Applicant/Acceptance Ratio: 4:1
Size of Incoming Class: 25
Tuition: $7,975 full-time (under review)
Books/Materials: $1,500 estimated

Comments: Courses are offered in Human Resources Management, Labour Management Relations, Collective Bargaining and Dispute Resolution, Organization Development Change, Labour Market and Social Policy. A Ph.D. program is also available.

JOURNALISM

The following fact sheets outline general information including academic requirements and application procedures for Journalism Schools in Canada. The data have been compiled in a concise format to assist students interested in these professional schools. Information was obtained from updates completed by each school, or in some cases from the school's Internet website.

Journalism Schools in Canada

Carleton University
Concordia University
University of King's College
Université Laval

University of Regina*
Ryerson Polytechnic University*
University of Western Ontario*

Comments

1. These fact sheets act as a guide only. Students are advised to refer to the individual calendars or to write to the schools for more detailed information.

2. Application deadlines vary. Dates indicated refer to fall admission unless otherwise noted.

3. Tuition fees represent annual costs unless otherwise noted.

4. All of the schools listed above may not be represented.

* This university has not updated its information. Please contact the university directly.

Carleton University

Supervisor of Graduate Studies
School of Journalism and Communication
Ottawa, ON K1S 5B6
Tel: 613-520-7404
Fax: 613-520-6690
E-mail: journalism@carleton.ca
Internet: www.carleton.ca/sjc

General Information:
Degree Offered: M.J.
Length: Semesters
Years: 1* or 2**
Language: English

Admission Requirements:
Previous Education: For admission
to first year, an upper - second class
honours in an undergraduate degree; for
admission to second year, a Bachelor of
Journalism (Honours) or undergraduate
degree in another field with at least 5
years professional journalism experience is
required
Prerequisite Courses: None
Average GPA: n/a
Range: B+ or 75 - 78% minimum in core
courses, B overall
Admission Test: n/a
Average Score: n/a
Score Report Deadline: n/a
Other Admission Criteria: Previous
journalistic experience, proven interest in
journalism, and solid references

Application Information:
Deadline: March 1
Application Fee: $75
Applicant/Acceptance Ratio: *8:1; **4:1
Size of Incoming Class: *20; **6-10
Tuition: $4,905.71
Books/Materials: $1,000

Comments: Second year is also open
in some cases to students with no prior
degree but with a long and distinguished
career in journalism.

Concordia University

Mike Gasher, Ph.D.
Director
Journalism Department
7141 Sherbrooke West
Montreal, QC H4B 1R6
Tel: 514-848-2424 ext. 2465
Fax: 514-848-2473
E-mail: gashmj@alcor.concordia.ca
Internet: www.concordia.ca

General Information:
Degree Offered: Postgraduate diploma
Length: 3 semesters
Years: 1
Language: English

Admission Requirements:
Previous Education: Undergraduate
degree in field other than Journalism
Prerequisite Courses: None
Average GPA: 3.18 approx.
Range: B
Admission Test: n/a
Average Score: n/a
Score Report Deadline: n/a
Other Admission Criteria: Application
forms, official transcript, academic
references, certified Birth Certificate,
interview (working knowledge of French
desirable, but not essential)

Application Information:
Deadline: December 15 (International
students), January 15 (Canadian students),
cleasses begin early June
Application Fee: $50
Applicant/Acceptance Ratio: 4:1
Size of Incoming Class: 24
Tuition: $1,800 (Quebec residents);
$4,800 (non-Quebec residents); $10,750
(international students)
Books/Materials: $400

Comments: Programs offered:
Broadcasting (radio and tv) Print, Online.
Applicants must submit a letter of 500
words describing their background,

interests, and aspirations in journalism. Transcripts should also be included with their application. Once received, students will be notified of the English test and interview dates. Director: Prof. Mike Gasher. Program 1 of 2

Concordia University
Journalism Department
7141 Sherbrooke West
Montreal, QC   H4B 1R6
Tel: 514-848-2424, ext. 2465
Fax: 514-848-2473
E-mail: admreg@alcor.concordia.ca
Internet: https://welcome.concordia.ca/
concordia/admiss/index.jsp

General Information:
Degree Offered: B.A.
Length: Semesters
Years: 3
Language: English

Admission Requirements:
Previous Education: OSSD with six Grade 12 U or M courses
Prerequisite Courses: None
Average GPA: 70%
Range: B minimum
Admission Test: English proficiency test administered by department; current events quiz
Average Score: n/a
Score Report Deadline: March 1
Other Admission Criteria: Typewritten letter of intent (250-300 words) describing applicant's background, interests, goals in journalism, and how you feel a journalism program will help you fulfill these goals.

Application Information:
Deadline: March 1
Application Fee: $50
Applicant/Acceptance Ratio: 5:1
Size of Incoming Class: 100 approx.
Tuition: $1,668.30 (residents of Quebec) plus $812-$931 student fee; $4,173.30

(residents of all other provinces) plus $812-$931 student fee
Books/Materials: $1,552 approx.

Comments: Programs offered: Major in Journalism, Specialization in Journalism, Specialization in Communication and Journalism. Students interested in the joint specialization must be accepted by both the Journalism and Communication Studies Departments. Program 2 of 2

University of King's College
School of Journalism
Halifax, NS   B3H 2A1
Tel: 902-422-1271
Fax: 902-423-3357
E-mail: tara.moorehead@ukings.ns.ca
Internet: www.ukings.ca

General Information:
Degree Offered: B.J.
Length: 2 semesters
Years: 1
Language: English

Admission Requirements:
Previous Education: Bachelor's Degree
Prerequisite Courses: None
Average GPA: 80 approx.
Range: B or 70 - 75% minimum
Admission Test: Not required
Average Score: n/a
Score Report Deadline: n/a
Other Admission Criteria: Some knowledge of French, skills in autobiographical writing, and clippings/audio/video

Application Information:
Deadline: March 1
Application Fee: $70
Applicant/Acceptance Ratio: 4:1
Size of Incoming Class: 40
Tuition: $8,991
Books/Materials: $300

Comments: Program 1 of 2

University of King's College

School of Journalism
Halifax, NS   B3H 2A1
Tel: 902-422-1271
Fax: 902-423-3357
E-mail: tara.moorehead@ukings.ns.ca
Internet: www.ukings.ca

General Information:
Degree Offered: B.J. (Honours)
Length: 8 semesters
Years: 4
Language: English

Admission Requirements:
Previous Education: Five senior level university preparatory classes
Prerequisite Courses: English
Average GPA: n/a
Range: 70% especially in English, no single mark below 60
Admission Test: Not required
Average Score: n/a
Score Report Deadline: n/a
Other Admission Criteria: Some knowledge of French, skills in autobiographical writing, and clippings

Application Information:
Deadline: March 1
Application Fee: $45
Applicant/Acceptance Ratio: 4:1
Size of Incoming Class: 40
Tuition: $7,246 - $7,975
Books/Materials: $1,000

Comments: Program 2 of 2

University of Regina

School of Journalism
Regina, SK   S4S 0A2
Tel: 306-585-4420
Fax: 306-585-4867
E-mail: journalism@uregina.ca
Internet: www.uregina.ca/journal

General Information:
Degree Offered: B.A.; B. Journalism
Length: 4 semesters
Years: 2
Language: English

Admission Requirements:
Previous Education: Two years in a pre-journalism program in the Faculty of Arts or equivalent credit or an undergraduate degree
Prerequisite Courses: In the pre-journalism stage students must complete at least 60 credit hours (2 full years) including: (a) 2 courses in English at the 100 level; (b) LGC 100 or a unversity-level course in Math; (c) One course in a language other than English beyond "Language 30" or equivalent; (d) One course in a natural science involving laboratory work; (e) One course from the Faculty of Fine Arts; (f) One course in humanitites in addition to those used to satisfy the English, language, and logic requirements; (g) 3 of the following 4 courses: (1) a history course emphasizing Canadian history, (2) a course in political science emphasizing Canadian politics and government, (3) an economics course at the 100 level, (4) SOSC 100 or equivalent course dealing with the media in the social science context; (h) Electives - not more than 14 introductory courses may be used in this program.
Average GPA: n/a
Range: 70% minimum
Admission Test: English Proficiency Test, short essay, interview, selection
Average Score: Pass/Fail
Score Report Deadline: n/a
Other Admission Criteria: Proficiency in English must be well above average
Application Information:
Deadline: January 31
Application Fee: $50
Applicant/Acceptance Ratio: 4:1
Size of Incoming Class: 26

Tuition: $2,000 per semester plus material and student union fees
Books/Materials: $400

Comments: A Bachelor of Journalism is also available for students with a previous degree. See calendar for details. Journalism degrees are also available through affiliated colleges - Campion and First Nations University of Canada. The first 2 years of the program is offered by the Faculty of Arts. Students must therefore register in Arts but designate their program as pre-journalism. Students who have completed pre-journalism will apply for admission to the professional program. Students who are enrolled in an Arts program at another university and wish to transfer to the University of Regina should have their transcripts and a letter of intent sent to the Registrar for evaluation. Students who are planning on taking their Arts classes at a university other than the University of Regina should contact Shelley Kessel to ensure that the classes are equivalent.

Ryerson Polytechnic University
Admissions/Liaison/Curriculum Advising
350 Victoria Street
Toronto, ON   M5B 2K3
Tel: 416-979-5036
E-mail: inquire@ryerson.ca
Internet: www.ryerson.ca/prospective

General Information:
Degree Offered: B.A.A. (Journalism)
Length: n/a
Years: 2
Language: English

Admission Requirements:
Previous Education: Bachelor's degree from an accredited English-language university
Prerequisite Courses: Senior level English course
Average GPA: n/a

Range: n/a
Admission Test: n/a
Average Score: n/a
Score Report Deadline: n/a
Other Admission Criteria: A questionnaire; brief biographical sketch; and portfolio of any published journalistic work, maximum 6 items

Application Information:
Deadline: March 1
Application Fee: $80
Applicant/Acceptance Ratio: 5:1
Size of Incoming Class: 60
Tuition: $3,338.04
Books/Materials: $1,000 - $1,300

Comments: *Application Fee: An additional $40 evaluation fee must be submitted directly to Ryerson for all applicants who are not current Ontario high school students. Program 1of 2

Ryerson Polytechnic University
Admissions/Liaison/Curriculum Advising
350 Victoria Street
Toronto, ON   M5B 2K3
Tel: 416-979-5036
E-mail: inquire@ryerson.ca
Internet: www.ryerson.ca/prospective

General Information:
Degree Offered: B.A.A. (Journalism)
Length: 8 semesters
Years: 4
Language: English

Admission Requirements:
Previous Education: O.S.S.D. with six Grade 12 U/M credits
Prerequisite Courses: Grade 12 U English (ENG4U)
Average GPA: 70%
Range: n/a
Admission Test: n/a
Average Score: n/a
Score Report Deadline: n/a
Other Admission Criteria: Applicants are

required to answer a questionnaire on their journalism and life experience and submit a 300-word essay on a topic to be provided. A portfolio of published work is encouraged. Instructions will be sent by mail by the Office of Undergraduate Admissions as part of the admissions process. These will be used in the selection process. A minimum keyboarding skill of 30 words per minute is also required.

Application Information:
Deadline: March 1
Application Fee: $80 subject to change
Applicant/Acceptance Ratio: 12:1
Size of Incoming Class: 120
Tuition: $3,338.04
Books/Materials: $1,200

Comments: Program 2 of 2

University of Western Ontario
Faculty of Information and Media Studies
North Campus Building
London, ON   N6A 5B7
Tel: 519-661-3542
Fax: 519-661-3506
E-mail: journalism@uwo.ca
Internet: www.fims.uwo.ca

General Information:
Degree Offered: M.A. (Journalism)
Length: 3 semesters
Years: 1
Language: English

Admission Requirements:
Previous Education: An Honours Bachelor's degree or equivalent
Prerequisite Courses: None
Average GPA: B++ or 79% approx.
Range: B minimum in last 2 years of study
Admission Test: Not required
Average Score: n/a
Score Report Deadline: n/a
Other Admission Criteria: Letters of reference, clippings, and/or tapes, 1,000

word autobiographical sketch, transcripts, and résumé

Application Information:
Deadline: January 15
Application Fee: $50
Applicant/Acceptance Ratio: 6:1
Size of Incoming Class: 45
Tuition: $2,563.91 per semester as of May 2004
Books/Materials: $500*

Comments: *Four-week internship is a mandatory part of curriculum; budget for extra living expenses for this internship.

LAW

The following fact sheets outline general information including academic requirements and application procedures for Law Schools in Canada. The data have been compiled in a concise format to assist students interested in these professional schools. Information was obtained from updates completed by each school, or in some cases from the school's Internet website.

Please refer to the section on "Admissions Tests" for information on the Law School Admission Test (LSAT) which is required for most law schools.

Law Schools in Canada

University of Alberta
University of British Columbia
University of Calgary*
Dalhousie University
Université Laval
University of Manitoba
McGill University
Université de Moncton
Université de Montréal*
University of New Brunswick*

University of Ottawa
Queen's University*
University of Saskatchewan*
Université de Sherbrooke
University of Toronto
University of Victoria
University of Western Ontario
University of Windsor
York University

Comments

1. These fact sheets act as a guide only. Students are advised to refer to the individual calendars or to write to the schools for more detailed information.

2. Application deadlines vary. Dates indicated refer to fall admission unless otherwise noted.

3. Tuition fees represent annual costs unless otherwise noted.

4. All of the schools listed above may not be represented.

This university has not updated its information. Please contact the university directly.

University of Alberta
Admissions Secretary
Faculty of Law
Edmonton, AB   T6G 2H5
Tel: 780-492-3067

General Information:
Degree Offered: LL.B.
Length: Terms
Years: 3 (part-time program - 6)
Language: English

Admission Requirements:
Previous Education: University degree or the equivalent of 2 years of undergraduate work acceptable to the University of Alberta*
Prerequisite Courses: Not required
Average GPA: 3.7/ 4.0 or A- or 80 - 84%
Range: 7.8 - 8.8 or 3.4 - 4.2**
Admission Test: LSAT
Average Score: 159-161 (Mature, Native, 2-year applicants not included)
Score Report Deadline: December test date
Other Admission Criteria: Two official copies of all post-secondary academic transcripts, Faculty of Law Supplement Form.

Application Information:
Deadline: November 1
Application Fee: $100
Applicant/Acceptance Ratio: 8:1
Size of Incoming Class: 175
Tuition: $9,772
Books/Materials: $1,500

Comments: *All applicants must have a minimum of 2 full years (60 credit hours) toward a degree recognized by the University of Alberta. Applicants applying with only the minimum of 2 years must have the equivalent of a 3.4 gpa and minimum LSAT score in the 90 percentile. All university requirements must be met by February 1 of the year for which admission is being sought.

** For degreed applicants, no minimum GPA required. For 2-year, 3.7 required. Mature and Native applicants need not necessarily have the minimum GPA of 3.7 and LSAT of 90% as regular non-degreed applicants but they must have the minimum of 60 credit hours toward a degree and they must write the LSAT. Aboriginal & Mature Applicants normally must have a minimum of two years leading towards any degree or equivalent acceptable to a university in Alberta, completed prior to or in the winter session preceding the September in which admission is sought (i.e. by April 30th). Consideration may be given to Applicants with a minimum of one year leading to a degree or equivalent, if they exhibit evidence of past achievements in non-academic areas indicative of an ability to succeed in law school.

Mature and Aboriginal applicants must also submit the following: resume, personal statement (2 pages), and two letters of reference. Aboriginal applicants must submit proof of Aboriginal ancestry.

University of British Columbia
Faculty of Law
1822 East Mall
Vancouver, BC   V6T 1Z1
Tel: 604-822-6303
Fax: 604-822-8108
E-mail: admissions@law.ubc.ca
Internet: www.law.ubc.ca/prospective/llb

General Information:
Degree Offered: LL.B.
Length: Semesters
Years: 3
Language: English

Admission Requirements:
Previous Education: Minimum of 3 full years (90 credit hours) at a recognized university, with a minimum overall

standing of 65%. If a student is currently in third year, an offer would be conditional upon successful completion with the same overall academic average
Prerequisite Courses: n/a
Average GPA: 3.8
Range: 82%
Admission Test: LSAT
Average Score: 164
Score Report Deadline: February
Other Admission Criteria: Official transcripts, personal statement letter

Application Information:
Deadline: February 1
Application Fee: $80
Applicant/Acceptance Ratio: 10:1
Size of Incoming Class: 180
Tuition: $9,550.87 (first year)
Books/Materials: $1,400 - $1,600

University of Calgary
Admissions Office, Faculty of Law
Murray Fraser Hall, Room 4380A, 2500
University Drive N.W.
Calgary, AB   T2N 1N4
Tel: 403-220-7222
E-mail: law@ucalgary.ca
Internet: www.law.ucalgary.ca

General Information:
Degree Offered: LL.B.; LL.B./MBA; LL.B./MEDes
Length: Semesters
Years: 3
Language: English

Admission Requirements:
Previous Education: Successful completion of 2 years or the equivalent of 2 years of a full program of studies leading to a degree at a university in Alberta or its equivalent. The Faculty advises however that virtually all candidates hold an undergraduate degree
Prerequisite Courses: Not required
Average GPA: 3.5 or B+/A-

Range: n/a
Admission Test: LSAT
Average Score: 69th percentile
Score Report Deadline: December test
Other Admission Criteria: Evidence of analytical ability, maturity and motivation, work experience and community involvement; official copies of all university transcripts; 3 letters of reference (2 of these should be academic)

Application Information:
Deadline: February 1
Application Fee: $65
Applicant/Acceptance Ratio: 11:1
Size of Incoming Class: 75
Tuition: $4,750 per year
Books/Materials: $2,000

Comments: We welcome applications from Native students. Other law degrees include a Master of Laws degree focusing on Natural Resources Law, and joint law programs offered with a Master's of Business Administration (LLB/MBA), and a Master's of Environmental Design (LLB/MEDes)

Dalhousie University
6061 University Avenue
Halifax, NS   B3H 4H9
Tel: 902-494-3495
Fax: 902-494-1316
E-mail: law.admissions@dal.ca
Internet: www.dal.ca/law

General Information:
Degree Offered: LL.B.
Length: September - May
Years: 3
Language: English

Admission Requirements:
Previous Education: B.A., B.Comm., B.Sc., or equivalent degree from Dalhousie University or from another degree-granting college or university recognized by the Senate

Prerequisite Courses: Not required
Average GPA: 3.7 or A approx.
Range: 3 - 4.3
Admission Test: LSAT
Average Score: 78th percentile
Score Report Deadline: February writing
Other Admission Criteria: Academic references; supporting documents; interview may be requested

Application Information:
Deadline: November 30 (early deadline) and February 28
Application Fee: $70
Applicant/Acceptance Ratio: 9:1
Size of Incoming Class: 157
Tuition: $12,475
Books/Materials: $1,200

Comments: Degrees also offered: LL.B./Master of Public Administration; LL.B./Master of Library and Information Sciences; LL.B./Master of Business Administration; LL.B./Master of Health Services Administration; and a Master of Laws.

Université Laval
Faculté de droit
Pavillon Charles-De Koninck
1030, av. Des Sciences-Humaines
Québec, QC   G1V 0A6
Tel: 418-656-3036
E-mail: fd@fd.ulaval.ca
Internet: www.ulaval.ca/fd

General Information:
Degree Offered: LL.B. (Civil Law)
Length: Semesters
Years: 3
Language: français

Admission Requirements:
Previous Education: Québec DEC or equivalent
Prerequisite Courses: Not required
Average GPA: n/a
Range: n/a

Admission Test: Not required
Average Score: n/a
Score Report Deadline: n/a
Other Admission Criteria: Official copies of the Québec Diplôme d'études collégiales (DEC) and/or all university academic transcripts

Application Information:
Deadline: March 1 for Fall semester November 1 for Winter semester
Application Fee: $30
Applicant/Acceptance Ratio: 2:1
Size of Incoming Class: 330 (265 admitted in September and 65 in January)
Tuition: $1,820
Books/Materials: $8.25 du crédit

Comments: Master of Law and Doctorate of Law programs are also offered.

University of Manitoba
Marie Jivan
Student Services Centre
Admissions & Financial Aid
Faculty of Law, Robson Hall
Winnipeg, MB   R3T 2N2
Tel: 204-480-1485
Fax: 204-474-7580
E-mail: marie_jivan@umanitoba.ca
Internet: www.umanitoba.ca/law

General Information:
Degree Offered: LL.B.
Length: September - April
Years: 3
Language: English

Admission Requirements:
Previous Education: Two years of university or 60 credit hours of courses leading to a degree at the University of Manitoba or an acceptable equivalent
Prerequisite Courses: None
Average GPA: 3.9
Range: 3.50 - 4.40
Admission Test: LSAT

Average Score: 160
Score Report Deadline: March of year of application
Other Admission Criteria: Supplementary information, other than grades and LSAT scores, is used only in the assessment of individual consideration applicants

Application Information:
Deadline: November 1
Application Fee: $90
Applicant/Acceptance Ratio: 9:1
Size of Incoming Class: 101
Tuition: $8,600
Books/Materials: $2,500

Comments: The Applicant Information Bulletin is the official statement on requirements. Request most recent edition for specific information such as deadline for LSAT scores. Special admission processes for Aboriginal and Individual Consideration applicants. For Individual Consideration category, contact Student Services.

McGill University
Admissions Officer
Faculty of Law
3644 Peel Street, Room 418
Montreal, QC   H3A 1W9
Tel: 514-398-6602
Fax: 514-398-8453
E-mail: undergradadmissions.law@mcgill.ca
Internet: www.law.mcgill.ca

General Information:
Degree Offered: Integrated B.C.L./LL.B. - all students do both degrees
Length: 105 Credits
Years: 3 to 4 years
Language: English and French

Admission Requirements:
Previous Education: Quebec College of General and Vocational Education (CEGEP); further studies at the undergraduate level may be required for admission to certain bars of the Common Law provinces; 2 years of undergraduate study in a recognized university program
Prerequisite Courses: Not required
Average GPA: Average Cote R 34.185 CEGEP students; 83% or A- or 3.7 university students
Range: Cote R 31.260-37.429 CEGEP students and 72%-91% university students
Admission Test: Law School Admission Test (LSAT – not mandatory, but will be considered if a candidate has taken it or will be taking it)
Average Score: 160 (81.3 percentile)
Score Report Deadline: As early as possible (last LSAT accepted is the February one, however, candidates are strongly encouraged to do so by December of the year prior to the year for which they seek admission)
Other Admission Criteria: Two letters of reference, official copies of all university academic transcripts, personal statement, resume, and substantial comprehension and reading ability in French and English

Application Information:
Deadline: November 1; March 1 for CEGEP students currently completing their DEC. The Admissions Committee starts reviewing files November 1, and reviews all files completed by November 1.
Application Fee: $60 for CEGEP candidates and $80 for all others
Applicant/Acceptance Ratio: 9:1
Size of Incoming Class: 170
Tuition: $3,036.22 for residents of Quebec; $5,951.42 for residents of all other Canadian provinces; and $13,082.02 for International candidates
Books/Materials: n/a

Université de Moncton
Vice-doyen Robert L. LeBlanc
Faculté de droit
Moncton, NB E1A 3E9
Tel: 506-858-4564
Fax: 506-858-4534
E-mail: edr@umoncton.ca
Internet: www.umoncton.ca/Droit/

General Information:
Degree Offered: LL.B., LL.M.
Length: Semesters
Years: 3 (LL.B.); 1-3 (LL.M.)
Language: français
Admission Requirements:
Previous Education: Titulaire d'un diplôme universitaire ou personne ne restant qu'une année d'études universitaire et ayant maintenu une moyenne cumulative exceptionnelle (3,5 sure 4,3)
Prerequisite Courses: Pas exigé
Average GPA: 3.3/4.3 or B or 74%
Range: 2.8 - 4.0
Admission Test: Pas exigé
Average Score: n/a
Score Report Deadline: n/a
Other Admission Criteria: Bonne connaissance de l'anglais et du français. Un test de français peut être exigé

Application Information:
Deadline: March 31
Application Fee: $39
Applicant/Acceptance Ratio: 2.5:1
Size of Incoming Class: 45
Tuition: $5,136
Books/Materials: n/a

Comments: Joint Civil and Common law degrees are offered as well as an LL.B./Master of Business Administration, LL.B./Master of Administration Publique. Soon, LL.B./Master of Environmental Studies

Université de Montréal
Vice-Doyen au Développement Académique
Faculté de droit
C.P. 6128, succursale Centre-ville
Montréal, QC H3C 3J7
Tel: 514-343-2428
E-mail: info1ercycle@droit.umontreal.ca
Internet: www.droit.umontreal.ca/faculte/

General Information:
Degree Offered: LL.B.
Length: Trimesters
Years: 3
Language: français

Admission Requirements:
Previous Education: DEC or equivalent
Prerequisite Courses: Not required
Average GPA: 78%
Range: 60%+
Admission Test: Not required
Average Score: n/a
Score Report Deadline: n/a
Other Admission Criteria: Sufficient knowledge of the French language

Application Information:
Deadline: March 1
Application Fee: $30
Applicant/Acceptance Ratio: 5:1
Size of Incoming Class: 335
Tuition: $2,200 yearly
Books/Materials: $750 minimum yearly

Comments: Admission is determined by academic record

University of New Brunswick
Law Admissions Office, Faculty of Law
Ludlow Hall
P.O. Box 44271
Fredericton, NB E3B 6C2
Tel: 506-453-4693
Fax: 506-458-7722
E-mail: lawadmit@unb.ca
Internet: www.law.unb.ca

General Information:
Degree Offered: LL.B.
Length: Semesters
Years: 3
Language: English

Admission Requirements:
Previous Education: Must have completed at least 3 years university or equivalent at a recognized university
Prerequisite Courses: Not required
Average GPA: 3.6/4.3 or A-
Range: 3.0 - 4.3
Admission Test: LSAT; 40% of Admissions Index
Average Score: 158/180
Score Report Deadline: February
Other Admission Criteria: Official copies of all university academic transcripts. Exceptions to general admissions policies exist for Aboriginals and discretionary category applicants

Application Information:
Deadline: March 1 - Applicants strongly urged to apply early
Application Fee: $50
Applicant/Acceptance Ratio: 9:1
Size of Incoming Class: 80
Tuition: $6,972
Books/Materials: $1,500

Comments: A joint LLB/MBA degree is also offered over a 4 year period.

University of Ottawa
Faculty of Law
Fauteux Hall
57 Louis Pasteur
Ottawa, ON K1N 6N5
Tel: 613-562-5800, ext. 3270
(common law) 613-562-5703

General Information:
Degree Offered: LL.B., L.L.L.
Length: 6 semesters
Years: 3
Language: French and English (L.L.L. French only)

Admission Requirements:
Previous Education: A minimum of 3 years of university studies; priority is given to those applicants who have completed 4 years of studies
Prerequisite Courses: None
Average GPA: 80%
Range: n/a
Admission Test: LSAT (English Common Law only)
Average Score: No set minimum; highest LSAT score is used
Score Report Deadline: December
Other Admission Criteria: In addition to academic performance, the Admissions Committee may take into consideration achievements in extracurricular activities, personal or professional experiences, racial, linguistic or cultural factors and challenges such as a physical or learning disability or adverse economic circumstances.

Application Information:
Deadline: November 1 (Common Law English); March 1 (Civil Law); February 1 (Common Law French)
Application Fee: $85 (Civil Law); $175 (+ $75 for each law school selection) (Common Law)
Applicant/Acceptance Ratio: 21:1 English and 4:1 French
Size of Incoming Class: 210 English and 60 French
Tuition: $10,483.38 (Common Law); $4,076 (Civil Law)
Books/Materials: $1,100

Comments: The University of Ottawa also offers: Licence en Droit Civil – 3-year program; Licence en Droit Civil LL.B./L.L.L. – one-year program after the LL.B. degree; a joint MBA/LL.B. – 4-year program; a joint LL.B./M.A. in International Affairs with Carleton University – 4-year program; LL.B./J.D. – 4-year program with Michigan State University College of Law and American University Washington

College of Law in Washington, DC; and Programme de driot Canadien (PDC) – 3-year program offered primarily in French. *Apply directly to University of Ottawa for Civil Law; to apply to Common Law, request application material from the Ontario Law School Application Service.

Queen's University
Ms. Jane E. Emrich
Director of Admissions
Faculty of Law
Kingston, ON   K7L 3N6
Tel: 613-533-2220
E-mail: llb@post.queensu.ca
Internet: http://qsilver.queensu.ca/law

General Information:
Degree Offered: LL.B.
Length: Semesters
Years: 3
Language: English

Admission Requirements:
Previous Education: See "Comments"
Prerequisite Courses: Not required
Average GPA: 77% or B+
Range: n/a
Admission Test: LSAT
Average Score: 78th percentile
Score Report Deadline: January
Other Admission Criteria: A substantial number of places are committed to applicants having important qualities not necessarily related to academic achievement and promise

Application Information:
Deadline: November 1
Application Fee: $50 plus $150 fee to OLSAS
Applicant/Acceptance Ratio: III:I
Size of Incoming Class: 160
Tuition: $10,663 for 2004
Books/Materials: $1,700-1,950 if leasing a computer budget $1,000-1,500 more per year

Comments: Previous Education: (a) a degree in Arts, Science, Commerce, Engineering, Journalism, Nursing, Medicine, or any equivalent degree from a recognized university; or (b) successful completion of a minimum of two full years academic work at a recognized university after completing secondary schooling in Canada or any equivalent university studies.All applicants to Ontario law schools must apply through OLSAS (Ontario Law School Application Service) at www.ouac.on.ca/olsas/. Ontario Universities Application Centre, P.O. Box 1328, 650 Woodlawn Road West, Guelph, ON, N2H 7P4.

University of Saskatchewan
Admissions Committee
College of Law
15 Campus Drive
Saskatoon, SK   S7N 5A6
Tel: 306-966-5045
Internet: http://law.usask.ca

General Information:
Degree Offered: LL.B.
Length: Semesters
Years: 3
Language: English

Admission Requirements:
Previous Education: A university degree from a recognized institution or 2 full years of academic work beyond the senior matriculation level at a recognized university or the equivalent of such work
Prerequisite Courses: Not required
Average GPA: 3.43 or B+ or 78%
Range: 2.69 - 4.27
Admission Test: LSAT
Average Score: 157th percentile
Score Report Deadline: February examination
Other Admission Criteria: Official copies of all university academic transcripts and official certificates equivalent to

Senior matriculation of the province of Saskatchewan indicating the subjects completed and the standing obtained in each subject

Application Information:
Deadline: February 1
Application Fee: $50
Applicant/Acceptance Ratio: 9:1
Size of Incoming Class: 110
Tuition: $6,515
Books/Materials: $3,600 over 3 years

Comments: A slight preference given to residents of Sask., N.W.T., Yukon, P.E.I. and Nfld. If additional information is required, please contact the secretary to the Admissions Committee, College of Law (306) 966-5874. LL.M. program also offered.

University of Toronto
Admissions Office*
Faculty of Law
78 Queen's Park
Toronto, ON   M5S 2C5
Tel: 416-978-3716
Fax: 416-978-7899
E-mail: law.admissions@utoronto.ca
Internet: www.law.utoronto.ca

General Information:
Degree Offered: J.D.
Length: 6 Semesters
Years: 3
Language: English

Admission Requirements:
Previous Education: Non-mature candidates must have successfully completed 3 years of an approved course leading to a degree at a recognized university by the end of May in the year of entry. However, prospective applicants should be aware that almost all of our students have completed a four-year degree.
Prerequisite Courses: Not required

Average GPA: 3.8 or A- or 84%
Range: 78% - 95%
Admission Test: LSAT
Average Score: 95th percentile
Score Report Deadline: February 2009 test for entry 2009-2010 academic year
Other Admission Criteria: Personal statement, OLSAS application form, official copies of all university academic transcripts

Application Information:
Deadline: November 1**
Application Fee: $185 plus $75 per law school
Applicant/Acceptance Ratio: 11:1
Size of Incoming Class: 170
Tuition: $21,767 (academic fee only)
Books/Materials: $1,000

Comments: It is strongly recommended that applicants consult the Faculty of Law website for more detailed information on admission policies. For further information call 416-978-3716 or e-mail law. admissions@utoronto.ca. *All applicants to Ontario law schools must apply online: Ontario Law School Application Service, Ontario Universities Application Centre, 170 Research Lane, Guelph, ON, N1G 5E2, E-mail: olsas@ouac.on.ca, Internet: www.ouoc.on.ca/olsas/.** Please contact the Admissions Office for information on obtaining a late application.

University of Victoria
Admissions Office, Faculty of Law
P.O. Box 2400, Stn CSC
Victoria, BC   V8W 3H7
Tel: 250-721-8151
Fax: 250-721-6390
E-mail: lawadmss@uvic.ca
Internet: www.law.uvic.ca

General Information:
Degree Offered: LL.B.*
Length: 6 semesters
Years: 3
Language: English

Admission Requirements:
Previous Education: Minimum of 3 years university (Regular Category) or qualify as an applicant in Aboriginal or Special Access Category
Prerequisite Courses: None
Average GPA: 3.90/4.33 or high A- or 84%
Range: 3.55 - 4.25
Admission Test: LSAT
Average Score: 162 or 88th percentile
Score Report Deadline: February test
Other Admission Criteria: Official copies of all university academic transcripts are required. Work experience, extra-curriculars, community service, and other personal factors are considered.

Application Information:
Deadline: February 1
Application Fee: $75
Applicant/Acceptance Ratio: 10:1
Size of Incoming Class: 105
Tuition: $7,860
Books/Materials: $1,000

Comments: * Many joint programs exist that combine a law degree with another degree. For example, Master's of Business Administration (LLB/MBA), Master's of Public Administration (LLB/MPA), Master's of Arts in Indigenous Governance (LLB/M.A.I.G.) and Civil Law (LLB/BCL). As well, the school has a graduate program offering both LL.M. and Ph.D. degrees.

University of Western Ontario
Admissions Office
Faculty of Law
London, ON   N6A 3K7
Tel: 519-661-3347
Fax: 519-661-2063
E-mail: lawapp@uwo.ca
Internet: www.law.uwo.ca

General Information:
Degree Offered: LL.B.

Length: Semesters
Years: 3
Language: English

Admission Requirements:
Previous Education: For General Category admission, a degree from a recognized university. For Discretionary Categories (Aboriginal, Access and Mature), candidates must have an LSAT score of above the 60th percentile and it is recommended that candidates complete three years of undergraduate study before admission
Prerequisite Courses: None
Average GPA: 82% or A- or 3.7
Range: 75% - 96%
Admission Test: LSAT
Average Score: 162 or 82nd percentile
Score Report Deadline: February test
Other Admission Criteria: Official copies of all university academic transcripts, personal statement, academic references, extra-curricular activities, graduate work, community involvement, and oustanding work experience. TOEFL score may be requested where English is a second language

Application Information:
Deadline: November 1
Application Fee: $175 plus $75 per law school
Applicant/Acceptance Ratio: 12:1
Size of Incoming Class: 165
Tuition: $13,300
Books/Materials: $1,500

Comments: All applicants to Ontario Law Schools must complete an online application through the Ontario Law School Application Services at www.ouac.on.ca/olsas. Ontario Law School Application Services, Ontario Universities Application Centre, 170 Research Lane, Guelph, ON N1G 5E2, Tel: 519-823-1940, Fax: 519-823-5232, Email: olsas@ouac.on.ca

University of Windsor
Faculty of Law
401 Sunset Avenue
Windsor, ON   N9B 3P4
Tel: 519-253-3000 ext. 2925
Fax: 519-973-7064
E-mail: uwlaw@uwindsor.ca
Internet: www.uwindsor.ca/law

General Information:
Degree Offered: LL.B.; J.D./LL.B.;
M.B.A./LL.B.
Length: 2 semesters/year (Sept. to May)
Years: 3 (LL.B), 3 (J.D./LL.B), 4
(M.B.A./LL.B.)
Language: English

Admission Requirements:
Previous Education: Two full years of
academic work at a recognized university
after senior matriculation
Prerequisite Courses: None
Average GPA: n/a
Range: n/a
Admission Test: LSAT
Average Score: n/a
Score Report Deadline: February test
Other Admission Criteria: Official copies
of all university academic transcripts,
academic and non-academic reference
letters, and a personal profile

Application Information:
Deadline: November 1
Application Fee: $150 plus $50 per law
school
Applicant/Acceptance Ratio: 2:1
Size of Incoming Class: 155
Tuition: $10,708 plus compulsory fees
Books/Materials: $2,000 approx.

Comments: The objective of the
admission policy of the Faculty of Law,
University of Windsor is to select those
students who will excel in the study of
law and have the potential to contribute
creatively and meaningfully to the law
school and the community. No one factor
is determinative of admission to the
law school. Please check the website for
criteria.
*All applicants to Ontario Law Schools
must obtain an application from: Ontario
Law School Application Service, Ontario
Universities Application Centre, 170
Research Lane, Guelph, Ontario, N1G 5E2,
E-mail: olsas@ouac.on.ca, Website: www.
ouac.on.ca/olsas

York University
Admissions Officer
Osgoode Hall Law School
4700 Keele Street
North York, ON   M3J 1P3
Tel: 416-736-5712
E-mail: admission@osgoode.yorku.ca
Internet: www.osgoode.yorku.ca

General Information:
Degree Offered: LL.B.
Length: Semesters
Years: 3
Language: English

Admission Requirements:
Previous Education: 3 years
undergraduate study at a recognized
degree granting university
Prerequisite Courses: Not required
Average GPA: 3.7 or A or 80%
Range: 3.65 - 4.0
Admission Test: LSAT
Average Score: 85%
Score Report Deadline: February Test of
the entering year. Recommend LSAT be
written by the December Test sitting of the
year preceding entry.
Other Admission Criteria: Official copies
of all postsecondary academic transcripts.

Application Information:
Deadline: November 3
Application Fee: $185 (OLSAS) plus $75
(per law school)
Applicant/Acceptance Ratio: approx.
10:1

Size of Incoming Class: 290
Tuition: $15,000
Books/Materials: $1,000

Comments: *All applicants to Ontario Law
Schools must obtain an application from:
Ontario Law School Application Service
Ontario Universities Application Centre
170 Research Lane, Guelph, ON, N1G 5E2
Email: olsas@ouac.on.ca
Website: www.ouac.on.ca

LIBRARY & INFORMATION SCIENCE

The following fact sheets outline general information including academic requirements and application procedures for Library & Information Science Schools in Canada. The data have been compiled in a concise format to assist students interested in these professional schools. Information was obtained from updates completed by each school, or in some cases from the school's Internet website.

Library & Information Science Schools in Canada

University of Alberta   Université de Montréal
University of British Columbia   University of Toronto
Dalhousie University   University of Western Ontario
McGill University

Comments

1. These fact sheets act as a guide only. Students are advised to refer to the individual calendars or to write to the schools for more detailed information.

2. Application deadlines vary. Dates indicated refer to fall admission unless otherwise noted.

3. Tuition fees represent annual costs unless otherwise noted.

4. All of the schools listed above may not be represented.

University of Alberta

Admissions Committee
School of Library and Information Studies
3 - 20 Rutherford South
Edmonton, AB   T6G 2J4
Tel: 780-492-4578
Fax: 780-492-2430
E-mail: slis@ualberta.ca
Internet: www.slis.ualberta.ca

General Information:
Degree Offered: M.L.I.S.
Length: Semesters
Years: 2
Language: English

Admission Requirements:
Previous Education: Four-year baccalaureate from an accredited institution
Prerequisite Courses: Courses to be distributed among the Social Sciences, Biological Sciences and Physical Sciences, Literature and other areas of the Humanities
Average GPA: 3.0/4.0 approx.
Range: 3.0 to 4.0
Admission Test: See "Comments"
Average Score: GRE - 1725; TOEFL - 600
Score Report Deadline: February 1
Other Admission Criteria: A personal statement of interests and professional goals is also considered, as are 3 letters of reference

Application Information:
Deadline: February 1
Application Fee: $100 beginning Sept 2004
Applicant/Acceptance Ratio: 3:1
Size of Incoming Class: 45
Tuition: $5,360 yearly (full-time)
Books/Materials: $300

Comments: Applicants with degrees only from other countries may be required to take the Graduate Record Examination Aptitude Tests administered by the Educational Testing Service (ETS). Students should arrange for the ETS to report results to the School of Library and Information Studies.
All non-Canadians for whom English is not the major language must first write and pass satisfactorily either the Michigan English Language Assessment Battery – MELAB (The Director, Testing and Certification Division, English Language Institute, University of Michigan, Ann Arbor, Michigan 48104, U.S.A.) or the Test of English as a Foreign Language - TOEFL (Educational Testing Service, Princeton, New Jersey 08540, U.S.A.) before formal admission will be considered.

University of British Columbia

School of Library, Archival and Information Studies
470-1961 East Mall
Vancouver, BC   V6T 1Z1
Tel: 604-822-2404
Fax: 604-822-6006
E-mail: slais@interchange.ubc.ca
Internet: www.slais.ubc.ca

General Information:
Degree Offered: M.L.I.S.*, M.A.S.**; Joint M.L.I.S./M.A.S.; MACL (Master of Arts in Children's Literature)***
Length: 4 Semesters (6 for Joint Program)
Years: 2 (3 for Joint Program)
Language: English

Admission Requirements:
Previous Education: Bachelor's Degree
Prerequisite Courses: None
Average GPA: 3.33 in last 2 years of a 4-year degree
Range: 3.33 to 4.0
Admission Test: Not required
Average Score: n/a
Score Report Deadline: n/a
Other Admission Criteria: Basic computer competencies, academic records, work history, letters of reference, and by

personal or written interviews, work experience in library or archival work, teaching, academic studies, or some similar intellectual pursuit

Application Information:
Deadline: February 1
Application Fee: $90 (CDN), $150 (CDN) for international applicants
Applicant/Acceptance Ratio: 2:1
Size of Incoming Class: *50; **20; ***10
Tuition: $4,029 per annum; $7,200 for International Students; ***$3,940
Books/Materials: $1,000

Dalhousie University
Administrative Assistant
School of Information Management
Halifax, NS   B3H 3J5
Tel: 902-494-3656
Fax: 902-494-2451
E-mail: slis@is.dal.ca
Internet: www.sim.management.dal.ca

General Information:
Degree Offered: MLIS, MLIS/LLB, MLIS/MBA, MLIS/MPA
Length: Semesters
Years: 2
Language: English

Admission Requirements:
Previous Education: Bachelor's degree
Prerequisite Courses: Recognized academic degree (90 credits, i.e., B.A., B.Sc., B.Comm, etc.)
Average GPA: B+ provides greater certainty of consideration
Range: B or 70 - 74% minimum
Admission Test: Not required
Average Score: n/a
Score Report Deadline: n/a
Other Admission Criteria: 2 references (one academic), transcripts, statement of "Interest in the Profession"

Application Information:
Deadline: April 1
Application Fee: $70
Applicant/Acceptance Ratio: 5:1
Size of Incoming Class: 38-42
Tuition: $7751 for the standard 8 courses (4 per term); please see website for further information
Books/Materials: $800

Comments: About 2/3 of each class are from the Atlantic Region, 1/6 are from the rest of Canada, 1/6 are foreign students. Interested inquirers should check the website www.sim.management.dal.ca. Applications should be submitted early in the fall. Incoming class completed by mid-April. Scholarships awarded by the end of April. Acceptable applicants thereafter are placed on a waiting list pending possible withdrawals from the class.

McGill University
School of Information Studies
3459 McTavish Street
Montreal, QC   H3A 1Y1
Tel: 514-398-4204
Fax: 514-398-7193
E-mail: sis@mcgill.ca
Internet: www. mcgill.ca/sis

General Information:
Degree Offered: M.L.I.S.
Length: 16 courses, non-thesis, 48 credits
Years: 2
Language: English

Admission Requirements:
Previous Education: Undergraduate degree
Prerequisite Courses: Computer experience desirable
Average GPA: 3.4 or 82% approx. for incoming class
Range: 70% or 3.0/4.0 minimum or Second Class Upper Division required
Admission Test: Not required

Average Score: n/a
Score Report Deadline: n/a
Other Admission Criteria: Two official copies of transcripts showing degree awarded, letter from applicant, application form, 2 letters of reference and $80 application fee. For Visa students a TOEFL (minimum of 600)

Application Information:
Deadline: April 1 (March 1 for Visa students)
Application Fee: $80
Applicant/Acceptance Ratio: 3:1
Size of Incoming Class: 70
Tuition: $55.61 per credit for Quebec students, $171.36 for other Canadian students,
Cdn. $465.50 per credit for Visa students, $800 per term student services, etc.
Books/Materials: $500+/year

Comments: Accredited by the American Library Association; Other programs: Graduate Certificate, Graduate Diploma, Ph.D. (Ad Hoc)

Université de Montréal
Secrétariat
École de bibliothéconomie et des sciences de l'information
3150 rue Jean Brillant, porte C-2004
Montréal, QC   H3C 3J7
Tel: 514-343-6044
Fax: 514-343-5753

General Information:
Degree Offered: M.S.I.
Length: 4 semestres
Years: 2
Language: français

Admission Requirements:
Previous Education: B.A. ou B.Sc.
Prerequisite Courses: n/a
Average GPA: 70% ou B ou 3/4
Range: 2.7 - 3.0 minimum
Admission Test: Voir "Comments"

Average Score: Minimum 70%
Score Report Deadline: 30 juin
Other Admission Criteria: Excellente connaissance du français et bonne connaissance de l'anglais écrit. Excellente connaissance du système d'exploitation Windows 95 pour micro-ordinateurs.

Application Information:
Deadline: 1er février (1ere cohorte) et 1er mai (2e cohorte)
Application Fee: $100
Applicant/Acceptance Ratio: 3:1
Size of Incoming Class: 60
Tuition: $1,920/année
Books/Materials: $200

Comments: Admission: examen en français obligatoire pour tous test de microinformatique (obtenir un score de A- ou plus)

University of Toronto
Faculty of Information Studies
140 St. George Street
Toronto, ON   M5S 3G6
Tel: 416-978-3234
Internet: www.fis.utoronto.ca

General Information:
Degree Offered: M.I.St.
Length: Sessional
Years: 2 years full-time
Language: English

Admission Requirements:
Previous Education: A 4-year Bachelor's degree from an approved university
Prerequisite Courses: n/a
Average GPA: An overall B average with at least a mid-B in the final year
Range: n/a
Admission Test: n/a
Average Score: n/a
Score Report Deadline: n/a
Other Admission Criteria: Two letters of reference; resume; applicant statement. All applicants educated outside Canada

whose primary language is not English must demonstrate facility in the English language. This requirement is a condition of admission and must be met by the application deadline.

Application Information:
Deadline: Please refer to their website for information regarding deadlines
Application Fee: $160
Applicant/Acceptance Ratio: 3:1
Size of Incoming Class: 140
Tuition: $7,500 (approx.)
Books/Materials: $300 minimum

Comments: The Faculty of Information Studies (FIS) combines strengths in the stewardship and curation of cultural heritage (libraries, archives, and museums) with leadership in the future of information practice as society is transformed by the rise of digital technologies. The two-year Master of Information Studies program allows students to explore the breadth of information, and to focus on one or more areas of interest: library and information science, archival studies, and information systems. The Combined Juris Doctor/ Master of Information Studies program is offered jointly by the Faculty of Law and the Faculty of Information Studies at the University of Toronto. In four years, students receive two degrees, information studies and law. Program 1 of 2.

University of Toronto
Faculty of Information Studies
140 St. George Street
Toronto, ON   M5S 3G6
Tel: 416-978-3234
Internet: www.fis.utoronto.ca

General Information:
Degree Offered: M.M.St.
Length: Sessional
Years: 2 years full-time (20 consecutive months)

Language: English

Admission Requirements:
Previous Education: A 4-year Bachelor's degree from an approved university
Prerequisite Courses:
Average GPA: An overall B+/A- average
Range: n/a
Admission Test: n/a
Average Score: n/a
Score Report Deadline: n/a
Other Admission Criteria: Two letters of reference; resume; applicant statement. All applicants educated outside Canada whose primary language is not English must demonstrate facility in the English language. This requirement is a condition of admission and must be met by the application deadline.

Application Information:
Deadline: Please refer to their website for information regarding deadlines
Application Fee: $160
Applicant/Acceptance Ratio: 5:1
Size of Incoming Class: 30-35
Tuition: $8,500 (approx.)
Books/Materials: $300 minimum

Comments: The Faculty of Information Studies (FIS) combines strengths in the stewardship and curation of cultural heritage (libraries, archives, and museums) with leadership in the future of information practice as society is transformed by the rise of digital technologies. The two-year Master of Museum Studies program prepares students for future involvement in museums and related cultural agencies. The program examines the theoretical body of knowledge of museology as a necessary context for professional practice. Program 2 of 2.

University of Western Ontario

Faculty of Information and Media Studies
North Campus Building
London, ON   N6A 5B7
Tel: 519-661-3542
Fax: 519-661-3506
E-mail: mlisinfo@uwo.ca
Internet: www.fims.uwo.ca

General Information:
Degree Offered: Master of Library and
Information Science
Length: Minimum 3 terms
Years: Minimum 1 year
Language: English

Admission Requirements:
Previous Education: Honors degree or
equivalent (twenty full academic credits)
with an average of at least 70% in the last
two years of full-time study (or over the
last 10 full academic courses, if part-time)
Prerequisite Courses: None
Average GPA: 77%
Range: B average in last two years of study
Admission Test: Not required
Average Score: n/a
Score Report Deadline: n/a
Other Admission Criteria: Transcripts,
resume, two letters of recommendation,
list of computer skills, statement of intent

Application Information:
Deadline: Changes each term. Please visit
website for exact date.
Application Fee: $50
Applicant/Acceptance Ratio: n/a
Size of Incoming Class: varies (intake in
Jan, Sept and May)
Tuition: $2,751.35
Books/Materials:

Comments: Intake 3 times per year:
Program starts in January, September and
May. Co-operative work/study option
available. Part-time option available.
Limited number of distance courses
available.

MEDICINE

The following fact sheets outline general information including academic requirements and application procedures for Medical Schools in Canada. The data have been compiled in a concise format to assist students interested in these professional schools. Information was obtained from updates completed by each school, or in some cases from the school's Internet website.

Please refer to the section on "Admissions Tests" for information on the Medical College Admissions Test (MCAT) which is a requirement of most medical schools.

Medical Schools in Canada

University of Alberta	Newfoundland*
University of British Columbia	Université de Montréal*
University of Calgary	University of Ottawa
Dalhousie University*	Queen's University*
Université Laval*	University of Saskatchewan*
University of Manitoba	Université de Sherbrooke
McGill University	University of Toronto*
Memorial University of	University of Western Ontario*

Comments

1. These fact sheets act as a guide only. Students are advised to refer to the individual calendars or to write to the schools for more detailed information.

2. Application deadlines vary. Dates indicated refer to fall admission unless otherwise noted.

3. Tuition fees represent annual costs unless otherwise noted.

4. All of the schools listed above may not be represented.

* *This university has not updated its information. Please contact the university directly.*

University of Alberta

Faculty of Medicine and Dentistry
2-45 Medical Sciences Building
Edmonton, AB   T6G 2H7
Tel: 780-492-6350
Fax: 780-492-9531
E-mail: admission@med.ualberta.ca
Internet: www.med.ualberta.ca/ugme

General Information:
Degree Offered: M.D.
Length: 4 years
Years: 4
Language: English

Admission Requirements:
Previous Education: Minimum 2 years university within a degree program (5 full-courses equivalent per year)
Prerequisite Courses: Full courses in Organic and Inorganic Chemistry, English, Physics, Biology, and a half-course in Statistics, and a ½ course in Biochemistry.
Average GPA: 3.5 - 4.0 for 4-year+ students (3.3 for 4-year AB; 3.5 for 4-year NONAB); 3.7 - 4.0 for second and third year students
Range: 3.3 - 4.0
Admission Test: MCAT
Average Score: 10.0 out of 15 or higher
Score Report Deadline: Fall test before admission year
Other Admission Criteria: Interview, personal attributes, and letters of reference

Application Information:
Deadline: November 1
Application Fee: $60
Applicant/Acceptance Ratio: 12:1 - 1,200 applications
Size of Incoming Class: 133
Tuition: $6,387.72 and $4,000 differential fee
Books/Materials: $900 plus $800 for instruments

Comments: The University of Alberta does not accept Grade 13 (specifically English) as a university equivalent

University of British Columbia

Admissions
Faculty of Medicine
317-2194 Health Sciences Mall
Vancouver, BC   V6T 1Z3
Tel: 604-822-4482
Fax: 604-822-6061
Internet: www.med.ubc.ca/admissionsmd

General Information:
Degree Offered: M.D.
Length: 8 semesters
Years: 4
Language: English

Admission Requirements:
Previous Education: Minimum 3 full years of university
Prerequisite Courses: One-year university course in each of the following: English, Biology, General Chemistry, Organic Chemistry, Biochemistry
Average GPA: 5.0/9.0, 2.8/4.0, or 2.8/4.33
Range: 70% or B minimum (UBC) (under review)
Admission Test: MCAT
Average Score: n/a
Score Report Deadline: Fall prior to application deadline
Other Admission Criteria: Performance in interview, 3 letters of reference, submission of non-academic autobiographical statement and list of extra-curricular activities.
Criteria to be evaluated include motivation, maturity, integrity, emotional stability, realistic self-appraisal, social concern and responsibility, reliability, creativity, scientific and intellectual curiosity, attitude toward continued learning, problem-solving and decision-making aptitude, ability to communicate verbally and in writing, leadership potential, capacity to understand and cooperate with others, concern for human welfare, and demonstrated high level of performance in any aspect of human endeavour

Application Information:
Deadline: September 2
Application Fee: $105 for BC residents (under review); $155 for out-of-province applicants plus $30 for non-BC transcript processing
Applicant/Acceptance Ratio: 6:1
Size of Incoming Class: 256
Tuition: $15,000 approx.
Books/Materials: $5,500 approx.

University of Calgary

Admissions Office
Faculty of Medicine
3330 Hospital Drive N.W.
Calgary, AB   T2N 4N1
Tel: 403-220-4262
Fax: 403-210-8148
E-mail: ucmedapp@ucalgary.ca
Internet: www.med.ucalgary.ca/admissions

General Information:
Degree Offered: M.D.
Length: *
Years: 3
Language: English

Admission Requirements:
Previous Education: Minimum 2 full years of university
Prerequisite Courses: Recommended: Biochemistry, Biology, Calculus, Chemistry, English, Organic Chemistry, Physics, Physiology, Psychology
Average GPA: 3.72
Range: 3.2 - 4.0
Admission Test: MCAT
Average Score: 11 in each of biological and physical sciences, 10 in verbal reasoning and Q in the writing sample
Score Report Deadline: Year before desired entry
Other Admission Criteria: Letters of reference, essays, extra-curricular activities, and interview

Application Information:
Deadline: October 15
Application Fee: $120
Applicant/Acceptance Ratio: 15:1
Size of Incoming Class: 135
Tuition: $13,744
Books/Materials: Year 1: $3,528; Years 2 & 3: $2,205

Comments: *Length: First year, 10 months; second year, 8 months; and third year, 13 months.

Dalhousie University

Co-ordinator, Admissions and Student Affairs
Clinical Research Centre
5849 University Avenue
Room C-132
Halifax, NS   B3H 4H7
Tel: 902-494-1874
Fax: 902-494-6369
E-mail: medical.communications@dal.ca
Internet: www.medicine.dal.ca

General Information:
Degree Offered: M.D.
Length: Semesters
Years: 4
Language: English

Admission Requirements:
Previous Education: Completed undergraduate degree
Prerequisite Courses: n/a
Average GPA: 80%+ for non-maritime applicants and 77%+ for maritime applicants for the last 2 years of university with a heavy course load
Range: n/a
Admission Test: MCAT
Average Score: 8 for maritimers and 10 for non-maritimers on all numerical sections
Score Report Deadline: One year prior to admission
Other Admission Criteria: Interview

Application Information:
Deadline: October 31 of the year prior
Application Fee: $70
Applicant/Acceptance Ratio: 8:1
Size of Incoming Class: 82*
Tuition: $11,718
Books/Materials: $1,750 per year

Comments: *Preference of admission is given to residents of Nova Scotia, New Brunswick, and Prince Edward Island.

Université Laval
Comité d'admission
Faculté de médecine
Québec, QC G1K 7P4
Tel: 418-656-2492

General Information:
Degree Offered: M.D.
Length: 9 semesters
Years: 4-5
Language: français

Admission Requirements:
Previous Education: DEC - profil des sciences de la santé
Prerequisite Courses: Mathématiques, Physique, Chimie, et Biologie
Average GPA: 3.6 - 4.0
Range: 3.4 - 4.0
Admission Test: Aucun
Average Score: n/a
Score Report Deadline: Voir "Comments"
Other Admission Criteria:
Appréciation par simulation (APS); Note autobiographique standardisée

Application Information:
Deadline: 1er mars (pour les colléges), 15 fevrier (pour les universitaires)
Application Fee: $55
Applicant/Acceptance Ratio: 5:1
Size of Incoming Class: 196
Tuition: $2,500 citoyen canadien; $13,000 autres
Books/Materials: $2,000

Comments: *Score Report Deadline: 1er fevrier (candidats hors Canada); 1er mars (candidats Canadiens); 106 places réservées aux Cégépiens Québécois; 83 places réservées aux universitaires Québécois; 5 places pour candidats hors Québec; 2 places pur candidates étrangers.

University of Manitoba
Beth Jennings
Student Services Administrator
260 - 727 McDermot Avenue
Winnipeg, MB R3E 3P5
Tel: 204-789-3499
Fax: 204-789-3929
E-mail: registrar_med@umanitoba.ca
Internet: www.umanitoba.ca/medicine/admissions

General Information:
Degree Offered: M.D.
Length: August - May
Years: 4
Language: English

Admission Requirements:
Previous Education: Bachelor's degree
Prerequisite Courses: Biochemistry and Humanities/Social Sciences, plus additional requirements as outlined in the Applicant Information Bulletin
Average GPA: 4.0
Range: 3.6 - 4.5
Admission Test: MCAT
Average Score: 10.5
Score Report Deadline: October of admission year
Other Admission Criteria: Preference given to Manitoba residents. Interview required.

Application Information:
Deadline: n/a
Application Fee: $90 non-refundable
Applicant/Acceptance Ratio: 10:1
Size of Incoming Class: 110

Tuition: $7,585
Books/Materials: $3,200

Comments: The Applicant Information Bulletin is the official statement on requirements. For more information visit their website at www.umanitoba.ca/medicine/admissions

McGill University
Admissions Office
Faculty of Medicine
3655 promenade Sir-William-Osler
Montreal, QC   H3G 1Y6
Tel: 514-398-3517
Fax: 514-398-4631
E-mail: admissions.med@mcgill.ca
Internet: www.mcgill.ca/medicine

General Information:
Degree Offered: M.D., C.M.; joint program: MDCM & MBA
Length: n/a
Years: 4
Language: English

Admission Requirements:
Previous Education: Bachelor's degree (4-year degree, full time)
Prerequisite Courses: Minimum 6 semester hours in general Biology, Chemistry and Physics, and minimum 3 semester hours in Organic Chemistry. All must be at a university level with laboratory or practical work in each. Distance/correspondance education courses are not accepted. Prerequisite courses completed more than 8 years from date of application must be repeated. Exception may be made for applicants with advanced degrees in the material concerned. Courses in biochemistry, cell/molecular biology, and statistics are recommended, but not required for admission.
Average GPA: 3.8
Range: 3.5-4.0

Admission Test: Medical College Admission Test (MCAT)
Average Score: 33 (range: 30-45)
Score Report Deadline: Fall
Other Admission Criteria:
Application Information:
Deadline: January 15 for residents of Quebec; November 15 (of year prior to admissions) for residents in all other provinces and terrritories and International applicants
Application Fee: $80
Applicant/Acceptance Ratio: approximately 8 places are available for out-of-province Canadian students and International students
Size of Incoming Class: 177
Tuition: $4,748 for residents of Quebec; $10,327 for residents of all other provinces and territories; $23,691 for International students
Books/Materials: $1,500 approx.

Comments: Application for admission must be made online. Medical students are expected to have facility with computers and Internet access. Please see www.medicine.mcgill.ca/admissions for full details.

Memorial University of Newfoundland
Admissions Office
Faculty of Medicine
Room 1751, Health Sciences Centre
St. John's, NL   A1B 3V6
Tel: 709-737-6615
Fax: 709-777-8422
E-mail: munmed@mun.ca
Internet: www.med.mun.ca/med

General Information:
Degree Offered: M.D.
Length: 10 semesters
Years: 4
Language: English

Admission Requirements:
Previous Education: Bachelor's Degree
Prerequisite Courses: Two courses in English
Average GPA: n/a
Range: n/a
Admission Test: Medical College Admission Test (MCAT)
Average Score: n/a
Score Report Deadline: n/a
Other Admission Criteria: Interview; Two reference letters or the Pre-Health Professions Advisor Report are required. Additional references will not be considered by the Admissions Committee.

Application Information:
Deadline: October 15 of the year prior
Application Fee: $75
Applicant/Acceptance Ratio: 12:1
Size of Incoming Class: 60
Tuition: Year 1 & 2: $13,000; Year 3 & 4: $13,000
Books/Materials: $1,386** first year, $669 second year, $751 third year, $852 fourth year

Comments: *Students may apply without a degree. The requirements are 20 courses, including two courses in English, from a recognized University/College, and the MCAT. It is preferred that the 20 courses be in a recent program of study and full course loads. Applicants applying with these requirements must be exceptional in all areas of the application in order to be considered. **First year books and materials includes $650 for medical instruments. Non-Canadians pay $30,000 per year.

Université de Montréal
Faculté de Médecine-Admission
Pavillon principal
C.P. 6128, Centre-ville
Montréal, QC   H3C 3J7
Tel: 514-343-6265

General Information:
Degree Offered: M.D.
Length: 11 semestres
Years: 4
Language: français
Admission Requirements:
Previous Education: Diplôme d'études collégiales ou autre diplôme d'études postsecondaires
Prerequisite Courses: Concentration en sciences de la santé ou l'équivalent; cours obligatoires: Mathématiques 103, 203; Physique 101, 201, 301; Chimie 101, 201, 202; et Biologie 301, 401
Average GPA: n/a
Range: n/a
Admission Test: Test de connaissance de la langue française: 83%
Average Score: Test de connaissance de la langue française: 83%
Score Report Deadline: n/a
Other Admission Criteria: entrevues

Application Information:
Deadline: 1er mars
Application Fee: $30
Applicant/Acceptance Ratio: 15:1
Size of Incoming Class: 149
Tuition: $1,130 par trimestre
Books/Materials: $1,000 pour année

Comments: Note: Être citoyen canadien ou résident permanent à la date limite fixée pour le dépôt de la demande d'admission. La Faculté pourra admettre, hors contingentement et par entente intergouvernementale, 3 candidats francophones du Nouveau-Brunswick, et 3 candidats munis d'un visa d'étudiant.

University of Ottawa
Office of the Registrar
Admissions - Faculty of Medicine
451 Smyth Road, Room 2046
Ottawa, ON   K1H 8M5
Tel: 613-562-5409
Fax: 613-562-5651
E-mail: admissmd@uottawa.ca
Internet: www.medicine.uottawa.ca

General Information:

Degree Offered: M.D.
Length: 8 semesters
Years: 4
Language: French or English

Admission Requirements:

Previous Education: Three years of full-time university studies
Prerequisite Courses: One full course in Biology or Zoology (including laboratory); one full course in Humanities; 2 of the following 3 chemistry courses: General Biochemistry (without laboratory session), General Chemistry (with laboratory), and Organic Chemistry (with laboratory)
Average GPA: 75% minimum
Range: n/a
Admission Test: None required
Average Score: n/a
Score Report Deadline: n/a
Other Admission Criteria: No candidates will be admitted without a successful interview. Quality of grades and results of the assessment of the detailed autobiographical sketch are the selection tools for invitation to an interview.

Application Information:

Deadline: Please see deadlines published at www.ouac.on.ca/omsas
Application Fee: $200 plus $75 school fee
Applicant/Acceptance Ratio: n/a
Size of Incoming Class: 143
Tuition: $15,288.35 + incidental fees of $571.98
Books/Materials: $2,000+

Comments: The Faculty of Medicine also conducts programs in graduate studies leading to Master and Doctorate degrees in different fields; a program in Continuing Medical Education; a program leading to a Bachelor of Medical Science degree for eligible applicants registered in Medicine; and a Postgraduate Medical Education Program.

Queen's University

School of Medicine
Undergraduate Medical Education
Kingston, ON   K7L 3N6
Tel: 613-533-2542
Fax: 613-533-3190
Internet: http://meds.queensu.ca

General Information:

Degree Offered: M.D.
Length: 147 weeks
Years: 4
Language: English

Admission Requirements:

Previous Education: Three full years in any university program
Prerequisite Courses: The equivalent of a full year university course in each of the following (a) biological sciences (e.g. anatomy, biochemistry, biology, botany, genetics, immunology, microbiology, physiology, zoology); (b) physical sciences (e.g. general chemistry, geology, organic chemistry, physics); (c) humanities (e.g. classics, English, French, foreign languages, film studies, drama, music, history, philosophy, religion) OR social sciences (e.g., anthropology, economics, geography, political science, psychology, sociology)
Average GPA: Based on applicant pool
Range: n/a
Admission Test: MCAT
Average Score: For 2004 minimum sum of 32, N on WS, 9 on VR, 9 on BS and PS
Score Report Deadline: MCAT must be written prior to October 1
Other Admission Criteria: Must be a Canadian citizen, a Permanent Resident, or a child of Queen's alumni residing outside of Canada

Application Information:

Deadline: October 1 of year prior to anticipated registration
Application Fee: $175 for application to

one Ontario medical school plus $75 for each additional school selection
Applicant/Acceptance Ratio: 4:1
Size of Incoming Class: 100
Tuition: $14,300 includes student fees
Books/Materials: $3,400 first year

Comments: Place of residence, location of university, age, gender, race and religion are not factors considered in the selection process. The following steps are used to identify the group to be invited for an interview and for assessment of personal qualities: 1. A cumulative GPA based on all years of undergraduate study, or last two years GPA, 2. The result of the MCAT. Candidates will be ranked for offers and wait listed as determined by the assessment of letters of reference, Personal Information Form, autobiographic sketch, and interview.

University of Saskatchewan
Admissions Secretary
College of Medicine
B103 Health Sciences Building
107 Wiggins Road
Saskatoon, SK   S7N 5E5
Tel: 306-966-8554
Fax: 306-966-6164
E-mail: med.admissions@usask.ca
Internet: www.usask.ca/medicine

General Information:
Degree Offered: M.D.
Length: Semesters
Years: 4
Language: English

Admission Requirements:
Previous Education: Two years pre-medicine
Prerequisite Courses: An overall average of at least 70% in the following: prerequisites: Biochemistry 200.3 and 211.3, Biology 110.6, Chemistry 112.3, Organic Chemistry 250.3, English 110.6, Physics 111.6, and a full social science or humanities course
Average GPA: 87.70%
Range: At least 78% in the 2 best full undergraduate years; out-of-province students should have at least 80%
Admission Test: MCAT required
Average Score: Minimum Scores: 8/15 in sciences and verbal reasoning sections; N in writing skills - one 7 or M will be accepted
Score Report Deadline: Scores must be available by the application deadline
Other Admission Criteria: 3 reference letters from each applicant

Application Information:
Deadline: Dec 1 - Saskatchewan Residents
Dec 1 - Out-of-Province Residents
Application Fee: $40 - Saskatchewan Residents; $75 - Out-of-Province Residents
Transcript Fee: $25 - Canadian University
$50 - University outside of Canada
Applicant/Acceptance Ratio: 10:1
Size of Incoming Class: 60
Tuition: $10,000 plus $150 student fee
Books/Materials: $6,000

Comments: Up to 6 of the 60 positions may be offered to out-of-province students

---

Université de Sherbrooke
Admissions Office
Faculty of Médicine
3001 - 12th Avenue North
Sherbrooke, QC   J1H 5N4
Tel: 819-564-5208
Fax: 819-820-6809
E-mail: admission-med@usherbrooke.ca
Internet: www.usherbrooke.
ca/doctorat_medecine

General Information:
Degree Offered: M.D.*
Length: Semestres
Years: 4
Language: français (teaching)

Admission Requirements:
Previous Education: (DEC) Diploma
of Collegial Studies in Sciences or Post-
Secondary Diploma
Prerequisite Courses: Mathematics,
Chemistry, Biology, Physics
Average GPA: n/a
Admission Test: TAAMUS (Test d'aptitudes
à l'apprentissage de la medécine à
l'Université de Sherbrooke) et MEM (Mini
Entrevues Multiples)
Average Score: n/a
Score Report Deadline: n/a
Other Admission Criteria: Admission
selection is based on scholastic records
and a learning skills test

Application Information:
Deadline: March 1 (college students),
January 15 (all other applicants)
Application Fee: $70
Applicant/Acceptance Ratio: n/a
Size of Incoming Class: 192-196
Tuition: $8,900 (first year)
Books/Materials: $2,000 (first year)

Comments: *Other programs offered
include B.Sc., Nursing, M.Sc., and Ph.D.

University of Toronto
Admissions Office
Faculty of Medicine
Room 2135, Medical Sciences Building
Toronto, ON   M5S 1A8
Tel: 416-978-2717
Fax: 416-971-2163
Internet: www.library.utoronto.
ca/medicine

General Information:
Degree Offered: M.D.
Length: Semesters
Years: 4
Language: English

Admission Requirements:
Previous Education: Minimum 3 years of
a degree program at a Canadian university
(15 full credits)
Prerequisite Courses: Two full courses in
Life Sciences and one full course in Social
Sciences or Humanities or Languages. It
is recommended, although not required,
that applicants complete a university-level
course in Biometrics or Statistics.
Average GPA: 3.6
Range: n/a
Admission Test: MCAT
Average Score: *9 (on Verbal Reasoning,
Biological and Physical Sciences); N (on
Writing Sample)
Score Report Deadline: October 1
Other Admission Criteria: References;
personal interview; First Aid & C.P.R.
certification

Application Information:
Deadline: October 1
Application Fee: $175 plus $75 University
of Toronto fee (non-refundable)
Applicant/Acceptance Ratio: 9:1
Size of Incoming Class: 198
Tuition: $17,287.50
Books/Materials: $1,600 first year

Comments: *Low marks (below 9 in any
subtest and below N essay marks) will be
unacceptable to the Faculty and jeopardize
the success of the application.

University of Western Ontario
Admissions/Student & Equity Affairs
Faculty of Medicine & Dentistry
Medical Sciences Building
London, ON   N6A 5C1
Tel: 519-661-3744
Fax: 519-661-3797
E-mail: admissions@med.uwo.ca
Internet: www.fmd.uwo.ca/

General Information:
Degree Offered: M.D.
Length: Semesters
Years: 4
Language: English

Admission Requirements:

Previous Education: Completed or be currently enrolled in a program leading to an undergraduate degree at a recognized university and expect to have completed a minimum of 15 full or equivalent courses by the end of the academic year.

Prerequisite Courses: One full or equivalent course in Biology, Organic Chemistry and one additional science not related to Biology or Chemistry. There are also 3 full or equivalent non-science courses required, 2 of which must be from different disciplines, one at the first-year level and one from second year or above, chosen from one of the subjects in first year. One must be an essay course.

Average GPA: 3.7

Range: A

Admission Test: MCAT

Average Score: BS-10, PS-9, VR-9, WS-Q

Score Report Deadline: MCAT must be written prior to October 15 application deadline

Other Admission Criteria: Personal interview, references, proficiency in English, basic life support training

Application Information:

Deadline: October 15

Application Fee: $175 plus $75 for each school selected (subject to annual review)

Applicant/Acceptance Ratio: n/a

Size of Incoming Class: 133

Tuition: $14,233.23

Books/Materials: $2,500

Comments: An M.D./Ph.D. combined program is also offered. Refer to the University of Western Ontario Academic Calendar for further details. Applicants must be Canadian citizens or permanent residents on the closing date for application. Admission to the Faculty of Medicine and Dentistry is based primarily on the academic undergraduate record, MCAT scores, and the interview score.

Although careful assessment is made of the academic record throughout all years at university, the academic marks obtained during the final and the best other full undergraduate year will be used to formulate your grade point average (five full or equivalent courses in each year, September to April, being considered). The structure of the medical curriculum at the University of Western Ontario is such that admission with advanced standing or transfer from another Canadian medical school can be considered only in very exceptional cases and subject to space being available. The Medical College Admission Test (MCAT) is required, MCAT results before the spring of 1991 will not be acceptable. No preference is given according to place of residence, age, or university attended. Applications to Medical School are available from the Ontario Medical School Application Service (OMSAS) in Guelph, Ontario. Applications are available in June and must be completed and returned to OMSAS before the deadline. The deadline for application admission to medical school is October 15, for the following September. All applicants must have an adequate knowledge of written and spoken English.

NURSING

The following fact sheets outline general information including academic requirements and application procedures for Nursing Schools in Canada. The data have been compiled in a concise format to assist students interested in these professional schools. Information was obtained from updates completed by each school, or in some cases from the school's Internet website.

Nursing Schools in Canada

University of Alberta
Athabasca University*
University of British Columbia*
University of Calgary*
Dalhousie University*
Université Laval
University of Manitoba
McGill University*
McMaster University*
Memorial University of Newfoundland
Université de Montréal
University of New Brunswick
University of Northern British Columbia*

University of Ottawa*
Université du Québec à Chicoutimi
Université du Québec à Rimouski
Université du Québec à Trois-Rivières
Université du Québec en Outaouais
Queen's University*
University of Saskatchewan*
Université de Sherbrooke
University of Toronto*
University of Victoria
University of Western Ontario*
University of Windsor*

Comments

1. These fact sheets act as a guide only. Students are advised to refer to the individual calendars or to write to the schools for more detailed information.

2. Application deadlines vary. Dates indicated refer to fall admission unless otherwise noted.

3. Tuition fees represent annual costs unless otherwise noted.

4. All of the schools listed above may not be represented.

* This university has not updated its information. Please contact the university directly.

University of Alberta

Dr. Katherine Moore
Associate Dean, Graduate Studies
Faculty of Nursing
3rd Floor Clinical Sciences Building
Edmonton, AB   T6G 2G3
Tel: 780-492-4338
Fax: 780-492-2551
E-mail: katherine.moore@ualberta.ca
Internet: www.uofaweb.ualberta.
ca/nursing

General Information:
Degree Offered: Master of Nursing (MN), Ph.D. in Nursing
Length: 4-12 Semesters
Years: 2-6
Language: English

Admission Requirements:
Previous Education: A baccalaureate degree in nursing (for MN); MN (for Ph.D.)
Prerequisite Courses: An undergraduate course (MN) or graduate course (for Ph.D.) in each of statistics and research methods, preferably completed within the past 6 years.
Average GPA: 3/4 on the 4 ppoint scale
Range: n/a
Admission Test: Not required
Average Score: n/a
Score Report Deadline: n/a
Other Admission Criteria: Normally, a minimum of one year of clinical nursing experience in the specialty area to which the student is applying. All non-Canadian applicants whose native language is not English and who have not previously received a degree (for which the language of instruction was English) from a university in Canada, the U.K., the U.S.A., Australia, or New Zealand must obtain a satisfactory score on an English language examination approved by the Faculty of Nursing, University of Alberta (e.g., 550

on the paper-based TOEFL; 213 on the computer-based test.)

Application Information:
Deadline: October 1for September admission (of the following year)
Application Fee: Please see www. gradstudies.ualberta.ca
Applicant/Acceptance Ratio: n/a
Size of Incoming Class: n/a
Tuition: Please see www.gradstudies. ualberta.ca
Books/Materials: Please see www. gradstudies.ualberta.ca

University of Alberta

Joan Liu
Recruitment Officer
Faculty of Nursing
4th Floor, Clinical Sciences Building
Edmonton, AB   T6G 2G3
Tel: 780-492-0952
Fax: 780-492-2551
E-mail: joan.liu@ualberta.ca
Internet: www.ua.nursing.ualberta.ca

General Information:
Degree Offered: B.ScN (Collaborative); B.ScN (Bilingual); B.ScN (Post RN); Registered Psychiatric Nurse (RPN)
Length: Semesters
Years: 4 years
Language: English (or French for B.ScN offered through Faculté St - Jean)

Admission Requirements:
Previous Education: B.ScN - HS courses (5 - Grade 12)
Prerequisite Courses: Eng 30, Bio 30, Chem or Science 30, PureMath, Math 31, or Physics 30, one additional subject
Average GPA: 78%
Range: n/a
Admission Test: Not required
Average Score: n/a
Score Report Deadline: n/a

Other Admission Criteria: Spoken English Language Proficiency, Record of Immunization, CPR Certification, Standard First Aid Certificate, medical examination

Application Information:
Deadline: February 1
Application Fee: $100
Applicant/Acceptance Ratio: n/a
Size of Incoming Class: n/a
Tuition: $6,545.82
Books/Materials: $800-1,000

Athabasca University
Master of Nursing Program
Centre for Nursing & Health Studies
1 University Drive
Athabasca, AB   T9S 3A3
Tel: 1-800-788-9041 ext. 6381 or
780-675-6381
Fax: 780-675-6468
E-mail: mhs@athabascau.ca
Internet: www.athabascau.ca/cnhs

General Information:
Degree Offered: MN
Length: Semesters
Years: n/a
Language: English

Admission Requirements:
Previous Education: 4-year Canadian baccalaureate degree program in nursing or the equivalent from an accredited university and have a minimum of 2 years professional nursing experience. Students seeking admission to the MN program who possess a 4-year baccalaureate degree in a field other than nursing with a minimum GPA of 3.0 (B) in the final 30 credits of undergraduate study must: 1) possess a minimum of 2 years full-time equivalent work experience as a registered nurse; 2) successfully complete the courses (or their equivalent) as outlined in Prerequisite Courses section before admission to the MN as a program student.

Prerequisite Courses: MATH 215 Introduction to Statistics or MATH 216 Computer-Oriented Approach to Statistics; HLST 320 Teaching and Learning for Health Professionals; NURS 324 Concepts and Theories in Nursing Practice; NURS 328 Understanding Research; NURS 434 Community Health Promotion
Average GPA: n/a
Range: n/a
Admission Test: n/a
Average Score: n/a
Score Report Deadline: n/a
Other Admission Criteria: Official transcripts, 3 letters of reference, up to date resume including details of professional work experience, see website for more details

Application Information:
Deadline: See website for details
Application Fee: $60
Applicant/Acceptance Ratio: n/a
Size of Incoming Class: n/a
Tuition: See website for details
Books/Materials: See website for details

University of British Columbia
Lily Yee
Outreach Secretary
School of Nursing
T201-2211 Westbrook Mall
Vancouver, BC   V6T 2B5
Tel: 604-822-7489
Fax: 604-822-7448
E-mail: lily@nursing.ubc.ca
Internet: www.nursing.ubc.ca

General Information:
Degree Offered: BSN
Length: Semesters
Years: 4 - students who enter from secondary school ; 2 - Students with advanced standing or previous bachelor degrees, and prerequisite courses
Language: English

Admission Requirements:

Previous Education: Applicants must meet the general admission requirements of the University, which include British Columbia Secondary School graduation or the equivalent with a minimum 67% average (2.6 on a 4-point scale) calculated on 4 Grade 12 courses only. Because of enrolment limitations the academic standing required for admission is higher than the published minimum.

Prerequisite Courses: British Columbia Secondary School course work must include the following: Biology 12, Chemistry 11, English 11, English 12, French 11 (or other language), Mathematics 11, Social Studies 11 and two additional examinable Grade 12 courses. Students entering directly from Senior Secondary School complete a minimum of 48 credits of support and elective courses before beginning the five-term Upper-Division component of the nursing program.

Average GPA: n/a
Range: n/a
Admission Test: n/a
Average Score: n/a
Score Report Deadline: n/a
Other Admission Criteria: A supplemental application form, due Feb. 28, is required for third-year entry. Post RN applicants must apply directly to the School of Nursing.

Application Information:

Deadline: Februrary 28
Application Fee: Visit website for details
Applicant/Acceptance Ratio: n/a
Size of Incoming Class: 50-60
Tuition: Visit website for details
Books/Materials: n/a

Comments: You can apply online at http://www.pas.bc.ca or you can call the Registrar's Office at 604-822-3014 to obtain a paper copy.

University of Calgary

Faculty of Nursing
Professional Faculties
2500 University Dr. N.W.
Calgary, AB   T2N 1N4
Tel: 403-220-6262
Fax: 403-284-4803
Internet: http://www.ucalgary.ca/NU/home.htm

General Information:

Degree Offered: Master of Nursing (MN)
Length: 6 semesters
Years: 1.5
Language: English

Admission Requirements:

Previous Education: Nurse Practitioner (NP)
Prerequisite Courses: Master's degree, normally in Nursing
Average GPA: Minimum 3.0
Range: all Master's courses
Admission Test: Not required
Average Score: n/a
Score Report Deadline: n/a
Other Admission Criteria:
Application Information:
Deadline: September 15 for the following January admission; February 1 for the following May or September admission
Application Fee: $60
Applicant/Acceptance Ratio:
Size of Incoming Class: Maxiumum 15
Tuition: $581/course plus $581 annual program fee
Books/Materials: n/a

University of Calgary

Faculty of Nursing
Professional Faculties
2500 University Dr. N.W.
Calgary, AB   T2N 1N4
Tel: 403-220-6262
Fax: 403-284-4803
Internet: http://www.ucalgary.ca/NU/home.htm

General Information:
Degree Offered: Master of Nursing/Nurse Practitioner (MN/NP)
Length: 7 semesters
Years: 2
Language: English

Admission Requirements:
Previous Education: Bachelor of Nursing (BN)
Prerequisite Courses: Undergraduate statistics and nursing research methodology
Average GPA: Minimum 3.0
Range: last 20 half-courses
Admission Test: Not required
Average Score: n/a
Score Report Deadline: n/a
Other Admission Criteria: Active nursing association registration and CPR, 2 years clinical experience

Application Information:
Deadline: September 15 for the following January admission
Application Fee: $60
Applicant/Acceptance Ratio: 50%
Size of Incoming Class: n/a
Tuition: $581/course
Books/Materials: n/a

University of Calgary
Faculty of Nursing
Professional Faculties
2500 University Dr. N.W.
Calgary, AB   T2N 1N4
Tel: 403-220-6262
Fax: 403-284-4803
Internet: http://www.ucalgary.ca/NU/home.htm

General Information:
Degree Offered: Master of Nursing (MN)
Length: 5 semesters
Years: 2
Language: English

Admission Requirements:
Previous Education: Bachelor of Nursing (BN) normally
Prerequisite Courses: Undergraduate statistics and nursing research methodology
Average GPA: Minimum 3.0
Range: last 20 half-courses
Admission Test: Not required
Average Score: n/a
Score Report Deadline: n/a
Other Admission Criteria: Active nursing association registration and CPR, 2 years clinical experience

Application Information:
Deadline: February 1 for the following September admission
Application Fee: $60
Applicant/Acceptance Ratio: 2/3 (68% admitted)
Size of Incoming Class: Varies
Tuition: Course-based is $581/course; thesis is $6,000 for the program for a 2 year period
Books/Materials: n/a

Dalhousie University
Dr. Joan Evans
Graduate Coordinator
Nursing Program
1st Floor, Forrest Building
5869 University Ave.
Halifax, NS   B3H 1W2
Tel: 902-494-2391
Fax: 902-494-3487
E-mail: nursing@dal.ca
Internet: www.dal.ca

General Information:
Degree Offered: MN
Length: Semesters
Years: 2
Language: English

Admission Requirements:
Previous Education: Bachelor of Nursing

Prerequisite Courses: Research, Statistics, Family Nursing, Community Nursing
Average GPA: n/a
Range: 3.0 - 4.3 minimum
Admission Test: n/a
Average Score: n/a
Score Report Deadline: n/a
Other Admission Criteria: 3 letters of reference, interview, curriculum vitae, statement of career goals, 2 years professional nursing experience

Application Information:
Deadline: April 1
Application Fee: $70
Applicant/Acceptance Ratio: n/a
Size of Incoming Class: n/a
Tuition: $7,460 per year
Books/Materials: n/a

University of Manitoba
Faculty of Nursing
Helen Glass Centre for Nursing
Winnipeg, MB   R3T 2N2
Tel: 204-474-7452
Fax: 204-474-7682
E-mail: nursing_info@umanitoba.ca
Internet: www.umanitoba.ca/nursing/programs/graduate

General Information:
Degree Offered: MN
Length: 2 years full time
Years: 6 years limit
Language: English

Admission Requirements:
Previous Education: Bachelor of Nursing (BN)
Prerequisite Courses: Statistics and Research Methods (C+ minimum in each)
Average GPA: 3.0 or Higher
Range: 3.0 - 4.5
Admission Test: n/a
Average Score: n/a
Score Report Deadline: n/a

Application Information:
Deadline: January 15
Application Fee: $75 ($90 for international students)
Applicant/Acceptance Ratio: 80%
Size of Incoming Class: 25
Tuition: $4,177 (1st year); $4,177 (2nd year)
Books/Materials: Varies

McGill University
School of Nursing
Wilson Hall
3506 University Street
Montreal, QC   H3A 2A7
Tel: n/a
Fax: 514-398-8455
E-mail: admissions@mcgill.ca
Internet: www.nursing.mcgill.ca

General Information:
Degree Offered: B.N., B.Sc. (N.)
Length: 8 Semesters
Years: 3
Language: English

Admission Requirements:
Previous Education: B.Sc. (N) for holders of a collegial diploma in Health Sciences or Natural Sciences (or its equivalent); BN for registered nurses who graduate from a college or diploma nursing program.
Prerequisite Courses: OAC Calculus or OAC Algebra and Geometry or MCB4U or MGA4U, and two of the following: OAC Biology or SBI4U, OAC Chemistry or SCH4U, OAC Physics or SPH4U, OAC or 4U English or French
Average GPA: n/a
Range: 75%
Admission Test: None
Average Score: n/a
Score Report Deadline: n/a
Other Admission Criteria: High school profile

Application Information:
Deadline: February 1
Application Fee: $60
Applicant/Acceptance Ratio: n/a
Size of Incoming Class: n/a
Tuition: $1,668.30 for residents of Quebec; $4,012.50 for residents in all other provinces
Books/Materials: $2,100 approx.

McMaster University
Admission Officer
Nursing Programme
Faculty of Health Sciences
1280 Main Street West
Health Sciences Centre
Room 3N10
Hamilton, ON   L8S 4L8
Tel: 905-525-9140 ext 22983
E-mail: macadmit@mcmaster.ca
Internet: www.fhs.mcmaster.ca/nursing

General Information:
Degree Offered: BScN
Length: Semesters
Years: 4
Language: English

Admission Requirements:
Previous Education: n/a
Prerequisite Courses: Six Grade 12 U/M courses or OAC equivalent courses, including English U, one of Geometry and Discrete Mathematics or Mathematics of Data Management or Advanced Functions and Introductory Calculus, and two of: Biology U, Chemistry U or Physics U
Average GPA: n/a
Range: 79% - 83%
Admission Test: n/a
Average Score: n/a
Score Report Deadline: n/a
Other Admission Criteria: n/a

Application Information:
Deadline: n/a
Application Fee: n/a
Applicant/Acceptance Ratio: n/a
Size of Incoming Class: n/a
Tuition: n/a
Books/Materials: n/a

Memorial University of Newfoundland
Academic Program Assistant
Graduate Programs and Research
School of Nursing
St. John's, NL   A1B 3V6
Internet: www.mun.ca/nursing

General Information:
Degree Offered: M.N. – Thesis Option, Practicum (Non-Thesis) Option, Nurse Practitioner Option, and Post Masters Nurse Practitioner Graduate Diploma
Length: Please see www.mun.ca/nursing
Years: Please see www.mun.ca/nursing
Language: English

Admission Requirements:
Previous Education: BN or equivalent
Prerequisite Courses: Undergraduate courses in statistics within the last 5 years; nursing research course
Average GPA: At least B standing in the BN program. Most students admitted have an A average
Range: n/a
Admission Test: n/a
Average Score: n/a
Score Report Deadline: n/a
Other Admission Criteria: Admission to the program is limited and competitive

Application Information:
Deadline: February 15 for September admission
Application Fee: Please see www.mun.ca/sgs
Applicant/Acceptance Ratio: n/a
Size of Incoming Class: Approximately 20
Tuition: Please see www.mun.ca/sgs
Books/Materials: Please see www.distance.mun.ca

University of New Brunswick

Faculty of Nursing
Admissions Office
P.O. Box 4400
Fredericton, NB   E3B 5A3
Tel: 506-453-4865
Fax: 506-453-5016
E-mail: registrar@unb.ca
Internet: www.unbf.ca/nursing

General Information:
Degree Offered: BN (Basic)
Length: n/a
Years: 4
Language: English

Admission Requirements:
Previous Education: Secondary School Diploma Prerequisite courses:Biology 12, Chemistry 12, English 12, Math 11, plus two electives (check website for options)
Prerequisite Courses: Biology 120, Chemistry 122, English 122, Math 111/112 (includes Geometry and applications in math plus Functions and Relations), plus two electives (check website for options)
Average GPA: n/a
Range: 70%+ (minimum)
Admission Test: Not required
Average Score: 80%+
Score Report Deadline: n/a
Other Admission Criteria: Official transcript; a completed life sketch form; completed nursing supplemental form (both forms found online at http://www.unbf.ca/nursing/prospective.html); proof of CPR certification

Application Information:
Deadline: March 31 (please note that this program is a competitive program with a rolling basis for admission; applicants are encouraged to apply in advance of the deadline)
Application Fee: $45
Applicant/Acceptance Ratio: n/a
Size of Incoming Class: n/a
Tuition: $5,482
Books/Materials: n/a

University of Northern British Columbia

Patricia Norris
Program Secretary
3333 University Way
Prince George, BC   V2N 4Z9
Tel: 250-960-6309
Fax: 250-960-5744
E-mail: norrisp@unbc.ca
Internet: www.unbc.ca/nursing

General Information:
Degree Offered: B.Sc.N.
Length: n/a
Years: 4
Language: English

Admission Requirements:
Previous Education: Secondary School Diploma
Prerequisite Courses: Grade 11 Math, Grade 12 English, Grade 12 Chemistry, Grade 12 Biology
Average GPA: n/a
Range: 65% or C+ minimum
Admission Test: Not required
Average Score: n/a
Score Report Deadline: n/a
Other Admission Criteria: Transcripts

Application Information:
Deadline: March 31
Application Fee: $25
Applicant/Acceptance Ratio: n/a
Size of Incoming Class: 57 to Prince George cohort, 18 to Quesnel cohort
Tuition: $134.32 per credit hour
Books/Materials: n/a

University of Ottawa

Admissions Officer
School of Nursing
Faculty of Health Sciences
451 Smyth Rd., Room 3051
Ottawa, ON   K1H 8M5
Tel: 613-562-5473
Fax: 613-562-5443
E-mail: gsecr@uottawa.ca
Internet: www.health.uottawa.ca/sn

General Information:
Degree Offered: B.Sc.N.
Length: Semesters
Years: 4
Language: English

Admission Requirements:
Previous Education: Visit their website for more information
Prerequisite Courses: n/a
Average GPA: n/a
Range: 72%
Admission Test: n/a
Average Score: n/a
Score Report Deadline: n/a
Other Admission Criteria: Transcripts

Application Information:
Deadline: n/a
Application Fee: $60
Applicant/Acceptance Ratio: n/a
Size of Incoming Class: n/a
Tuition: $4,575.19
Books/Materials: n/a

Queen's University

Dr. Ann Brown
Graduate Coordinator
School of Nursing
Faculty of Health Sciences
92 Barrie Street
Kingston, ON   K7L 3N6
Tel: 613-533-2668
E-mail: nursing@post.queensu.ca
Internet: http://meds.queensu.ca/nursing/

General Information:
Degree Offered: MSc
Length: 6 Semesters, consecutive
Years: 2
Language: English
Admission Requirements:
Previous Education: BNSc
Prerequisite Courses: Statistics, Research Methods, Nursing Theories
Average GPA: Upper 2nd Class
Range: B+ to A+
Admission Test: None
Average Score: n/a
Score Report Deadline: n/a
Other Admission Criteria: RN or eligible for License in Ontario

Application Information:
Deadline: Feburary 1st
Application Fee: $70 CDN
Applicant/Acceptance Ratio: Variable
Size of Incoming Class: 8 - 12
Tuition: $6,000 CDN
Books/Materials: $200

Comments: Research Focused

University of Saskatchewan

Dr. Gail Laing
Graduate Program Coordinator
College of Nursing
107 Wiggins Road
Saskatoon, SK   S7N 5E5
Tel: 306-966-6229
Fax: 306-966-1745
E-mail: laing@sask.usask.ca
Internet: www.usask.ca/nursing/masters/index.html

General Information:
Degree Offered: MN
Length: 1 to 2 years
Years: n/a
Language: English

Admission Requirements:
Previous Education: BScN or equivalent, RN or RPN

Prerequisite Courses: Research, Statistics
Average GPA: 70%
Range: n/a
Admission Test: n/a
Average Score: n/a
Score Report Deadline: n/a

Application Information:
Deadline: February 29
Application Fee: $50
Applicant/Acceptance Ratio: 2:1
Size of Incoming Class: 18
Tuition: $480 per 3 CU
Books/Materials: $200

University of Toronto
Admissions Officer
Office of Student Affairs
Faculty of Nursing
50 St. George St.
Toronto, ON   M5S 3H4
Tel: 416-978-8727
Fax: 416-978-8222
E-mail: inquiry.nursing@utoronto.ca
Internet: www.nursing.utoronto.ca

General Information:
Degree Offered: B.Sc.N.
Length: Semesters
Years: 2
Language: English

Admission Requirements:
Previous Education: Completion of at least 10 university full course equivalents prior to admission
Prerequisite Courses: One full course in Human Physiology or its equivalent; one full course equivalent in Life Sciences or Physical Sciences (e.g. Anatomy, Biology, Immunology, Pathology, Psychology, Astronomy, Chemistry, Geology, Physics, Physical Geography); one full course equivalent in Social Sciences (e.g. Anthropology, Economics, Political Science, Psychology, Sociology, Women's Studies); one full course equivalent in

Humanities (e.g. Art Cinema, Classics, Drama, English, History, Languages, Literature, Philosophy, Religion); one half course in statistics
Average GPA: 3.0
Range: mid-B minimum
Admission Test: None
Average Score: n/a
Score Report Deadline: n/a
Other Admission Criteria: Transcripts; personal statement providing information about goals and knowledge of nursing and thoughts on health care; one academic reference; one work related reference; resume

Application Information:
Deadline: March 1 (Ontario); February 1 (all other provinces)
Application Fee: n/a
Applicant/Acceptance Ratio: n/a
Size of Incoming Class: n/a
Tuition: $6,379.86
Books/Materials: n/a

University of Victoria
School of Nursing
Human and Social Development Building
P.O. Box 1700
Victoria, BC   V8W 2Y2
Tel: 250-721-7954
Fax: 250-721-6231
E-mail: dwalton@uvic.ca
Internet: www.nursing.uvic.ca

General Information:
Degree Offered: B.S.N.
Length: Semesters
Years: 4
Language: English

Admission Requirements:
Previous Education: Must have successfully completed all courses in the Collaboration for Academic Education in Nursing program (CAEN): terms 1-5 or for licenced RNs, completion of an accredited

RN diploma and active registration as a registered nurse.
Prerequisite Courses: See website for details
Average GPA: 3.0/9.0
Range: n/a
Admission Test: Not Required
Average Score: n/a
Score Report Deadline: n/a
Other Admission Criteria: University of Victoria, either CAEN terms 1-5 or application form; School of Nursing application form; two official transcripts demonstrating successful completion of an approved diploma nursing program; two official transcripts of all other post-secondary education; official verification of active practicing registration as a registered nurse (or the equivalent in the jurisdiction(s) in which the student is taking the program) if applicable; completion of a basic life-support level C course no more than 12 months prior to admission; a valid CPR level C certificate must be maintained for the duration of the Nursing program and there are mask fit requirements prior to undertaking any practice experience. It is recommended that applicants provide evidence of complete current immunizations upon admission to the program. All students must keep immunizations updated and provide documentation to practice agencies when required.

Application Information:
Deadline: March 31 and September 30
Application Fee: See website
Applicant/Acceptance Ratio: n/a
Size of Incoming Class: n/a
Tuition: n/a
Books/Materials: n/a

University of Western Ontario

Lori Johnson H.R.P.
School of Nursing
Faculty of Health Sciences
London, ON   N6A 5C1
Tel: 519-661-3409
Fax: 519-850-2514
E-mail: ljohns24@uwo.ca
Internet: www.uwo.ca/grad

General Information:
Degree Offered: Master of Science of Nursing (MScN)
Length: Semesters
Years: 2 years full time; 3 years part-time
Language: English

Admission Requirements:
Previous Education: MScN - Baccaulaurate prepared
Prerequisite Courses: Research and Statistics
Average GPA: 78%
Range: B+
Admission Test: TOEFL (for International Students only)
Average Score: 213 electronic version; 550 paper version
Score Report Deadline: In accordance with admission requirements
Other Admission Criteria: Visit their website at www.uwo.ca/fhs for more information

Application Information:
Deadline: February 15th for September admission
Application Fee: $50
Applicant/Acceptance Ratio: Varies
Size of Incoming Class: 15 - 20
Tuition: $2,400 approx. per term
Books/Materials: $400 - $800 approx. per term

University of Windsor

Faculty of Nursing
401 Sunset Avenue
Room 336, Toldo Health Education Centre
Windsor, ON   N9B 3P4
Tel: 519-253-3000 ext. 6129
Fax: 519-973-7084
E-mail: nursing@uwindsor.ca
Internet: www.uwindsor.ca/nursing

General Information:
Degree Offered: B.Sc.N. (Post-diploma)
Length: Semesters
Years: 2
Language: English

Admission Requirements:
Previous Education: Graduate from an approved basic Diploma program
Prerequisite Courses: University entrance-level English, Mathematics, Biology, and Chemistry
Average GPA: 2.7
Range: C- minimum
Admission Test: Not required
Average Score: n/a
Score Report Deadline: n/a
Other Admission Criteria: Interview may be required; letter of reference from current or most recent employer; an extended Police Clearance is mandatory and financial responsibility of the student; valid certificate first aid certificate and a basic rescuer (level C) course certificate in Cardio Pulmonary Resuscitation; yearly CPR recertification is required

Application Information:
Deadline: January 14
Application Fee: $40
Applicant/Acceptance Ratio: n/a
Size of Incoming Class: 150
Tuition: $4,797.60
Books/Materials: n/a

OCCUPATIONAL THERAPY

The following fact sheets outline general information including academic requirements and application procedures for Occupational Therapy Schools in Canada. The data have been compiled in a concise format to assist students interested in these professional schools. Information was obtained from updates completed by each school, or in some cases from the school's Internet website.

Occupational Therapy Schools in Canada

University of Alberta
University of British Columbia
Dalhousie University*
Université Laval*
University of Manitoba
McGill University*

McMaster University*
Université de Montréal
University of Ottawa
Queen's University*
University of Toronto*
University of Western Ontario

Comments

1. These fact sheets act as a guide only. Students are advised to refer to the individual calendars or to write to the schools for more detailed information.

2. Application deadlines vary. Dates indicated refer to fall admission unless otherwise noted.

3. Tuition fees represent annual costs unless otherwise noted.

4. All of the schools listed above may not be represented.

* This university has not updated its information. Please contact the university directly.

University of Alberta

Faculty of Rehabilitation Medicine
Department of Occupational Therapy
2-64 Corbett Hall
Edmonton, AB   T6G 2G4
Tel: 780-492-2499
Fax: 780-492-4628
E-mail: margaret.wood@ualberta.ca
Internet: www.ot.ualberta.ca

General Information:

Degree Offered: B.Sc. (O.T.); M.Sc. (O.T.)*
Length: 3 fall and winter sessions and 2 intersessions; 2 fall and winter sessions and 2 intersessions*
Years: 2
Language: English

Admission Requirements:

Previous Education: 4 year undergraduate degree
Prerequisite Courses: Statistics
Average GPA: varies by pool wanting admission (3.0 minimum)
Range: n/a
Admission Test: n/a
Average Score: n/a
Score Report Deadline: n/a
Other Admission Criteria: None

Application Information:

Deadline: February 1
Application Fee: Please see website – www.gradstudies.ualberta.ca
Applicant/Acceptance Ratio: 4:1
Size of Incoming Class: 85 + 15 Saskatchewan students
Tuition: Please see website – www.gradstudies.ualberta.ca
Books/Materials: $600 - $1,000 per year. Additional costs of fieldwork uniform, travel, and accommodations

Comments:

*Length of Program (Years): 24 months plus 4 year undergraduate degree from any discipline from an accredited university program.

University of British Columbia

Student Services Program Assistant
Department of Occupational Science and Occupational Therapy
T325 - Third Floor Koerner Pavilion
2211 Wesbrook Mall
Vancouver, BC   V6T 2B5
Tel: 604-822-7196
Fax: 604-822-7624
E-mail: mot.admissions@ubc.ca
Internet: www.ot.med.ubc.ca

General Information:

Degree Offered: Master of Occupational Therapy (MOT)
Length: 24 months completed over 6 terms
Years: 2
Language: English

Admission Requirements:

Previous Education: 4 year Bachelor's Degree
Prerequisite Courses: Human Anatomy (3 credits) at 300 level or higher; Social Sciences (3 credits), for example, sociology, anthropology, human geography; Behavioural Sciences (3 credits), for example, psychology, learning & cognition, brain & behaviour
Average GPA: 76% or higher
Range: 76% to 95%
Admission Test: Test of competency in written English if education is completed in a different language
Average Score: TOEFL 600 written, 250 computer; MELAB overall 81; IELTS minimum overall score of 6.5 (see website for further detail)
Score Report Deadline: February 1
Other Admission Criteria: A minimum of 70 hours of volunteer or paid work in a setting which includes persons with disabilities. A personal interview is required, and a preference is given to B.C. residents. Please contact department for current information.

Application Information:
Deadline: February 1
Application Fee: $90 online application fee plus $100 supplementary application fee directly to the Department of Occupational Science and Occupational Therapy
Applicant/Acceptance Ratio: 1:4
Size of Incoming Class: 40
Tuition: $11,673.29 (approx.)
Books/Materials: $1,600 (approx.)

Dalhousie University

School of Occupational Therapy
Halifax, NS   B3H 3J5
Tel: 902-494-8804
Fax: 902-494-1229
E-mail: occupational.therapy@dal.ca
Internet: www.occtherapy.dal.ca

General Information:
Degree Offered: Masters (Professional Entry)*
Length: 6 semesters
Years: 2
Language: English

Admission Requirements:
Previous Education: Bachelor's degree, minimum B average
Prerequisite Courses: 3 credits of prerequisite classes: 1 credit social sciences, 1/2 credit human anatomy, 1/2 credit human physiology, 1/2 credit statistics, 1/2 credit human development (psychology); 1/2 credit = 1 semester
Average GPA: B+ or 80% approx.
Range: n/a
Admission Test: Not required
Average Score: n/a
Score Report Deadline: n/a
Other Admission Criteria:
Autobiographical letter & academic reference, prior learning assessment for atypical applicants

Application Information:
Deadline: March 15
Application Fee: $70
Applicant/Acceptance Ratio: n/a
Size of Incoming Class: 48
Tuition: n/a
Books/Materials: $1,200 per year, Fieldwork expenses - travel and living expenses variable depending on placement location

Comments: Priority given to applicants from Atlantic Canada.
*Length of program (years) - 4 (3 professional years); * A post graduate, advanced MSc(OT) for qualified occupational therapists only is offered over 3 semesters online (5 credits with course work stream and research thesis stream).

Université Laval

Département de Readaptation
Faculté de médecine
Pavillon Ferdinand-Vandry
Bureau 3246
Cité universitaire
Québec, QC   G1K 7P4
Tel: 418-656-7923
Fax: 418-656-2733
E-mail: viviane.vaillencourt@fmed.ulaval.ca
Internet: www.fmed.ulaval.ca

General Information:
Degree Offered: B.Sc. de la santé (ergothérapie)
Length: 7 semesters
Years: 3-1/2
Language: français

Admission Requirements:
Previous Education: Diplôme d'études collégiales ou l'équivalent
Prerequisite Courses: Mathématiques 103 et 203; Biologie 301 et 401; Physique 101, 201 et 301; Chimie 101, 201 et 202
Average GPA: n/a
Range: n/a

Admission Test: Not required
Average Score: n/a
Score Report Deadline: n/a
Other Admission Criteria: Excellence du dossier scolaire (priorité aux candidats et candidates en provenance du Québec)*

Application Information:
Deadline: 1er mars
Application Fee: $75 ($35 applicables aux droits de soclarité)
Applicant/Acceptance Ratio: 7:1
Size of Incoming Class: 65**
Tuition: approx. $680 - $1,010, 12 - 18 crédits (soit $55.60/crédit & frais afférents)
Books/Materials: $200 par année en moyenne

Comments: * L'étudiant ou l'étudiante doit faire la preuve de la compétence relative au français. C'est à dire réussir un examen de français pour poursuivre son programme.
** Trois (3) places hors contingent, sont réservées aux étudiants et étudiantes du Nouveau-Brunswick en raison d'une entente particulière.

University of Manitoba
Lisa Mendez, Chair
Admissions and Selections Committee
Department of Occupational Therapy
School of Medical Rehabilitation
R106 - 771 McDermot Ave.
Winnipeg, MB   R3E 0T6
Tel: 204-977-5632
Fax: 204-789-3927
E-mail: mendezl@cc.umanitoba.ca
Internet: www.umanitoba.ca/medrehab

General Information:
Degree Offered: M.O.T. (Master of Occupational Therapy)
Length: 4 semesters
Years: 2 years
Language: English

Admission Requirements:
Previous Education: Previous undergraduate degree from a university recognized by the University of Manitoba
Prerequisite Courses: Must have a grade of 'C' or better on the following prerequisite courses: Introductory Psychology, Introductory Sociology, Human Anatomy, Human Physiology, Basic Statistics, Child Development (psychology) and Adult Development (psychology)
Average GPA: Must have maintained a 3 or better in the last 60 credit hours of study
Range: 3.0+
Admission Test: Not required
Average Score: n/a
Score Report Deadline: n/a
Other Admission Criteria: Interview

Application Information:
Deadline: April 1st
Application Fee: $75
Applicant/Acceptance Ratio: 2:1
Size of Incoming Class: 50
Tuition: $5,000
Books/Materials: $2,000

Comments: Limited enrolment faculty, first priority to Manitoba Applicants. Canadian Aboriginal persons who meet all the entrance requirements will be given priority for up to 15% of the enrolment number.

McGill University
School of Physical and Occupational Therapy, Davis House
3654 Promenade Sir-William-Osler
Montreal, QC   H3G 1Y5
Tel: 514-398-4500
Fax: 514-398-6360
E-mail: admissions@mcgill.ca
Internet: www.medicine.mcgill.ca/spot

General Information:
Degree Offered: B.Sc.(O.T.)
Length: 7 Semesters
Years: 3
Language: English

Admission Requirements:
Previous Education: Diploma of Collegial Studies (DCS) prior to start of classes; DCS, in Quebec
Prerequisite Courses: Biology, General Chemistry, Organic Chemistry, Mathematics, Physics, and a B.Sc. in Kinesiology
Average GPA: Above average
Range: n/a
Admission Test: Not required
Average Score: n/a
Score Report Deadline: n/a
Other Admission Criteria: All students must submit a letter attesting to 50 hours of volunteer or paid work in a health care facility or other appropriate setting, no later than August 1 of the entering year.

Application Information:
Deadline: January 15 - candidates studying outside Canada; February 1 - all other candidates
Application Fee: $60 non-refundable
Applicant/Acceptance Ratio: n/a
Size of Incoming Class: 60
Tuition: $1,668.30 for residents of Quebec; $4,401.30 for residents of all other provinces, plus the cost of student service fees
Books/Materials: $1,500 approx.

McMaster University
Office of the Registrar
1280 Main Street West
Hamilton, ON   L8S 4L8
Tel: 905-525-9140, ext. 22114

General Information:
Degree Offered: B.H.Sc.(O.T.)
Length: 24 months

Years: 2
Language: English

Admission Requirements:
Previous Education: Prior degree in any discipline
Prerequisite Courses: None
Average GPA: B- on last 2 years of academic work
Range: B- to A+
Admission Test: Not required
Average Score: n/a
Score Report Deadline: n/a
Other Admission Criteria:
Autobiographical material and interview

Application Information:
Deadline: December 1 for Application
January 15 for Supplementary Autobiographical material
Application Fee: $50
Applicant/Acceptance Ratio: 8:1
Size of Incoming Class: 60
Tuition: $3,972
Books/Materials: n/a

University of Ottawa
Faculty of Health Sciences
Graduate Secretariat, Admissions
451 Smyth
Ottawa, ON   K1H 8M5
Tel: 613-562-5700, ext. 8695
E-mail: sante.health@uottawa.ca
Internet: www.grad.uottawa.ca/sr

General Information:
Degree Offered: M.H.Sc. (Occupational Therapy)
Length: 6 semesters
Years: 2
Language: French offered to bilingual students
Admission Requirements:
Previous Education: Honours Bachelor's degree and prerequisite courses
Prerequisite Courses: University courses: Human Anatomy, Introduction to

Psychology, Child Development, Statistics, and one course in Sociology, Philosophy, or Antropology
Average GPA: 70% minimum
Range: n/a
Admission Test: Second Language Proficiency Test
Average Score: n/a
Score Report Deadline: n/a
Other Admission Criteria: Competence in English and French is compulsory. An immunization record is required by Aug 1.

Application Information:
Deadline: First Monday of February
Application Fee: 75
Applicant/Acceptance Ratio: 3:1
Size of Incoming Class: 32
Tuition: $2,511.16 per semester
Books/Materials: $400 - $800 first year

Queen's University
Admission Services
Richardson Hall
Kingston, ON   K7L 3N6
Tel: 613-533-2218
E-mail: admissn@post.queensu.ca
Internet: www.queensu.ca/admission

General Information:
Degree Offered: B.Sc.(O.T.)
Length: Semesters
Years: 3
Language: English
Admission Requirements:
Previous Education: See "Comments"
Prerequisite Courses: See "Comments"
Average GPA: n/a
Range: 70% minimum
Admission Test: Not required
Average Score: n/a
Score Report Deadline: n/a
Other Admission Criteria: Personal statement of experience

Application Information:
Deadline: February 25
Application Fee: n/a
Applicant/Acceptance Ratio: 6:1
Size of Incoming Class: 40
Tuition: $2,300
Books/Materials: $1,080 - $1,120

Comments: Occupational Therapy: University credit in Cellular Biology (or OAC Biology); Introductory Physics for Science Students (or OAC Physics) or Biomechanics; Introduction to/Principles of Psychology; Human Growth and Development Psychology (0.5 credit); Abnormal Psychology (0.5 credit); Introduction to Sociology; Research Methods (0.5 credit); Introduction to Statistics (0.5 credit); 1.5 course weight of university electives; and one English credit (100 level or above).

University of Toronto
Department of Occupational Therapy
500 University Ave.
Toronto, ON   M5G 1V7
Tel: 416-978-2765
Fax: 416-946-8570
E-mail: occupational.therapy@utoronto.ca
Internet: www.ot.utoronto.ca

General Information:
Degree Offered: M.Sc.(O.T.)
Length: Semesters
Years: 2
Language: English
Admission Requirements:
Previous Education: Four-year Bachelor's degree from a recognized university
Prerequisite Courses: Human growth and development (half credit); introductory physiology or introductory biology, human or vertebrae (half credit minimum); psychology (full credit); sociology or anthropology (half credit minimum); statistics (half credit minimum
Average GPA: 3.0

Range: 73% or mid-B minimum
Admission Test: Not required
Average Score: n/a
Score Report Deadline: n/a
Other Admission Criteria: All students
are ranked-ordered according to a
composite score. The score is derived
from marks & from a personal profile.
The personal profile is the non-academic
portion of your application. It consists of a
personal statement (responding to specific
questions), references, and a resume.

Application Information:
Deadline: Mid-January
Application Fee: $60
Applicant/Acceptance Ratio: 10:1
Size of Incoming Class: 70-80
Tuition: $6,737
Books/Materials: $500/year approx.

Application Information:
Deadline: January 15
Application Fee: $245
Applicant/Acceptance Ratio: 10:1
Size of Incoming Class: 52
Tuition: $2,751.35 per term (6 terms)
Books/Materials: $2,000 plus a fieldwork
placement fee, which is only required for
out of catchment placements

Comments: Candidates are urged to
visit occupational therapy facilities before
applying to gain a personal knowledge of
the profession. The final decision made by
the Admissions Committee is based only
on academic standing.

University of Western Ontario
Graduate Affairs Assistant
School of Occupational Therapy
Faculty of Health Sciences
Elborn College
London, ON   N6G 1H1
Tel: 519-661-2175
Fax: 519-661-3894
Internet: www.uwo.ca/fhs/ot

General Information:
Degree Offered: MSc(OT)
Length: 6 sessions
Years: 2
Language: English
Admission Requirements:
Previous Education: 4 year undergraduate
degree in any discipline
Prerequisite Courses: n/a
Average GPA: n/a
Range: n/a
Admission Test: Not required
Average Score: n/a
Score Report Deadline: n/a
Other Admission Criteria: Written
submission form

OPTOMETRY

The following fact sheets outline general information including academic requirements and application procedures for Optometry Schools in Canada. The data have been compiled in a concise format to assist students interested in these professional schools. Information was obtained from updates completed by each school, or in some cases from the school's Internet website.

Optometry Schools in Canada

University of Waterloo

Comments

1. These fact sheets act as a guide only. Students are advised to refer to the individual calendars or to write to the schools for more detailed information.

2. Application deadlines vary. Dates indicated refer to fall admission unless otherwise noted.

3. Tuition fees represent annual costs unless otherwise noted.

4. All of the schools listed above may not be represented.

University of Waterloo
School of Optometry
200 University Avenue West
Waterloo, ON   N2L 3G1
Tel: 519-888-4567, ext. 3178
Fax: 519-725-0784
Internet: www.optometry.uwaterloo.ca

General Information:
Degree Offered: O.D.
Length: Semesters
Years: 4
Language: English

Admission Requirements:
Previous Education: 3 Years of University science studies
Prerequisite Courses: *General Biology; General Chemistry; Physics; Calculus; English/Writing; Physiology (Human or Mammalian); Introductory Ethics; Organic Chemistry; Microbiology; Biochemistry; Statistics
Average GPA: 3.0
Range: 75%
Admission Test: Optometry Admission Test (O.A.T.)
Average Score: 370
Score Report Deadline: Please see website
Other Admission Criteria: Autobiographical sketch; interview; references

Application Information:
Deadline: Please see website
Application Fee: $115
Applicant/Acceptance Ratio: 3:1
Size of Incoming Class: 70
Tuition: $10,000
Books/Materials: $5,600 (equipment) + $3,400 (books)

Comments: *Check Optometry website for specific requirements on these courses. Human Anatomy, Embryology, Genetics, and Histology, Immunology, Linear Algebra or Trigonometry or Geometry are not required courses, but are highly recommended.

PHARMACY

The following fact sheets outline general information including academic requirements and application procedures for Pharmacy Schools in Canada. The data have been compiled in a concise format to assist students interested in these professional schools. Information was obtained from updates completed by each school, or in some cases from the school's Internet website.

Pharmacy Schools in Canada

University of Alberta
University of British Columbia
Dalhousie University
Université Laval
University of Manitoba

Memorial University of
Newfoundland
Université de Montréal
University of Saskatchewan*
University of Toronto

Comments

1. These fact sheets act as a guide only. Students are advised to refer to the individual calendars or to write to the schools for more detailed information.

2. Application deadlines vary. Dates indicated refer to fall admission unless otherwise noted.

3. Tuition fees represent annual costs unless otherwise noted.

4. All of the schools listed above may not be represented.

This university has not updated its information. Please contact the university directly.

University of Alberta
Faculty of Pharmacy & Pharmaceutical
Sciences
3126 Dentistry/Pharmacy Centre
Edmonton, AB   T6G 2N8
Tel: 780-492-3654
Fax:
E-mail: info@pharmacy.ualberta.ca
Internet: www.pharmacy.ualberta.ca

General Information:
Degree Offered: B.Sc. (Pharmacy)
Length: 2 four-month semesters
Years: 4 plus 1 year pre-professional
Language: English

Admission Requirements:
Previous Education: One pre-professional
year
Prerequisite Courses: A minimum of
6 units of course weight in General
Chemistry, Organic Chemistry and
English, as well as 3 units of course weight
in Biology, Biochemistry, Calculus and
Statistics.
Average GPA: 3.5
Range: n/a
Admission Test: Not required
Average Score: n/a
Score Report Deadline: n/a
Other Admission Criteria: Transcripts,
letter of intent

Application Information:
Deadline: March 1
Application Fee: $100
Applicant/Acceptance Ratio: 4:1
Size of Incoming Class: 130
Tuition: $3,828.00
Books/Materials: Year 1: $755; Year 2:
$850; Year 3: $1,530
Year 4: $300; Miscellaneous: $234.00

University of British Columbia
Director, Student Services
Faculty of Pharmaceutical Sciences
2146 East Mall
Vancouver, BC   V6T 1Z3
Tel: 604-822-4102
Fax: 604-822-3035
E-mail: manichol@interchange.ubc.ca
Internet: www.pharmacy.ubc.ca

General Information:
Degree Offered: B.Sc. (Pharmacy)
Length: Terms
Years: 4
Language: English

Admission Requirements:
Previous Education: Completion of one
year of sciences at a university or college
Prerequisite Courses: A full year each
(i.e. two semesters) of: first year university
biology with a lab, first year university
chemistry with a lab, first year university
English (for which UBC gives transfer
credit), first year university calculus, and
first year university physics with a lab
(also acceptable is a one semester physics
course that has a prerequisite requirement
of PHYS 12 and that includes a lab.
Average GPA: 75%
Range: 65% minimum
Admission Test: PCAT required (Pharmacy
College Admission Test)
Average Score: n/a
Transcript Deadline: June 15
Other Admission Criteria: Two letters
of reference, current resume, personal
statements. NB Supplemental Application
Form

Application Information:
Deadline: February 28, no exceptions
Application Fee: $60; $125 non-
refundable Application Fee
Applicant/Acceptance Ratio: 4:1
Size of Incoming Class: 150
Tuition: $7,800

Books/Materials: $800 approx. per annum

Comments: Admission is to first year only.

Dalhousie University
George A. Burbidge Pharmacy Building
College of Pharmacy
Halifax, NS   B3H 3J5
Tel: 902-494-2378
Fax: 902-494-1396
E-mail: pharmacy@dal.ca
Internet: www.pharmacy.dal.ca

General Information:
Degree Offered: B.Sc. (Pharmacy)
Length: Semesters
Years: 4
Language: English

Admission Requirements:
Previous Education: At least one year in a B.Sc. program at a recognized university
Prerequisite Courses: The following first-year Dalhousie courses (or their equivalent at other universities): Chemistry; Mathematics and Statistics; Biology; English; Social Science. Please see website for furthur information.
Average GPA: n/a
Range: B minimum
Admission Test: Not required
Average Score: n/a
Score Report Deadline: n/a
Other Admission Criteria: Official transcripts; interview

Application Information:
Deadline: February 1
Application Fee: $70
Applicant/Acceptance Ratio: Varies
Size of Incoming Class: 90
Tuition: $9,500
Books/Materials: $1,000 per year (approx.)

University of Manitoba
424 University Centre
Winnipeg, MB   R3T 2N2
Tel: 204-474-8808
Fax: 204-474-7554
E-mail: admissions@umanitoba.ca
Internet: www.umanitoba.ca/admissions

General Information:
Degree Offered: B.Sc. (Pharmacy)
Length: September - April
Years: 5 (includes pre-professional year)
Language: English

Admission Requirements:
Previous Education: One full year of university level study (4 prescribed courses and one Humanities option); 30 credit hours
Prerequisite Courses: 30 credit hours required including chemistry, biology, calculus and electives
Average GPA: 3.5
Range: 75%
Admission Test: Written essay/personal profile, problem-solving exercise
Average Score: 5/10 on essay
Score Report Deadline: n/a
Other Admission Criteria: Pharmacy applicants who are required by university regulation to demonstrate their proficiency in the English Language by writing the Test of English as a Foreign Language (TOEFL), CanTest, IELTS, or MELAB will also be required to achieve a score of not less than 200 in the Test of Spoken English (TSE). Please note that the Pharmacy College Admission Test (PCAT) is not a requirement.

Application Information:
Deadline: March 1
Application Fee: $90
Applicant/Acceptance Ratio: 6:1
Size of Incoming Class: 50
Tuition: $6,612
Books/Materials: $1,200

Memorial University of Newfoundland
School of Pharmacy
Health Science Centre
St. John's, NL   A1B 3V6
Tel: 709-777-7211
Fax: 709-777-7044
E-mail: pharminfo@mun.ca
Internet: www.mun.ca/pharmacy

General Information:
Degree Offered: B.Sc. (Pharmacy)
Length: 8 semesters
Years: 4
Language: English

Admission Requirements:
Previous Education: One year of university
Prerequisite Courses: Biology 1001, 1002, Chemistry 1050, 1051, English 1080, 1101 (or equivalent), Mathematics 1000, 1001, Physics 1020, 1021
Average GPA: 75% approx.
Range: 70% minimum
Admission Test: Not required
Average Score: n/a
Score Report Deadline: n/a
Other Admission Criteria: Two references; interview is usually required

Application Information:
Deadline: March 1
Application Fee: $75
Applicant/Acceptance Ratio: 4:1
Size of Incoming Class: 40
Tuition: Citizens of Canada and Permanent Residents - $85 per credit hour; International Students - $293 per credit hour;
$2,300 room and meals per semester
Books/Materials: $300 per semester

Comments: Application Processing Fee: $40 for all applicants
In addition: $40 for applicants with advanced standing & non-Canadian application fee (this fee is in addition to the Application Processing fee).

University of Saskatchewan
D.K.J. Gorecki, Ph.D.
College of Pharmacy and Nutrition
110 Science Place
Saskatoon, SK   S7N 5C9
Tel: 306-966-6328
Fax: 306-966-6377
E-mail: undergrad-pharmacy-nutrition@usask.ca
Internet: www.usask.ca/pharmacy-nutrition

General Information:
Degree Offered: B.S.P.
Length: Semesters
Years: 5
Language: English

Admission Requirements:
Previous Education: College of Arts & Science Pre-Pharmacy year
Prerequisite Courses: **Pre-Pharmacy year: Biology 110.6, Chemistry 112.3 and 250.3, English 110.6 (or two of English 111.3, 112.3, 113.3 or 114.3, or French 121.3 (or 122.3) and 125.3 or Literature 100.6), 12 credits of electives in humanities, social sciences or fine arts of which 6 credits must be from Psychology 110.6, Sociology 110.6, Philosophy 110.6 (or 120.3 and 133.3), or Native Studies 105.3 and 106.3
Average GPA: minimum of 70% required
Range: 70%+
Admission Test: Essay to Test Critical Skills and Personal Profile administered by the college
Average Score: n/a
Score Report Deadline: n/a
Other Admission Criteria: None

Application Information:
Deadline: February 15**
Application Fee: $75
Applicant/Acceptance Ratio: 5:1
Size of Incoming Class: 90**
Tuition: $5,500-$6,200 including student fees (subject to change)
Books/Materials: $1,000 per year

Comments: Admission is based on an admission score which consists of - Academic average (60%) + Test of Critical Skills (30%) + Personal Profile (10%). Non-resident students applying may be accepted into a limited quota. * Five-year program consists of one Pre-Pharmacy year and 4 years of Pharmacy. Please contact the college for more information before December 1st.

University of Toronto
Leslie Dan
Faculty of Pharmacy
144 College Street
Toronto, ON   M5S 3M2
Tel: 416-978-3967
Fax: 416-978-8511
E-mail: adm.phm@utoronto.ca
Internet: www.pharmacy.utoronto.ca/undergrad

General Information:
Degree Offered: Bachelor of Science in Pharmacy (BScPhm)
Length: n/a
Years: 4
Language: English

Admission Requirements:
Previous Education: A minimum of one full year (i.e. equivalent of 5 full credits) of university study. Applicants with more than one year of university study apply for first year of the Pharmacy program and are assessed for transfer credit upon admission. Candidates granted transfer credit have a reduced course load in one or more years, but are required to maintain full time status.
Prerequisite Courses: Englisg (ENG4U or former OAC); Biology (university level); Physics (SPH4U or former OAC or university level); Chemistry (university level, equivalent to U of T CHM138H + 139H or former CHM137Y); Calculus (university level), equivalent to U of T MAT135Y); Social Science or Humanities (university level)
Average GPA: 70% (B-) minimum cumulative university average is required to gain initial consideration in the initial screening of applicants. The minimum required average may be higher in the final selections.
Range: n/a
Admission Test: Pharmacy College Admissions Test (PCAT)
Average Score: n/a
Score Report Deadline: n/a
Other Admission Criteria: TBA

Application Information:
Deadline: December 12 for September admission; Apply online at www.pharmacy.utoronto.ca/undergrad
Application Fee: TBA
Applicant/Acceptance Ratio: 6.6:1
Size of Incoming Class: 240
Tuition: $11,752.12 (domestic); $23,761.12 (international); not including incidental fees
Books/Materials: TBA

Comments: Prerequisite courses taken at the university level must be full credit equivalents. For the 2009 admission cycle, the cumulative university average and performance on the PCAT will be considered. Furthur details regarding 2009 requirements will be posted on the Pharmcy website as of summer 2008. There may be additional requirements for future admission cycles.
Preference will be given to Canadian citizens or landed immigrants who have resided in the province of Ontario for at least one year immediately prior to September admission. A maximum of 10% of the first year places may be offered to non-Ontario applicants including international students. Due to the limited number of places available, it is not possible to admit all qualified

applicants. Therefore, in choosing courses, prospective applicants should follow a program of study which not only makes them eligible for admission to Phamacy but also offers an alternative to Pharmacy. Detailed information can be obtained from the Pharmacy website at www.pharmacy. utoronto.ca/undergrad.

PHYSICAL THERAPY

The following fact sheets outline general information including academic requirements and application procedures for Physical Therapy Schools in Canada. The data have been compiled in a concise format to assist students interested in these professional schools. Information was obtained from updates completed by each school, or in some cases from the school's Internet website.

Physical Therapy Schools in Canada

University of Alberta
University of British Columbia
Dalhousie University*
Université Laval
University of Manitoba*
McGill University*

McMaster University*
Université de Montréal
University of Ottawa
Queen's University*
University of Saskatchewan
University of Toronto

Comments

1. These fact sheets act as a guide only. Students are advised to refer to the individual calendars or to write to the schools for more detailed information.

2. Application deadlines vary. Dates indicated refer to fall admission unless otherwise noted.

3. Tuition fees represent annual costs unless otherwise noted.

4. All of the schools listed above may not be represented.

* This university has not updated its information. Please contact the university directly.

University of Alberta
Student Records Clerk
Faculty of Rehabilitation Medicine
3-50 Corbett Hall
Edmonton, AB   T6G 2G4
Tel: 403-492-5949
Internet: www.uofaweb.ualberta.ca/
rehabmed/pt

General Information:
Degree Offered: M.Sc. (P.T.)
Length: Semesters
Years: 2.5 years
Language: English

Admission Requirements:
Previous Education: 4 years B.Sc or other
recognized baccalaureate degree
Prerequisite Courses: English, Statistics,
Psychology, Human Anatomy, Human
Physiology
Average GPA: 8.0/9.0 on most recent 60
university half courses (92%/8.6 if non-
resident of Alberta)
Range: n/a
Admission Test: Not required
Average Score: n/a
Score Report Deadline: n/a
Other Admission Criteria: 30 hours of
paid or volunteer experience working with
individuals that have disabilities

Application Information:
Deadline: February 1
Application Fee: $100
Applicant/Acceptance Ratio: 8:1
Size of Incoming Class: 80
Tuition: $4,000
Books/Materials: $800-1,000

University of British Columbia
Claudia Buffone
Student Services Program Assistant
Department of Physical Therapy
T325 - Third Floor Koerner Pavilion
2211 Wesbrook Mall
Vancouver, BC   V6T 2B5
Tel: 604-822-7050
Fax: 604-822-7624
E-mail: claudia.buffone@ubc.ca
Internet: www.physicaltherapy.med.ubc.ca

General Information:
Degree Offered: Master of Physical
Therapy (M.P.T.)
Length: 26 months completed in 7 blocks
Years: 26 months
Language: English

Admission Requirements:
Previous Education: 4 year Bachelor's
Degree
Prerequisite Courses: Chemistry
12 or higher (3 credits), Statistics (3
credits), Physics 12 or higher (3 credits),
Psychology (3 credits), Anatomy (3
credits), Human Physiology (6 credits)
Average GPA: 76% or higher
Range: 75% - 95%
Admission Test: Test of competency in
written English
Average Score: n/a
Score Report Deadline: n/a
Other Admission Criteria: A minimum
of 70 hours of volunteer or paid work
in a setting which includes persons
with disabilities. A personal interview is
required, and priority is given to B.C.
residents. Please contact department for
current information.

Application Information:
Deadline: February 1
Application Fee: $90.00 for online
application + $100.00 supplementary
application fee directly to the Department
of Physical Therapy
Applicant/Acceptance Ratio: 1:5

Size of Incoming Class: 40
Tuition: $11,673.29 in 7 installments
Books/Materials: $1,700

Dalhousie University
School of Physiotherapy
Forrest Building
5869 University Avenue
Halifax, NS   B3H 3J5
Tel: 902-494-2524
E-mail: physiotherapy@dal.ca
Internet: www.dal.ca

General Information:
Degree Offered: B.Sc.PT.
Length: 8 semesters (including prerequisite year)
Years: 4
Language: English

Admission Requirements:
Previous Education: Four-year undergraduate degree
Prerequisite Courses: The following first-year Dalhousie courses (or their equivalent at other universities): Chemistry or Biology; Physics; one of Psychology or Sociology and Social Anthropology; Statistics; 1.5 Arts or Social Sciences electives, one of which fulfils the writing requirement
Average GPA: n/a
Range: 78 - 95%
Admission Test: Not required
Average Score: n/a
Score Report Deadline: n/a
Other Admission Criteria: Interview

Application Information:
Deadline: February 15
Application Fee: $45
Applicant/Acceptance Ratio: 8:1
Size of Incoming Class: 48
Tuition: $8,960
Books/Materials: Year 2: $900; Year 3: $1,200; Year 4: $700

Université Laval
Programme de physiothérapie
Faculté de médecine
Pavillon Ferdinand-Vandry
Ste-Foy, QC   G1K 7P4
Tel: 418-656-2131 poste 2492
Fax: 418-656-2733
E-mail: admission@fmed.ulaval.ca
Internet: www.fmed.ulaval.ca

General Information:
Degree Offered: Baccalauréat-Master Continuum
Length: 10 Semesters
Years: 4-1/2
Language: français

Admission Requirements:
Previous Education: Diplôme d'études collégiales ou l'équivalent - profile sciences de la santé
Prerequisite Courses: Mathématiques, Biologie, Physique, Chimie
Average GPA: 3.4
Range: 3.2 - 4.0
Admission Test: Test de connaissance du français
Average Score: n/a
Score Report Deadline: n/a
Other Admission Criteria: Excellence du dossier scolaire. Note autobiographique standardisée (NAS).
Priorité aux candidats en provenance du Québec.

Application Information:
Deadline: 1er mars
Application Fee: $30
Applicant/Acceptance Ratio: 9:1
Size of Incoming Class: 70
Tuition: $55.60 du crédit plus $8.25 du crédit de frais afférents (max $99.00) et $5.00 du crédit de frais de gestion (max $75.00)
Books/Materials: $2,000

University of Manitoba
Att: N. Iwaszczuk, Admissions Officer
Winnipeg, MB   R3T 2N2
Tel: 204-474-8815

General Information:
Degree Offered: B.M.R.(P.T.)
Length: August - April
Years: 3
Language: English

Admission Requirements:
Previous Education: First-year university (30 credit hours, Arts & Science)
Prerequisite Courses: Sociology 120, Psychology 120, Biology 123 or 125, and 2 additional full year courses or equivalent, including a 3 credit hour written English University 1 requirement
Average GPA: 3.914
Range: n/a
Admission Test: Not required
Average Score: n/a
Score Report Deadline: n/a
Other Admission Criteria: Interview. Limited enrolment faculty, first priority will be given to Manitoba residents

Application Information:
Deadline: March 1
Application Fee: $50; $60 Visa students
Applicant/Acceptance Ratio: 5:1
Size of Incoming Class: 30
Tuition: $4,819.00, plus $849.45 Clinical Education intersession
Books/Materials: Pending Senate approval, effective September 2000, 42 domestic; 6 international

Comments: A Master of Science in Rehabilitation is also offered. Special Consideration Category: Manitobans who apply through the SPSP and Access programs of the University of Manitoba

McGill University
Admissions, Recruitment and Registrar's Office
James Admininistration Bldg. Annex
847 Sherbrooke Street West
Montreal, QC   H3A 2T5
Tel: 514-398-3910
Fax: 514-398-4193
E-mail: admissions@mcgill.ca
Internet: www.mcgill.ca/applying

General Information:
Degree Offered: B.Sc.(P.T.)
Length: 7 Semesters (105 Credits)
Years: 3 following a Quebec Collegial Program in Sciences or equivalent
Language: English

Admission Requirements:
Previous Education: Quebec applicants: CEGEP Diploma of Collegial Studies; * See Comments section for more information
Prerequisite Courses: * See Comments section for more information
Average GPA: Depends on applicant pool
Range: n/a
Admission Test: Not required
Average Score: n/a
Score Report Deadline: n/a
Other Admission Criteria: All applicants much complete at least 50 hours of volunteer or paid work in a health care facility or other appropriate rehabilitation environment. A letter (or letters) or reference to attest to the service must be submitted prior to August 1 of the entering year. Visit their website for information on their Language Policy.

Application Information:
Deadline: Outside Canada - January 15; Out-of-Province - February 1; Quebec CEGEP - March 1
Application Fee: $60 non-refundable
Applicant/Acceptance Ratio: n/a
Size of Incoming Class: Limited enrollment

Tuition: Tuition is based on a 30 credit course load. Quebec residents (proof of residency required) who are Canadian citizens or Permanent residents: $1,668.30; Non-Quebec Canadian citizens and Permanent residents: $4,012.50; International students (depending on program and courses selected): $8,763 - $15,000. Note: amounts listed above do not include Student Service Fees.
Books/Materials: $1,000 approx.

Comments: * Quebec applicants who have obtained a CEGEP Diploma of Collegial Studies are expected to have taken the following prerequisite courses: Biololgy - 00UK, 00XU; Chemistry - 00UL, 00UM, 00XV; Mathematics - 00UN, 00UP; Physics - 00UR, 00US, 00UT. Applicants who have completed a minimum of one year of college/university studies (or equivalent) are expected to have taken the following university/college level courses: two terms of biology with labs; two terms of general chemistry with labs; one term of organic chemistry with labs; two terms of physics (mechanics, electricity and magnetism, waves and optics) with labs; one term of differential calculus; and one term of integral calculus. Applicants from the United Kingdom and Commonwealth countries must have completed two A-Level subjects with final grades of B or better, and two A-Level subjects with a final grade of C or better. A-Level subjects must include Biology, Chemistry, Mathematics and Physics. Applicants with a French Baccalaureate must have completed Series S, with a minimum overall average 12/20 and a minimum of 10/20 in each mathematics, biological and physical sciences course. Applicants may be required to complete additional courses in organic chemistry prior to admission. Applicants with an International Baccalaureate must have completed biology, chemistry, mathematics, and physics at Higher Level.

McMaster University
Admissions Coordinator
School of Rehabilitation Science
Institute for Applied Health Sciences
1400 Main Street West, Room 402
Hamilton, ON   L8S 1C7
Tel: 905-525-9140 ext. 27829
Fax: 905-524-0069
E-mail: otpt@mcmaster.ca
Internet: www-fhs.mcmaster.ca/rehab

General Information:
Degree Offered: M.Sc.PT - Master of Science (Physiotherapy)
Length: 24 months
Years: 2
Language: English

Admission Requirements:
Previous Education: 3 year baccalaureate degree (90 units/credits); 4 year baccalaureate degree (120 units/credits)
Prerequisite Courses: A full or half credit in one biological or life science course; a full or half credit in one social science or humanities course
Average GPA: 3.0
Range: 75% or B minimum
Admission Test: TOEFL test if English is not the applicant's first language
Average Score: 580 (paper); 237 (computer)
Score Report Deadline: n/a
Other Admission Criteria: Interview

Application Information:
Deadline: January 15
Application Fee: $150; Institutional Fee $60
Applicant/Acceptance Ratio: 15:1
Size of Incoming Class: 57
Tuition: $7,500 approx.
Books/Materials: $2,500 approx.

University of Ottawa
Faculty of Health Sciences
Graduate Secretariat, Admissions
451 Smyth
Ottawa, ON   K1H 8M5
Tel: 613-562-5700, ext. 8695
E-mail: sante.health@uottawa.ca
Internet: www.grad.uottawa.ca/sr

General Information:
Degree Offered: M.H.Sc. (Physiotherapy)
Length: 6 semesters
Years: 2
Language: French offered to bilingual students

Admission Requirements:
Previous Education: Honours Bachelor's degree and prerequisite courses
Prerequisite Courses: University courses: two courses in Human Anatomy, Introduction to Psychology, and Statistics. A third course in Anatomy is recommended.
Average GPA: 70% minimum
Range: n/a
Admission Test: Second Language Proficiency Test
Average Score: n/a
Score Report Deadline: n/a
Other Admission Criteria: Competence in English and French is compulsory. An immunization record is required by Aug 1.

Application Information:
Deadline: First Monday of February
Application Fee: $75
Applicant/Acceptance Ratio: 4:1
Size of Incoming Class: 32
Tuition: $2,511.16 per semester
Books/Materials: $400 - $800 first year

Queen's University
Admission Services
Richardson Hall
Kingston, ON   K7L 3N6
Tel: 613-533-2218
E-mail: admissn@post.queensu.ca
Internet: www.queensu.ca/admission

General Information:
Degree Offered: B.Sc. (P.T.)
Length: Semesters
Years: 3
Language: English

Admission Requirements:
Previous Education:
Prerequisite Courses: Physical Therapy: University credit in Cellular Biology; Introductory Physics for Science Students or Biomechanics; Introduction to/ Principles of Psychology; Human Growth and Development Psychology (0.5 credit); Introduction to Statistics (0.5 credit); and one English credit (100 level or above).
Average GPA: n/a
Range: n/a
Admission Test: n/a
Average Score: n/a
Score Report Deadline: n/a
Other Admission Criteria: Personal statement of experience

Application Information:
Deadline: February 20
Application Fee: n/a
Applicant/Acceptance Ratio: n/a
Size of Incoming Class: n/a
Tuition: $2,300
Books/Materials: n/a

University of Saskatchewan

Academic Program Assistant
School of Physical Therapy
1121 College Drive
Saskatoon, SK   S7N 0W3
Tel: 306-966-6579
Fax: 306-966-6575
Internet: www.medicine.usask.ca/pt

General Information:

Degree Offered: M.P.T
Length: Semesters
Years: 2 years and 6 weeks
Language: English

Admission Requirements:

Previous Education: 4-year baccalaureate in any discipline
Prerequisite Courses: Full courses in human physiology; half courses in statistics and human anatomy (prerequisite courses taken at universities other than University of Saskatchewan or University of Regina must be approved by the Admissions committee well in advance of application)
Average GPA: 83% in 2003
Range: GPA based on the last academic year in which a minimum course load of 30 credit units was taken
Admission Test: Not required
Average Score: n/a
Score Report Deadline: n/a
Other Admission Criteria: Admission/ selection process includes mandatory interview. Restricted to Saskatchewan, NWT, Yukon and Nunavut residents

Application Information:

Deadline: January 15
Application Fee: $75
Applicant/Acceptance Ratio: 4:1
Size of Incoming Class: 40
Tuition: $15,191 (estimated) tuition and student fees over the 2 years in 2007/2008
Books/Materials: $,5000 (estimated) over the 3 years

University of Toronto

Department of Physical Therapy
Faculty of Medicine
160-500 University Avenue
Toronto, ON   M5G 1V7
Tel: 416-978-2765
Fax: 416-946-8562
E-mail: physther.facmed@utoronto.ca
Internet: www.physicaltherapy.utoronto.ca

General Information:

Degree Offered: MScPT
Length: n/a
Years: 2
Language: English

Admission Requirements:

Previous Education: Four years of undergraduate study
Prerequisite Courses: One full-course equivalent in Human/Vertebrae Physiology; one full-course equivalent in Life and/or Physical Sciences; one full-course equivalent in Social Sciences or Humanities or Languages; one half-course or equivalent in Statistics or Research Methods. All prerequisite courses must be taken at a university level and must be completed within the last seven years.
Average GPA: A-
Range: n/a
Admission Test: CAP; see website for details
Average Score: n/a
Score Report Deadline: n/a

Application Information:

Deadline: mid-January
Application Fee: n/a
Applicant/Acceptance Ratio: 9:1
Size of Incoming Class: approx. 80
Tuition: $7,286 plus incidentals
Books/Materials: $1,500 over a two year period

PUBLIC ADMINISTRATION

The following fact sheets outline general information including academic requirements and application procedures for Public Administration Schools in Canada. The data have been compiled in a concise format to assist students interested in these professional schools. Information was obtained from updates completed by each school, or in some cases from the school's Internet website.

Public Administration Schools in Canada

University of Alberta*
Carleton University
Dalhousie University
McMaster University
Université de Moncton
Queen's University

University of Victoria
University of Western Ontario
University of Winnipeg with
University of Manitoba*
York University*

Comments

1. These fact sheets act as a guide only. Students are advised to refer to the individual calendars or to write to the schools for more detailed information.

2. Application deadlines vary. Dates indicated refer to fall admission unless otherwise noted.

3. Tuition fees represent annual costs unless otherwise noted.

4. All of the schools listed above may not be represented.

* This university has not updated its information. Please contact the university directly.

University of Alberta
Dept. of Public Health Sciences
13-103 Clinical Sciences Bldg.
Edmonton, AB   T6G 2G3
Tel: 780-492-6408
Fax: 780-492-0364
Internet: www.phs.ualberta.ca

General Information:
Degree Offered: M.P.H. Master of Public
Health (Health Policy Research)
Length: Semesters
Years: 2
Language: English

Admission Requirements:
Previous Education: Baccalaureate degree
Prerequisite Courses: Recent course in
Introductory Statistics
Average GPA: 7.2 on 9-point scale
Range: 6.5 on 9-point scale
Admission Test: GMAT or GRE
Average Score: GMAT: (30/30/500); GRE
(500/500/500/1500)
Score Report Deadline: September
Other Admission Criteria: Graduate
Studies Application Form, transcripts, 3
letters of reference, curriculum vitae, letter
of intent

Application Information:
Deadline: March 1
Application Fee: $100
Applicant/Acceptance Ratio: 6:1
Size of Incoming Class: 15
Tuition: $3,000 approx.
Books/Materials: $500 approx.

Comments: Program 1 of 3

University of Alberta
Dept. of Public Health Sciences
13-103 Clinical Sciences Bldg.
Edmonton, AB   T6G 2G3
Tel: 780-492-6408
Fax: 780-492-0364
Internet: www.phs.ualberta.ca

General Information:
Degree Offered: M.P.H. (Occupational
and Environment Health)
Length: Semesters
Years: 2
Language: English

Admission Requirements:
Previous Education: Baccalaureate
degree in Health Sciences, Environmental
Chemistry, or other relevant subject,
and related postgraduate training or
experience.
Prerequisite Courses: Recent course in
Introductory Statistics
Average GPA: 7.2 on 9-point scale
Range: 6.5 on 9-point scale
Admission Test:
Average Score:
Score Report Deadline: September
Other Admission Criteria: Graduate
Studies Application Form, transcripts, 3
letters of reference, curriculum vitae, letter
of intent

Application Information:
Deadline: March 1
Application Fee: $100
Applicant/Acceptance Ratio: 6:1
Size of Incoming Class: 15
Tuition: $3,000 approx.
Books/Materials: $500 approx.

Comments: Program 2 of 3

University of Alberta
Dept. of Public Health Sciences
13-103 Clinical Sciences Bldg.
Edmonton, AB   T6G 2G3
Tel: 780-492-6408
Fax: 780-492-0364
Internet: www.phs.ualberta.ca

General Information:
Degree Offered: M.P.H. Master of Public
Health (Health Policy and Management)
Length: Semesters
Years: 2
Language: English

Admission Requirements:
Previous Education: Baccalaureate degree
Prerequisite Courses: Recent course in Introductory Statistics
Average GPA: 7.2 on 9-point scale
Range: 6.5 on 9-point scale
Admission Test: GMAT or GRE
Average Score: GMAT (30/30/500); GRE (500/500/500/1500)
Score Report Deadline: September
Other Admission Criteria: Graduate Studies Application Form, transcripts, 3 letters of reference, curriculum vitae, letter of intent

Application Information:
Deadline: March 1
Application Fee: $100
Applicant/Acceptance Ratio: 6:1
Size of Incoming Class: 15
Tuition: $3,000 approx.
Books/Materials: $500 approx.

Comments: Program 3 of 3

Carleton University
School of Public Administration
1125 Colonel By Drive
Ottawa, ON   K1S 5B6
Tel: 613-520-2547
Fax: 613-520-2551
E-mail: public administration@carleton.ca

General Information:
Degree Offered: M.A. in Public Administration (Innovation, Science & Environment Concentration)
Length: 6 terms
Years: 2
Language: English

Admission Requirements:
Previous Education: Bachelor's degree in any discipline
Prerequisite Courses: University courses in micro and macro economic theory, and in Canadian government and politics
Average GPA: 9.0/B+

Range: 77 - 79%
Admission Test: n/a
Average Score: n/a
Score Report Deadline: n/a
Other Admission Criteria: Two References

Application Information:
Deadline: January 28 (for financial assistance);
May 1 (without funding)
Application Fee: $60
Applicant/Acceptance Ratio: n/a
Size of Incoming Class: 8 - 10
Tuition: n/a
Books/Materials: $500 - $600 per term

Comments: The M.A. in Public Administration can be completed in 2 years, full-time and up to 8 years on a part-time basis. Full-time Canadian students registered in the Co-op Option must satisfactorily complete at least two work terms in order to graduate with a co-op designation on their transcripts and diplomas.
Mid-career applicants must submit 2 references.
A one-year diploma in Public Administration (Innovation, Science & the Environment Concentration) is also available and can be completed on a full-time or part-time basis. Program 3 of 3.

Carleton University
School of Public Administration
1125 Colonel By Drive
Ottawa, ON   K1S 5B6
Tel: 613-520-2547
Fax: 613-520-2551
E-mail: public administration@carleton.ca

General Information:
Degree Offered: M.A. in Public Administration (International Development Concentration)
Length: 6 terms
Years: 2
Language: English

Admission Requirements:
Previous Education: Bachelor's degree in any discipline
Prerequisite Courses: University courses in micro and macro economic theory
Average GPA: 9.0/B+
Range: 77 - 79%
Admission Test: n/a
Average Score: n/a
Score Report Deadline: n/a
Other Admission Criteria: International students require a TOEFL of 550/213 and two references

Application Information:
Deadline: January 28 (for financial assistance)
Application Fee: n/a
Applicant/Acceptance Ratio: n/a
Size of Incoming Class: n/a
Tuition: n/a
Books/Materials: $500 - $600 per term

Comments: The M.A. in Public Administration can be completed in 2 years, full-time and up to 8 years on a part-time basis. Full-time Canadian students registered in the Co-op Option must satisfactorily complete at least two work terms in order to graduate with a co-op designation on their transcripts and diplomas. Mid-career applicants must submit 2 references. A one-year diploma in Public Administration (Development Concentration) is also available and can be completed on a full-time or part-time basis.
Program 2 of 3.

Carleton University
School of Public Administration
1125 Colonel By Drive
Ottawa, ON   K1S 5B6
Tel: 613-520-2547
Fax: 613-520-2551
E-mail: public administration@carleton.ca

General Information:
Degree Offered: M.A. in Public Administration (Public Management or Public Policy)
Length: 6 terms
Years: 2
Language: English

Admission Requirements:
Previous Education: Bachelor's degree in any discipline
Prerequisite Courses: University courses in micro and macro economic theory, and in Canadian government and politics
Average GPA: 9.0/B+
Range: 77 - 79%
Admission Test: n/a
Average Score: n/a
Score Report Deadline: n/a
Other Admission Criteria: Two academic references

Application Information:
Deadline: January 15 (for financial assistance)
May 1 (without funding)
Application Fee: $78
Applicant/Acceptance Ratio: n/a
Size of Incoming Class: n/a
Tuition: n/a
Books/Materials: $500 - $600 per term

Comments: The M.A. in Public Administration can be completed in 2 years, full-time and up to 8 years on a part-time basis. Full-time Canadian students registered in the Co-op Option must satisfactorily complete at least two work terms in order to graduate with a co-op designation on their transcripts and diplomas.
Mid-career applicants must submit 2 references. A one-year diploma in Public Administration (Canadian Concentration) is also available and can be completed on a full-time or part-time basis. Program 1 of 3.

Dalhousie University

Chair, Admission Committee
School of Public Administration
6100 University Avenue, Rm. 3010
Halifax, NS   B3H 3J5
Tel: 902-494-3742
Fax: 902-494-7023
E-mail: dalmpa@dal.ca
Internet: www.spa.management.dal.ca

General Information:
Degree Offered: M.P.A./G.D.P.A./M.P.A. (Management) online
Length: 4 and 2 semesters
Years: 2 and 1
Language: English

Admission Requirements:
Previous Education: Undergraduate degree (B.A., B.Sc. or B.Comm.)
Prerequisite Courses: None
Average GPA: A minimum of 3.3
Range: A minimum average grade of B+ (equivalent to a GPA of 3.3) in the last 2 years of studies
Admission Test: GMAT, if borderline GPA or non-Canadian
Average Score: 580
Score Report Deadline: Prefer April 15
Other Admission Criteria: Resume and academic references

Application Information:
Deadline: June 1 (program often filled earlier)
Application Fee: $70
Applicant/Acceptance Ratio: Varies from year to year
Size of Incoming Class: 50 FTE approx.
Tuition: Approx. $825 per course (incl. all fees); $1800 per course for online M.P.A. (M)
Books/Materials: $1,000 per year

Comments: Location of the School of Public Administration within Dalhousie's Faculty of Management offers students program linkages to graduate courses in Business Administration, Environmental Management, and Information Technology

McMaster University

Department of Political Science
Hamilton, ON   L8S 4M4
Tel: 905-525-9140, ext. 24741
Fax: 905-527-3071
E-mail: polisci@mcmaster.ca

General Information:
Degree Offered: M.A. (Public Policy and Administration)
Length: Terms
Years: 1
Language: English

Admission Requirements:
Previous Education: Honours degree in Political Science
Prerequisite Courses: n/a
Average GPA: B+
Range: n/a
Admission Test: None
Average Score: n/a
Score Report Deadline: n/a
Other Admission Criteria: None

Application Information:
Deadline: February 15
Application Fee: $90
Applicant/Acceptance Ratio: Varies
Size of Incoming Class: n/a
Tuition: $5,154 (Canadians and landed immigrants); $12,525 (Visa students) per year
Books/Materials: n/a

Comments: A Ph.D. in the field of Public Policy is also offered. The Department also offers an M.A. in the fields of Comparative, Canadian, International Relations, and Political Theory.

Université de Moncton

Sylvain Vézina, Dir.
Département d'administration publique
Moncton, NB E1A 3E9
Tel: 506-858-4177
Fax: 506-858-4506
E-mail: lucille.leger@umoncton.ca
Internet: www.umoncton.ca

General Information:

Degree Offered: M.A.P.
Length: 60 credits
Years: 2 (full-time); 5 (part-time)
Language: français

Admission Requirements:

Previous Education: Bachelor's degree or equivalent experience
Prerequisite Courses: None
Average GPA: B
Range: n/a
Admission Test: Not required
Average Score: n/a
Score Report Deadline: n/a
Other Admission Criteria: n/a

Application Information:

Deadline: June 1 (Canadian students); February 1 (International students)
Application Fee: $39
Applicant/Acceptance Ratio: 1:1
Size of Incoming Class: 12
Tuition: $191 CDN per credit (Canadian students); $299 CDN per credit (International students)
Books/Materials: $259 for international students until Sept 2004, starting Sept 2004, $274 for international students

Queen's University

School of Policy Studies
Kingston, ON K7L 3N6
Tel: 613-533-2159
Fax: 613-533-2135
E-mail: policy@post.queensu.ca
Internet: www.queensu.ca/sps/

General Information:

Degree Offered: M.P.A. (part-time M.P.A. program degree offered – 6 semesters/2 years)
Length: 3 semesters
Years: 1
Language: English

Admission Requirements:

Previous Education: Four-year undergraduate degree
Prerequisite Courses: None
Average GPA: 3.5 or B+ or 75%
Range: 3.3 - 4.0
Admission Test: n/a
Average Score: n/a
Score Report Deadline: n/a
Other Admission Criteria: TOEFL test from International students whose primary language is not English

Application Information:

Deadline: February 1
Application Fee: $85 non-refundable
Applicant/Acceptance Ratio: 5:1
Size of Incoming Class: 55
Tuition: $8,000
Books/Materials: $200 per course (part-time M.P.A. - $1080 per course)

University of Victoria

Att: Prof. J. Langford, Graduate Advisor
School of Public Administration
P.O. Box 1700
Victoria, BC V8X 2Y2
Tel: 250-721-8055
Fax: 250-721-8849
E-mail: padm@uvic.ca
Internet: http://publicadmin.uvic.ca

General Information:

Degree Offered: M.P.A. & M.P.A./L.L.B.
Length: Semesters
Years: 2 years for M.P.A. on-campus; M.P.A. online program (distance) is 2 years or longer, depending on pace
Language: English

Admission Requirements:
Previous Education: Required to have an undergraduate degree or equivalent academic qualification
Prerequisite Courses: n/a
Average GPA: B+ average (75-79%) in last two years of undergraduate degree
Range: n/a
Admission Test: GMAT and TOEFL (610/255) required of foreign applicants
Average Score: n/a
Score Report Deadline: n/a
Other Admission Criteria: Letter of Interest and resume

Application Information:
Deadline: February 15 for University Fellowship consideration; March 15 for Canadian applicants; December 15 for International applicants
Application Fee: $100 for Canadian applicants
Applicant/Acceptance Ratio: 3:1
Size of Incoming Class: 40 on-campus and 30 M.P.A. online
Tuition: Consult Faculty of Graduate Studies at http://web.uvic.ca/grar/website/continuing/feeregulations.html
Books/Materials: Varied

University of Western Ontario
Prof. Andrew Sancton, Director
Local Government Program
Faculty of Social Science
Social Science Centre
London, ON   N6A 5C2
Tel: 519-850-2985
Fax: 519-661-3904
E-mail: asancton@uwo.ca
Internet: www.localgovernment.uwo.ca

General Information:
Degree Offered: M.P.A.
Length: Semesters
Years: 12 months (full-time); 3 years (part-time)
Language: English

Admission Requirements:
Previous Education: Normally requires Honours Bachelor's degree
Prerequisite Courses: Equivalent of one full senior undergraduate course in local government, urban studies, public administration, or local government experience
Average GPA: 79%
Range: n/a
Admission Test: Not required
Average Score: n/a
Score Report Deadline: n/a
Other Admission Criteria: Local government experience an asset

Application Information:
Deadline: Mid-January (late applicants will be considered if space permits)
Application Fee: $75
Applicant/Acceptance Ratio: 85% acceptance rate
Size of Incoming Class: 10 to 15 full-time; 10 to 15 part-time (30 maximum)
Tuition: $6,000
Books/Materials: $150-$250

Comments: The M.P.A. program has a focus on public administration in local government and is designed to meet the needs of full-time students and part-time students, including those currently working in public administration. For this reason students take courses on weekends.

University of Winnipeg with University of Manitoba
Shirley McFaren
Graduate Secretary
Political Studies Department
Winnipeg, MB   R3T 5V5
Tel: 204-474-9733
Fax: 204-474-7585
Internet: www.umanitoba.ca/faculties/politicalstudies/

General Information:
Degree Offered: M.P.A.
Length: Semesters
Years: 2 and 1*
Language: English

Admission Requirements:
Previous Education: Bachelor's degree
Prerequisite Courses: None
Average GPA: 3.2
Range: 3.0+
Admission Test: None
Average Score: n/a
Score Report Deadline: n/a
Other Admission Criteria: None

Application Information:
Deadline: January 15 (under review)
Application Fee: $50
Applicant/Acceptance Ratio: 40
applications/20 full-time equivalent
admissions
Size of Incoming Class: 20 full-time
equivalent positions
Tuition: One Year Program (based on 24
c.h.) $4,103 approximately
Two Year Program (based on 48 c.h.)
$8,206 approximately
Books/Materials: n/a

Comments: * Candidates with an honours
undergraduate degree can apply for
advanced standing
Co-op Ed. Component: 2 - 13 weeks terms
are required. Co-op options available to
full time registered students only. Must
complete 24 credit hours of course work.
Co-op Work Term: $325 each term (two
terms required)

York University
Schulich School of Business
4700 Keele Street
Toronto, ON   M3J 1P3
Tel: 416-736-5060
Fax: 416-650-8174
E-mail: admissions@schulich.yorku.ca
Internet: http://www.yorku.ca/admissio/
graduate/gradprog/busadmin.asp

General Information:
Degree Offered: M.P.A.
Length: 60 credit hours
Years: 2 (full-time); 6 (part-time
- maximum)
Language: English

Admission Requirements:
Previous Education: Bachelor's degree in
any discipline. GMAT with a score of 600
(75th percentile) required for all degrees.
Two years relevant experience following
graduation is preferred.
Prerequisite Courses: None
Average GPA: B+
Range: B- to A+
Admission Test: GMAT
Average Score: 630
Score Report Deadline: n/a
Other Admission Criteria: Experience,
recommendations, and extra-curricular
activities

Application Information:
Deadline: Canadian full-time applicants
- April 1; Canadian part-time applicants
- May 1; International applicants - March 1
Application Fee: $100
Applicant/Acceptance Ratio: n/a
Size of Incoming Class: n/a
Tuition: $8,257.11 full-time; $3,325.00
part-time (per term)
Books/Materials: $1,000 to $2,000
depending on program

SOCIAL WORK

The following fact sheets outline general information including academic requirements and application procedures for Social Work Schools in Canada. The data have been compiled in a concise format to assist students interested in these professional schools. Information was obtained from updates completed by each school, or in some cases from the school's Internet website.

Social Work Schools in Canada

University of British Columbia
University of Calgary
Carleton University*
Dalhousie University
Lakehead University
Université Laval
University of Manitoba
McGill University*
McMaster University*
Memorial University of
Newfoundland*

Université de Moncton
Université de Montréal*
Université d'Ottawa
University of Regina
Ryerson Polytechnic University*
Université de Sherbrooke
University of Toronto*
University of Western Ontario
Wilfrid Laurier University
University of Windsor
York University*

Comments

1. These fact sheets act as a guide only. Students are advised to refer to the individual calendars or to write to the schools for more detailed information.

2. Application deadlines vary. Dates indicated refer to fall admission unless otherwise noted.

3. Tuition fees represent annual costs unless otherwise noted.

4. All of the schools listed above may not be represented.

* *This university has not updated its information. Please contact the university directly.*

University of British Columbia
School of Social Work
The Jack Bell Building
2080 West Mall
Vancouver, BC   V6T 1Z2
Tel: 604-822-2255
Fax: 604-822-8656
Internet: www.socialwork.ubc.ca

General Information:
Degree Offered: B.S.W.
Length: 60 credits
Years: 2
Language: English

Admission Requirements:
Previous Education: At least 60 credits
of a Bachelor of Arts degree at UBC or its
equivalent, or a Baccalaureate degree
Prerequisite Courses: 6 credits of English
(exempt if applicant holds a Canadian
degree); at least 18 credits of course
work selected from the subject areas of:
Economics, Sociology, Anthropology,
Psychology, Political Science, Canadian
History, Geography, Women's Studies, First
Nation's studies
Average GPA: 2.7
Range: 68%
Admission Test: n/a
Average Score: n/a
Score Report Deadline: n/a
Other Admission Criteria: Transcripts;
resume; suitability for a career in social
work as demonstrated by employment
and/or volunteer history, letters of
reference and through interviews

Application Information:
Deadline: January 31
Application Fee: $60
Applicant/Acceptance Ratio: 3:1
Size of Incoming Class: 30
Tuition: $4,257 per 30 credits; student
fees: $654
Books/Materials: $1280

Comments: Program 1 of 3

University of British Columbia
School of Social Work
The Jack Bell Building
2080 West Mall
Vancouver, BC   V6T 1Z2
Tel: 604-822-2255
Fax: 604-822-8656
Internet: www.socialwork.ubc.ca

General Information:
Degree Offered: M.S.W.
Length: 12 months
Years: 1
Language: English

Admission Requirements:
Previous Education: B.S.W. (Advanced)
Prerequisite Courses: At least three
credits in statistics
Average GPA: n/a
Range: A minimum B+ standing (76% at
UBC) in third and fourth year level courses
Admission Test: Not required
Average Score: n/a
Score Report Deadline: n/a
Other Admission Criteria: Preference may
be given to applicants with 2 years of post-
B.S.W. work experience.

Application Information:
Deadline: January 15
Application Fee: $90
Applicant/Acceptance Ratio: 3:1
Size of Incoming Class: 30
Tuition: $3,939.16
Books/Materials: $800

Comments: Program 2 of 3

University of British Columbia
School of Social Work
The Jack Bell Building
2080 West Mall
Vancouver, BC   V6T 1Z2
Tel: 604-822-2255
Fax: 604-822-8656
Internet: www.socialwork.ubc.ca

General Information:
Degree Offered: M.S.W. (Foundation)
Length: 24 months
Years: 2
Language: English

Admission Requirements:
Previous Education: B.A. in a relted discipline
Prerequisite Courses: At least three credits in statistics, research methods, and UBC SOWK 200 and 201 (or equivalent)
Average GPA: n/a
Range: A minimum B+ standing (76% at UBC) in third and fourth year level courses
Admission Test: Not required
Average Score: n/a
Score Report Deadline: n/a
Other Admission Criteria: Applicants require two full years of social service volunteer or work experience

Application Information:
Deadline: January 15
Application Fee: $90
Applicant/Acceptance Ratio: 3:1
Size of Incoming Class: 15
Tuition: $3,939.16 per year
Books/Materials: $800

Comments: Program 3 of 3

University of Calgary
Student Services
Faculty of Social Work
2500 University Drive N.W.
Calgary, AB   T2N 1N4
Tel: 403-220-6945
Fax: 403-282-7269
E-mail: socialwk@ucalgary.ca
Internet: http://fsw.ucalgary.ca

General Information:
Degree Offered: M.S.W.
Length: Sessions
Years: 1 - 2*
Language: English

Admission Requirements:
Previous Education: B.S.W. or 4 year degree with 2 years experience
Prerequisite Courses: n/a
Average GPA: 3.5 approx. on last 10 full courses or equivalents
Range: 3.0 minimum
Admission Test: Not required
Average Score: n/a
Score Report Deadline: n/a
Other Admission Criteria: Professional and/or volunteer experience, study plan and 3 references

Application Information:
Deadline: January 31
Application Fee: $100
Applicant/Acceptance Ratio: 3:1
Size of Incoming Class: 50
Tuition: $630 per course; $4,922 per year
Books/Materials: $1,000

Comments: *One to 2 years on average (4 years from registration is the permissible maximum for thesis students, although students seldom require this long). Six year maximum for course-based students. Program 1 of 2

University of Calgary
Student Services
Faculty of Social Work
2500 University Drive N.W.
Calgary, AB   T2N 1N4
Tel: 403-220-6945
Fax: 403-282-7269
E-mail: socialwk@ucalgary.ca
Internet: http://fsw.ucalgary.ca

General Information:
Degree Offered: M.S.W., Ph.D. Social Work
Length: Sessions
Years: 2 - 4 years
Language: English

Admission Requirements:
Previous Education: Bachelor's degree in related field

Prerequisite Courses: n/a
Average GPA: Minimum GPA is 3.0 approximately
Range: n/a
Admission Test: Not required
Average Score: n/a
Score Report Deadline: n/a
Other Admission Criteria: Relevant experience, required essay, and 3 letters of reference, detailed resume

Application Information:
Deadline: January 31 (MSW), April 1 (BSW)
Application Fee: $100
Applicant/Acceptance Ratio: Varies
Size of Incoming Class: Varies
Tuition: $630 per course; $4,922 per year
Books/Materials: $1,000

Comments: Students are admitted to study sites in Calgary, Edmonton, and Lethbridge. Program 2 of 2

Carleton University
School of Social Work
1125 Colonel By Drive
509 Dunton Tower
Ottawa, ON   K1S 5B6
Tel: 613-520-5601
Fax: 613-520-7496
E-mail: linda.guay@carleton.ca
Internet: www.carleton.ca/ssw

General Information:
Degree Offered: B.S.W. Honours
Length: Semesters
Years: 4
Language: English

Admission Requirements:
Previous Education: OSSD or equivalent
Prerequisite Courses: n/a
Average GPA: 75%+
Range: 65%+
Admission Test: Not required
Average Score: n/a
Score Report Deadline: n/a

Other Admission Criteria: Personal statement, references, transcripts, and work/volunteer experience

Application Information:
Deadline: Feb 1 (2 applications: Social Work application - Feb 1 and General University Application - March 1)
Application Fee: $85; apply through Ontario University Application Centre then all applications are sent to the university of their choice (3 choices)
Applicant/Acceptance Ratio: 4:1
Size of Incoming Class: 80
Tuition: $4,908 for two terms (fall and winter)
Books/Materials: n/a

Comments: Further information: Linda Guay, Undergraduate Student Administrator (613) 520-5601

Carleton University
School of Social Work
1125 Colonel By Drive
509 Dunton Tower
Ottawa, ON   K1S 5B6
Tel: 613-520-5601
Fax: 613-520-7496
E-mail: susan.brady@carleton.ca
Internet: www.carleton.ca/ssw

General Information:
Degree Offered: M.S.W.
Length: 3 semesters
Years: 1
Language: English

Admission Requirements:
Previous Education: B.S.W.
Prerequisite Courses: One full credit in Basic Research Methods
Average GPA: 78 - 83%
Range: B+ minimum (in majors or honours),
B- overall
Admission Test: Not required
Average Score: n/a

Score Report Deadline: n/a
Other Admission Criteria: Work/volunteer experience, personal statement, and reference letters
TOEFL score: 550 (if English is second language)

Application Information:
Deadline: December 1st for following September
Application Fee: $60
Applicant/Acceptance Ratio: 4:1
Size of Incoming Class: 30
Tuition: $1,995 per term (subject to change)
Books/Materials: Books: $550; supplies $350; field trips $200

Comments: Further information: Sue Brady, School Administrator (613) 520-5603

Carleton University
School of Social Work
1125 Colonel By Drive
509 Dunton Tower
Ottawa, ON   K1S 5B6
Tel: 613-520-5601
Fax: 613-520-7496
E-mail: susan.brady@carleton.ca
Internet: www.carleton.ca/ssw

General Information:
Degree Offered: M.S.W.
Length: 5 semesters
Years: II
Language: English

Admission Requirements:
Previous Education: B.A. (Honours - 4 yr. Post-secondary program) or equivalent
Prerequisite Courses: One full credit in Basic Research Methods
Average GPA: 78 - 83%
Range: B+ minimum (in majors or honours),
B- overall
Admission Test: Not required

Average Score: n/a
Score Report Deadline: n/a
Other Admission Criteria: Work/volunteer experience, personal statement, and reference letters
TOEFL score: 550 (if English is second language)

Application Information:
Deadline: December 1st for following September
Application Fee: $60
Applicant/Acceptance Ratio: 4:1
Size of Incoming Class: 30
Tuition: $1,995 per term (subject to change)
Books/Materials: Books: $550; supplies $350; field trips $200

Comments: Further information: Sue Brady, School Administrator (613) 520-5603

Dalhousie University
School of Social Work
Halifax, NS   B3H 3J5
Tel: 902-494-3760
Fax: 902-494-6709
Internet: www.socialwork.dal.ca

General Information:
Degree Offered: B.S.W.
Length: Semesters
Years: 2 to 3
Language: English

Admission Requirements:
Previous Education: Minimum of five university credits (60 hours) completed at a minimum B- average
Prerequisite Courses: Social Sciences
Average GPA: 2.70
Range: 70% or B- minimum
Admission Test: Not required
Average Score: n/a
Score Report Deadline: n/a
Other Admission Criteria: References, Personal Statement, Personal Suitability for

Social Work, related social human service/social activism work and/or volunteer experience

Application Information:
Deadline: February 15
Application Fee: $70
Applicant/Acceptance Ratio: 4:1
Size of Incoming Class: 80
Tuition: $6,690 full time; $666 for one half-credit course
Books/Materials: $1,000

Comments: Distance delivery study is also available on a part-time basis.

Dalhousie University
School of Social Work
Halifax, NS   B3H 3J5
Tel: 902-494-3760
Fax: 902-494-6709
Internet: www.socialwork.dal.ca

General Information:
Degree Offered: M.S.W.
Length: Semesters
Years: 1 (full time); 3 (part-time)
Language: English

Admission Requirements:
Previous Education: B.S.W.
Prerequisite Courses: n/a
Average GPA: 3.0
Range: B minimum
Admission Test: Not required
Average Score: n/a
Score Report Deadline: n/a
Other Admission Criteria: For B.S.W. graduates, a minimum of two years related social work experience, preferably after completion of the B.S.W. degree. References, Statement of Scholarly Interest, and resume are also required.

Application Information:
Deadline: December 1
Application Fee: $70
Applicant/Acceptance Ratio: 3:1

Size of Incoming Class: 45
Tuition: $7,976 (full time)
Books/Materials: $1,000

Comments: The M.S.W. degree program is also available on a part-time basis by distance education delivery to residents of Canada. An additional distance delivery fee of $204 is required for each half-credit.

Lakehead University
Admissions and Recruitment
955 Oliver Road
Thunder Bay, ON   P7B 5E1
Tel: 807-343-8500 or 1-800-465-3959
E-mail: admissions@lakeheadu.ca
Internet: www.lakeheadu.ca

General Information:
Degree Offered: HBSW
Length: n/a
Years: 1
Language: English

Admission Requirements:
Previous Education: B.A., B.Sc. or equivalent
Prerequisite Courses: n/a
Average GPA: Admission Requirement - 70%
Range: n/a
Admission Test: n/a
Average Score: n/a
Score Report Deadline: n/a
Other Admission Criteria: Submission of the Supplement Information Form, three letters of reference (forms), resume of volunteer and work experience, and completion of the Personal Statement

Application Information:
Deadline: Early January
Application Fee: $110 plus $40 Document Evaluation Fee
Applicant/Acceptance Ratio: n/a
Size of Incoming Class: n/a
Tuition: $8,046
Books/Materials: n/a

Comments: This is an after degree program which runs one calendar year. Program begins in July and ends in June of the following year.

Université Laval

Directeur du programme de maîtrise
École de service social
Pavillon Charles-de-Koninck
Ste-Foy, QC   G1K 7P4
Tel: 418-656-2131, poste 5568
Fax: 418-656-3567
E-mail: jocelyne.mangrain@svs.ulaval.ca
Internet: www.ulaval.ca

General Information:
Degree Offered: M.Serv.Soc.
Length: 4 à 6 trimestres (minimum)
Years: 4 (maximum)
Language: français

Admission Requirements:
Previous Education: Maîtrise en service social ou un baccalauréat dans une discipline connexe **Prerequisite Courses:** Scolarité complimentaire requise pour les diplômés d'autres disciplines que le service social (33 crédits de 1er cycle en service social)
Average GPA: 3.0/4.3
Range: n/a
Admission Test: Not required
Average Score: n/a
Score Report Deadline: n/a
Other Admission Criteria: Présenter un projet de maîtrise

Application Information:
Deadline: 1er mars
Application Fee: $55
Applicant/Acceptance Ratio: 3:2
Size of Incoming Class: 50
Tuition: $62.27/crédit plus frais afférents
Books/Materials: $250

Comments: Cinq domaines de spécialisation: Famille-enfance-jeunesse, Mouvements sociaux et intervention communautaire, Groupes de développement personnel et social, Gérontologie sociale, Santé et santé mentale. Deux cheminements: Cheminement Projet d'intervention, et essai; Cheminement mémoire. Temps partiel ou temps complet.

University of Manitoba

Faculty of Social Work
521 Tier Building
Winnipeg, MB   R3T 2N2
Tel: 204-474-7050
Fax: 204-474-7594
E-mail: social_work@umanitoba.ca
Internet: www.umanitoba.ca/social_work

General Information:
Degree Offered: B.S.W.
Length: Semesters
Years: 4
Language: English

Admission Requirements:
Previous Education: 30 credit hours
Prerequisite Courses: n/a
Average GPA: 2.5 (minimum)
Range: C+
Admission Test: Not required
Average Score: n/a
Score Report Deadline: n/a
Other Admission Criteria: Transcripts

Application Information:
Deadline: March 1
Application Fee: $90
Applicant/Acceptance Ratio: 3:1
Size of Incoming Class: 75
Tuition: $3,900
Books/Materials: $1,100

University of Manitoba

Faculty of Social Work
521 Tier Building
Winnipeg, MB R3T 2N2
Tel: 204-474-7050
Fax: 204-474-7594
E-mail: social_work@umanitoba.ca
Internet: www.umanitoba.ca/social_work

General Information:

Degree Offered: M.S.W.
Length: Semesters
Years: 2 calendar years (6 years maximum)
Language: English

Admission Requirements:

Previous Education: B.S.W.
Prerequisite Courses: n/a
Average GPA: 3.0 (minimum)
Range: B
Admission Test: n/a
Average Score: n/a
Score Report Deadline: n/a
Other Admission Criteria: Related
work experience, educational study plan
(complete details enclosed in application
packages), transcripts

Application Information:

Deadline: January 15
Application Fee: $75
Applicant/Acceptance Ratio: 2:1
Size of Incoming Class: 35-40
Tuition: $4177.00
Books/Materials: $1,500 approx.

McGill University

Graduate Admissions
School of Social Work
3506 University Street
Montreal, QC H3A 2A7
Tel: 514-398-7070
Fax: 514-398-4760
E-mail: graduate.socialwork@mcgill.ca
Internet: www.mcgill.ca/socialwork

General Information:

Degree Offered: M.S.W.*
Length: 3 semesters
Years: 1 - 1 ½
Language: English

Admission Requirements:

Previous Education: B.S.W.
Prerequisite Courses: Introductory course
in statistics
Average GPA: 3.4/4.0
Range: 3.0+
Admission Test: Not required
Average Score: n/a
Score Report Deadline: n/a
Other Admission Criteria: Clearly defined
area of specialized interest. Professional
experience strongly preferred.

Application Information:

Deadline: February 1
Application Fee: $60
Applicant/Acceptance Ratio: 2:1
Size of Incoming Class: 50 - 55
Tuition: Available on the Internet at www.
mcgill.ca/student-accounts/
Books/Materials: $300 - $500/year

Comments: *There are thesis and non-
thesis options. All students conduct and
report on an independent inquiry as a
requisite for the M.S.W. (The thesis or
for the non-thesis option, a smaller-scale
research project or theoretical paper). All
students in the non-thesis option take
a 12-credit practicum. Applications are
available online through the School's
website (www.mcgill.ca/socialwork) as of
late September of each year.

McMaster University

School of Social Work
Room 319, Kenneth Taylor Hall
1280 Main Street West
Hamilton, ON   L8S 4M4
Tel: 905-525-9140, ext. 23795
Fax: 905-577-4667
E-mail: socwork@mcmaster.ca
Internet: www.socsci.mcmaster.ca/socwork

General Information:
Degree Offered: B.A./B.S.W.
Length: Terms
Years: 4*
Language: English

Admission Requirements:
Previous Education: Completion of any level one university programme
Prerequisite Courses: See "Comments"
Average GPA: C+ or 67%
Range: C+ or 67% minimum
Admission Test: Required
Average Score: n/a
Score Report Deadline: n/a
Other Admission Criteria: Evidence of personal suitability as evaluated by one or a combination of written statements, tests, or interviews. All prerequisite work must be completed by April of the year in which application is made.

Application Information:
Deadline: March 1
Application Fee: $85 to OUAC (full-time) or $30 (part-time)
$50 to McMaster University
Applicant/Acceptance Ratio: 3:1
Size of Incoming Class: 40
Tuition: $4835.56 in 2003/04
Books/Materials: $1,500 plus travel to field placements

Comments: *Includes prerequisite introductory year.
Completion of any Level 1 program, including two of Psy 1A03 and 1AA3 (or 1A06), Sociol 1A06, Social Work 1A06,

normally with a CA of at least 6.0 and evidence of personal suitability, which may be evaluated by one or a combination of written statements, tests, or interviews.
Program 1 of 3

McMaster University

School of Social Work
Room 319, Kenneth Taylor Hall
1280 Main Street West
Hamilton, ON   L8S 4M4
Tel: 905-525-9140, ext. 23795
Fax: 905-577-4667
E-mail: socwork@mcmaster.ca
Internet: www.socsci.mcmaster.ca/socwork

General Information:
Degree Offered: B.S.W.
Length: Terms
Years: 2*
Language: English

Admission Requirements:
Previous Education: Completion of an undergraduate degree from a recognized university
Prerequisite Courses: See "Comments"
Average GPA: C+ or 67%
Range: C+ or 67%
Admission Test: Required
Average Score: n/a
Score Report Deadline: n/a
Other Admission Criteria: Evidence of personal suitability as evaluated by one or a combination of written statements, tests, or interviews. All prerequisite work must be completed by April of the year in which application is made.

Application Information:
Deadline: March 1
Application Fee: $85 to OUAC (full-time) or $30 (part-time)
$50 to McMaster University
Applicant/Acceptance Ratio: 3:1
Size of Incoming Class: 25
Tuition: $3,953.86 per year in 2003/04 ($1,775.04 summer)

Books/Materials: $1,500 plus travel to field placements

Comments: *Two academic years and the summer in between
Completion of an undergraduate degree from a recognized university, including two of Introductory Psychology, Sociology, or Social Work (equivalent to the McMaster courses Psy 1A06 and 1AA3 (or 1A06), Sociol 1A06, Social Work 1A06) normally with an average of at least 6.0 or its equivalent, and evidence of personal suitability which may be evaluated by one or a combination of written statements, interviews, or tests. Program 2 of 3.

McMaster University
School of Social Work
Room 319, Kenneth Taylor Hall
1280 Main Street West
Hamilton, ON   L8S 4M4
Tel: 905-525-9140, ext. 23795
Fax: 905-577-4667
E-mail: infomsw@mcmaster.ca
Internet: www.socsci.mcmaster.ca/socwork

General Information:
Degree Offered: M.S.W.
Length: 12 months
Years: 1 full-time*; 3 part-time**
Language: English
Admission Requirements:
Previous Education: See "Comments"
Prerequisite Courses: See "Comments"
Average GPA: n/a
Range: B+ or 77% minimum in senior level social work and related courses (statistics and research methods)
Admission Test: Not required
Average Score: n/a
Score Report Deadline: n/a
Other Admission Criteria: See calendar

Application Information:
Deadline: January 5
Application Fee: $75

Applicant/Acceptance Ratio: 3:1
Size of Incoming Class: *20; **20
Tuition: $4,862 in 2003/04
Books/Materials: $650

Comments: There are 2 streams within the M.S.W. program:
1. Analysis of Practice: Applicants holding a B.S.W. Admission Requirements: Introductory Statistics, Introductory Social Research Methods, B+ standing in senior level social work and related courses (statatistics and research methods), minimum of 2 senior level social welfare policy courses, two years' full-time experience in social work, normally post-B.S.W.; 2. Analysis of Policy: B.S.W. Admission Requirements: Introductory Statistics, and Social Research Methods, B+ standing in senior level social work and related courses (statatistics and research methods), minimum of two senior level social welfare policy courses. Program 3 of 3.

Memorial University of Newfoundland
Dr. Elizabeth Dow
Director, School of Social Work
St. John's, NL   A1B 3X8
Tel: 709-737-8165
Fax: 709-737-2408
E-mail: ccluett@mun.ca
Internet: www.mun.ca/socwrk

General Information:
Degree Offered: B.S.W.
Length: Semesters
Years: 4
Language: English

Admission Requirements:
Previous Education: 45 credit hours
Prerequisite Courses: Six credit hours in English; nine credit hours in Psychology (at least three of which must be chosen from Psychology 2010, 2011, or 2012 or

equivalent); three credits in Sociology;, three credits in either Anthropology, Geography, or Political Science; Social Work 2510 and/or 2700; three credit hours chosen from Philosophy 2800-2810 or Women's Studies 2000; further courses from Schedule A in the Social Work section of the Calendar to make up 45 credit hours
Average GPA: n/a
Range: A minimum of 65%
Admission Test: Not required
Average Score: n/a
Score Report Deadline: n/a
Other Admission Criteria: Relevant experience
Application Information:
Deadline: March 1
Application Fee: $30
Applicant/Acceptance Ratio: 2:1
Size of Incoming Class: n/a
Tuition: $697 per semester (full-time)
Books/Materials: $750 per year

Comments: Program 1 of 2.

Memorial University of Newfoundland
Graduate Program Coordinator
School of Social Work
St. John's College
St. John's, NL   A1C 5S7
Tel: 709-737-8165
Fax: 709-737-2408
E-mail: dodrisco@mun.ca
Internet: http://www.mun.ca/socwrk

General Information:
Degree Offered: M.S.W.
Length: 3 semesters
Years: 1
Language: English

Admission Requirements:
Previous Education: B.S.W. or equivalent
Prerequisite Courses: Undergraduate courses in Research and Statistics

Average GPA: n/a
Range: B minimum in the last 60 undergraduate credit hours
Admission Test: Not required
Average Score: n/a
Score Report Deadline: n/a
Other Admission Criteria: Two years post-B.S.W. professional experience; official transcript of the applicant's previous academic record submitted directly from the institution(s) attended; a statement of previous professional employment; a list of any published or unpublished works; and a declaration of program emphasis and educational objectives; and three letters of appraisal, to be submitted by three references capable of assessing the applicant's previous academic and/or practice performance. Letters of appraisal are to be submitted directly to the School of Graduate Studies.

Application Information:
Deadline: February 28
Application Fee: $30
Applicant/Acceptance Ratio: 2:1
Size of Incoming Class: 18
Tuition: $697 per semester for 6 semesters full-time;
$462 per semester for 9 semesters part-time plus a continuance fee of $316 per semester
Books/Materials: $750 per year

Comments: Program offered through both part-time and full-time study. Program 2 of 2.

Université de Moncton
École de travail social
Moncton, NB   E1A 3E9
Tel: 506-858-4181

General Information:
Degree Offered: M. travail social
Length: Semestres
Years: 1
Language: français

Admission Requirements:
Previous Education: Baccalauréat en service social ou dans un domaine connexe
Prerequisite Courses: Les politiques sociales, les mouvements sociaux, et la recherche-action
Average GPA: n/a
Range: 3.0+
Admission Test: n/a
Average Score: n/a
Score Report Deadline: n/a
Other Admission Criteria: Un projet de formation, entrevue, connaissance des 2 langues, (de préférence) 2 années d'expérience de travail en service social

Application Information:
Deadline: 8 juin
Application Fee: $39
Applicant/Acceptance Ratio: 2:1
Size of Incoming Class: 6
Tuition: $5,520
Books/Materials: n/a

Université de Montréal
École de service social
C.P. 6128
Succursale Centre-ville
Montréal, QC   H3C 3J7
Tel: 514-343-6605

General Information:
Degree Offered: M.Sc. service social
Length: 3 terms and writing (report) - 225010
4 terms and writing (report) - 225012
Years: n/a
Language: français

Admission Requirements:
Previous Education: B.Sc. Service social - 225010 ou Baccalauréat dans un domaine connexe - 225012
Prerequisite Courses: n/a
Average GPA: Moyenne de 3,2 aux études de 1er cycle

Range: n/a
Admission Test: Pas exigé
Average Score: n/a
Score Report Deadline: n/a
Other Admission Criteria: Fournir son curriculum vitae et répondre aux questions du supplément à la demande d'admission

Application Information:
Deadline: 1er novembre pour l'hiver
1er février pour l'automne
Application Fee: $30
Applicant/Acceptance Ratio: 2:1
Size of Incoming Class: 30 - 40
Tuition: $918 (plein temps/par trimestre)
Books/Materials: n/a

Université d'Ottawa
École de service social
Faculty of Social Sciences
1 Stewart (132)
Ottawa, ON   K1N 6N5
Tel: 613-562-5494
Fax: 613-562-5495
E-mail: servsoc@uottawa.ca
Internet: www.sciencessociales.uottawa.ca/svs

General Information:
Degree Offered: M.S.S.
Length: Semesters (3 or 6 based on admission path)
Years: 2
Language: French

Admission Requirements:
Previous Education: Admission path (6 semesters): Bachelor's degree, honours or with a major in Social Sciences, Health Sciences, or the equivalent; Admission path (3 semesters): Bachelor's degree in Social Work
Prerequisite Courses: 2 full courses in research methodology
Average GPA: 70% minimum
Range: n/a
Admission Test: n/a

Average Score: n/a
Score Report Deadline: n/a
Other Admission Criteria: Work experience in Social Work or related to the profession

Application Information:
Deadline: February 1
Application Fee: $75
Applicant/Acceptance Ratio: 3:1
Size of Incoming Class: 30
Tuition: Please see www.uottawa. ca/academic/info/index/english
Books/Materials: n/a

University of Regina
Faculty of Social Work
Regina, SK   S4S 0A2
Tel: 306-585-4554

General Information:
Degree Offered: B.S.W.
Length: Semesters
Years: 4
Language: English

Admission Requirements:
Previous Education: High school or equivalent
Prerequisite Courses: n/a
Average GPA: 65
Range: n/a
Admission Test: Not required
Average Score: n/a
Score Report Deadline: n/a
Other Admission Criteria:

Application Information:
Deadline: January 15, September 15
Application Fee: Not required
Applicant/Acceptance Ratio: n/a
Size of Incoming Class: n/a
Tuition: $407.55 per course (3 credit hours)
Books/Materials: $300 per year

Comments: Must be admitted to the University of Regina before application to BSW will be considered.

Ryerson Polytechnic University
Admissions/Liaison/Curriculum Advising
350 Victoria Street
Toronto, ON   M5B 2K3
Tel: 416-979-5036
E-mail: inquire@ryerson.ca
Internet: www.ryerson.ca/prospective

General Information:
Degree Offered: B.S.W.
Length: n/a
Years: 4
Language: English

Admission Requirements:
Previous Education: O.S.S.D. with six Grade 12 U/M courses
Prerequisite Courses: Grade 12 U English
Average GPA: n/a
Range: 70%
Admission Test: n/a
Average Score: n/a
Score Report Deadline: n/a
Other Admission Criteria: Applicants are invited to submit/write an admissions essay. The admissions essay will be used as a supplementary component of the admissions process. A resume of work and volunteer experience and not more than two letters of reference are invited.

Application Information:
Deadline: March 1
Application Fee: $85*
Applicant/Acceptance Ratio: 9:1
Size of Incoming Class: 136
Tuition: $3,338.04
Books/Materials: $1,000 - $1,300

Comments: *An additional $40 evaluation fee must be submitted directly to Ryerson for all applicants who are not current Ontario high school students.

University of Toronto

Admissions Office, Faculty of Social Work
246 Bloor Street West
Toronto, ON   M5S 1A1
Tel: 416-978-3257
Fax: 416-978-7072
E-mail: admissions.fsw@utoronto.ca
Internet: www.socialwork.utoronto.ca

General Information:

Degree Offered: M.S.W.
Length: Semesters
Years: 2 year full-time MSW program*;
1 year full-time MSW program with
advanced standing**
Language: English

Admission Requirements:

Previous Education: *A 4-year bachelor's
degree or equivalent from the University
of Toronto or an approved university,
and normally shall have achieved a
mid-B average in each of the last two
years of full-time study (or equivalent).
** Graduated with a BSW degree from
a university of recognized standing, and
normally shall have achieved a mid-B
average in each of the last two years of
full-time study (or equivalent)
Prerequisite Courses: All applicants must
have completed satisfactorily at least
three full courses, or their equivalent, in
the social sciences, to include a half-
credit course in research methodology,
preferably in the social sciences.
Average GPA: n/a
Range: n/a
Admission Test: n/a
Average Score: n/a
Score Report Deadline: n/a
Other Admission Criteria: Experience
(voluntary or paid) in the social services
and knowledge of critical social issues are
recommended. Suitability for professional
practice will also be considered. Must
show evidence of facility in the English
language. If your primary language is not
English and you graduated from a non-
Canadian university where the language
of instruction and examination was not
English, then you must demonstrate your
facility in English by completing on of the
following tests: TOEFL Computer-Based
Test Score of 237 and Essay Rating Score
of 5; IELTS Score of 7; MELAB Score of 85

Application Information:

Deadline: December 15
Application Fee: $90 submitted to School
of Graduate Studies; $40 submitted to
Faculty of Social Work
Applicant/Acceptance Ratio: 4:1 - two-
year full-time MSW Program; 3:1 - MSW
Program with Advanced Standing
Size of Incoming Class: 75 - two-year
full-time MSW Program; 60 - MSW
Program with Advanced Standing for
Full-time Studies; 25 - MSW Program with
Advanced Standing for Part-time Studies
Tuition: For Sept. 2004 -TBA; For Sept.
2003 - $6,841.62 domestic, $13,874.09
international
Books/Materials: $1,000 approx.

Comments: Documentation required for
application: SGS Form A & B; Application
fees; Transcripts of Academic Records:
One official transcript of your academic
record from each university and college
attended must be provided; MSW
Program Application Form; Resume; 3
References; Written Statement; Checklist.
Applications available mid-September from
the website. Visit their website or calandar
for additional information.

University of Western Ontario
Att: Bette-Jane Genttner
BSW Admissions Coordinator
School of Social Work
King's University College
266 Epworth Avenue
London, ON   N6A 2M3
Tel: 1-800-265-4406, ext. 4328 or
519-433-3491
Fax: 519-433-8691
E-mail: genttner@uwo.ca
Internet: www.uwo.ca/kings

General Information:
Degree Offered: B.S.W.
Length: 4 semesters
Years: 2
Language: English

Admission Requirements:
Previous Education: 10 full course equivalents
Prerequisite Courses: 3 social work prerequisites, 3 social sciences, one arts course
Average GPA: 70%
Range: n/a
Admission Test: Not required
Average Score: n/a
Score Report Deadline: n/a
Other Admission Criteria: Resume; volunteer work; other languages and diversity experience; two references; and a group interview.

Application Information:
Deadline: February 1
Application Fee: n/a
Applicant/Acceptance Ratio: 3:1
Size of Incoming Class: 45 - 50 (includes full time and part-time students)
Tuition: under review
Books/Materials: n/a

Comments: We also offer an Advanced Generalist M.S.W. program, both full and part-time.

University of Western Ontario
Att: Suzanne Book
Practicum and Graduate Program Assistant
School of Social Work
King's University College
266 Epworth Avenue
London, ON   N6A 2M3
Tel: 1-800-265-4406, ext. 4518 or
519-433-3491
Fax: 519-433-8691
E-mail: sbook3@uwo.ca
Internet: www.uwo.ca/kings

General Information:
Degree Offered: M.S.W. (full time and part-time)
Length: 9 semesters (full time); 3 semesters (part-time)
Years: 3 (full time); 10 months (part-time)
Language: English

Admission Requirements:
Previous Education: B.S.W. (or equivalent if from another country, confirmed by the CASW)
Prerequisite Courses: B.S.W. and full-course equivalent in Research Methodology and Statistics
Average GPA: 70% in the last 20 courses; 75% in the professional Social Work courses
Range: n/a
Admission Test: Not required
Average Score: n/a
Score Report Deadline: n/a
Other Admission Criteria: Resume, study plan, two references

Application Information:
Deadline: December 1
Application Fee: $50
Applicant/Acceptance Ratio: n/a
Size of Incoming Class: 25-35 (full time and part-time combined)
Tuition: n/a
Books/Materials: n/a

Wilfrid Laurier University

Michelle Corbett, Admissions Coordinator
or Susan Mintz, Marketing & Recruitment
Coordinator
Faculty of Social Work
120 Duke Street West
Kitchener, ON   N2H 3W8
Tel: 519-884-0710, ext. 5242
Fax: 519-888-9732
E-mail: socialwork@wlu.ca
Internet: www.wlu.ca/fsw

General Information:
Degree Offered: M.S.W.
Length: 5 semesters*; 3 semesters**
Years: *2; **1 Advanced Standing (and
equivalent programs taken part-time) *4
yrs, **2 yrs
Language: English

Admission Requirements:
Previous Education: *Bachelor's degree;
(Normally a four year bachelor's degree)
**accredited B.S.W. degree
Prerequisite Courses: Four full courses in
Social Sciences and a half course in each of
Statistics and Research Methodology
Average GPA: B
Range: B to A level performance
Admission Test: Not required
Average Score: n/a
Score Report Deadline: n/a
Other Admission Criteria: Evidence of
experience in human service organizations;
awareness of contemporary social issues
and social work values; demonstrated
ability to communicate effectively

Application Information:
Deadline: *January 15; **December 1
Application Fee: $100
Applicant/Acceptance Ratio: *4:1; **4:1
Size of Incoming Class: *80-90; **25 - 30
Tuition: Approx. $2,320 per term
Books/Materials: n/a

University of Windsor

Social Work Admissions
Office of the Registrar
Windsor, ON   N9B 3P4
Tel: 519-253-3000
Fax: 519-973-7036
E-mail: socwork@uwindsor.ca
Internet: www.uwindsor.ca

General Information:
Degree Offered: B.S.W. (Hons.)
Length: Semesters
Years: 4 full-time
Language: English

Admission Requirements:
Previous Education: OSSD, or Mature
student eligibility
Prerequisite Courses: English
Average GPA: 70% for Admission to Year
I and II
Range: n/a
Admission Test: University admission
procedures (Application to OUAC)
Average Score: n/a
Score Report Deadline: n/a
Other Admission Criteria: Limited and
competitive admission to Year III

Application Information:
Deadline: March 1 for Admission to Year
III
Application Fee: $105 to Ontario
University Application Centre (OUAC)
Applicant/Acceptance Ratio: 3:1 for
Admission to Year III
Size of Incoming Class: 60 (Year III)
Tuition: $2,500 per term
Books/Materials: $500 - $700

Comments: Students may be admitted
to Year I and II pre-Social Work from
secondary school or as Mature Students.
Students may be admitted to the Year III
and IV Professional Social Work program
from pre-Social Work or from a BA
program in another discipline.

York University
Office of Graduate Admissions
P.O. Box GA2300, 4700 Keele Street
Toronto, ON   M3J 1P3
Tel: 416-736-5000
Internet: www.yorku.ca/admissio/graduate
/gradprog/socwork.asp
General Information:
Degree Offered: M.S.W.
Length: Full Time - 3 terms; Part-time - 6 terms
Years: Full Time - 1 year; Part-time - 2 years
Language: English

Admission Requirements:
Previous Education: B.S.W.
Prerequisite Courses: B average required in last two years of BSW or equivalent honours undergraduate social work degree
Average GPA: n/a
Range: B minimum
Admission Test: Not required
Average Score: n/a
Score Report Deadline: n/a
Other Admission Criteria: Must complete Supplementary Programme Information Form; English Requirements: TOEFL (Paper Based: 600, Computer Based: 250); YELT (York English Language Test) - Band: 1

Application Information:
Deadline: January 16
Application Fee: $80
Applicant/Acceptance Ratio: n/a
Size of Incoming Class: n/a
Tuition: Full Time - Domestic - $1,595.01 per term; Part-time - Domestic - $797.51 per term
Books/Materials: $1,000 to $2,000 depending on program

Comments: The M.S.W. at York University is offered on a part-time and full-time basis in the evening and it was developed for people who are already working in the field of social work.

SPEECH-LANGUAGE PATHOLOGY

The following fact sheets outline general information including academic requirements and application procedures for Speech-Language Pathology Schools in Canada. The data have been compiled in a concise format to assist students interested in these professional schools. Information was obtained from updates completed by each school, or in some cases from the school's Internet website.

Speech-Language Pathology Schools in Canada

University of Alberta	Université de Montréal
University of British Columbia	University of Ottawa
Dalhousie University*	University of Toronto
McGill University*	University of Western Ontario

Comments

1. These fact sheets act as a guide only. Students are advised to refer to the individual calendars or to write to the schools for more detailed information.

2. Application deadlines vary. Dates indicated refer to fall admission unless otherwise noted.

3. Tuition fees represent annual costs unless otherwise noted.

4. All of the schools listed above may not be represented.

This university has not updated its information. Please contact the university directly.

University of Alberta
Department of Speech Pathology and
Audiology
Faculty of Rehabilitation Medicine
2-70 Corbett Hall
Edmonton, AB   T6G 2G4
Tel: 780-492-5990
Fax: 780-492-9333
Internet: http://www.uofaweb.ualberta.ca/
spa

General Information:
Degree Offered: M.Sc. (course-based);
Thesis option
Length: 6 semesters
Years: 2
Language: English

Admission Requirements:
Previous Education: Four-year
undergraduate degree in a related field
Prerequisite Courses: Obtain list from
department website
Average GPA: competitive
Range: 3.5 minimum in the last 2 years of
undergraduate work
Admission Test: GRE; TOEFL and TSE
required for non-native speakers of English
Average Score: n/a
Score Report Deadline: February 15
Other Admission Criteria: Refer
to calendar and contact Faculty of
Rehabilitation Medicine, Department of
Speech Pathology and Audiology directly.
See "Comments"

Application Information:
Deadline: February 15
Application Fee: n/a
Applicant/Acceptance Ratio: 4:1
Size of Incoming Class: 43 (Quota)
Tuition: $9,025 approx/year (3 semesters)
includes tuition, general, and compulsory
fees
Books/Materials: $2,200 (Year 1); $1,000
(Year 2)

Comments: This is a clinical graduate
program which commenced in 1992.
This allows students with a 4-year
undergraduate degree in a related field to
apply. There is the option to go to a thesis
route during the first term of the program.

University of British Columbia
Admissions Advisor
School of Audiology & Speech Sciences
5804 Fairview Avenue
Vancouver, BC   V6T 1Z3
Tel: 604-822-5591
Fax: 604-822-6569
Internet: www.audiospeech.ubc.ca

General Information:
Degree Offered: M.Sc. Audiology &
Speech Sciences
Length: 24 months
Years: 2
Language: English

Admission Requirements:
Previous Education: B.A./B.Sc.; 4-year
undergraduate degree in Linguistics or
Psychology
Prerequisite Courses: Please visit the
website for details as this program is now
split into two majors – Speech Language
Pathology and Audiology. All prerequisites
must be completed in order to be
competitive in the large applicant pool.
Average GPA: 80% - 83% approx. in
prerequisite course work
Range: 76% minimum in last 2 years of
degree required by Graduate Studies
Admission Test: none required
Average Score: n/a
Score Report Deadline: n/a
Other Admission Criteria: Minimum of
12 credits of first-class standing during last
2 years of undergraduate degree, 3 letters
of reference (2 from college professors), a
letter of intent, and clinical observational
experience prior to application

Application Information:
Deadline: February 28
Application Fee: $90
Applicant/Acceptance Ratio: 6:1
Size of Incoming Class: 35
Tuition: $3,939.16 each for first and second year plus $500 per year student levied fees
Books/Materials: $1,000

Comments: Applicants are strongly urged to apply early. Applications past the February 28 deadline will be processed only if the program is not yet full. Applicants who may qualify for Graduate Entrance Scholarships must complete applications by January 15. It is recommended that prospective students ascertain that their undergraduate course of studies is appropriate, preferably prior to their final year of study. Contact the Admissions Advisor as noted above for such assessment.

Dalhousie University
School of Human Communication Disorders
5599 Fenwick Street
Halifax, NS   B3H 1R2
Tel: 902-494-7052
Fax: 902-494-5151
E-mail: hcdwww@dal.ca
Internet: www.dal.ca

General Information:
Degree Offered: M.Sc.
Length: Semesters
Years: 3
Language: English

Admission Requirements:
Previous Education: Baccalaureate degree
Prerequisite Courses: Recommended courses include: Research Methods, Human Biology, Anatomy, Physiology, Psychology and Linguistics
Average GPA: n/a

Range: 3.4 - 4.0 or B overall minimum
Admission Test: Not required
Average Score: n/a
Score Report Deadline: n/a
Other Admission Criteria: Two letters of recommendation from professors and a personal statement

Application Information:
Deadline: January 15
Application Fee: $70
Applicant/Acceptance Ratio: 7:1
Size of Incoming Class: 30
Tuition: $7,872 per year
Books/Materials: $950/year

McGill University
School of Communication Sciences and Disorders
Beatty Hall, 1266 Pine Avenue West
Montreal, QC   H3G 1A8
Tel: 514-398-4137
Fax: 514-398-8123
E-mail: scsd@mcgill.ca
Internet: www.mcgill.ca/commsci

General Information:
Degree Offered: M.Sc.A. (Applied)
Length: 4 semesters and 1 practicum
Years: 2 ½ (2 calendar years)
Language: English

Admission Requirements:
Previous Education: Undergraduate degree
Prerequisite Courses: One full-year course in Statistics; one full-year course in Linguistics; six credits in Psychology
Average GPA: 3.0/4.0
Range: B minimum
Admission Test: None
Average Score: n/a
Score Report Deadline: n/a
Other Admission Criteria: Two letters of reference from professors, relevant experience, statement of interest, and two copies of official transcripts

Application Information:
Deadline: February 1
Application Fee: $60
Applicant/Acceptance Ratio: 8.5:1
Size of Incoming Class: 20 - 25
Tuition: Quebec residents - $2,504;
non-Quebec residents - $4,004
Books/Materials: $800 per year

Comments: Programs offered: Speech-Language Pathology and Audiology (admissions to the Audiology program have been suspended for the 2000-2001 academic year).
*Prerequisites for Speech-Language Pathology and Audiology are virtually the same. They are 1. Statistics (6 credits) - A full-year course in Statistics which could be offered by a Psychology, Sociology, Education, Mathematics, or Epidemiology Department. The course should have covered Analysis of Variance.
2. Linguistics (6 credits) - A full year course in Linguistics which could include courses in any of the following: General Phonetics, Linguistics Applied to Language Learning, Phonology, Morphology, Syntax, Field Methods in Linguistics; Linguistic Theory or Neurolinguistics. 3. Psychology (12 credits) - The division of credits should be as follows if possible: 3 credits from Physiological Psychology, Human Behaviour and the Brain, or Neuropsychology; 3 credits from Perception, Attention and Memory, Cognitive Science, or Thinking; 3 credits from Child Development, Language Learning in Children, Abnormal Psychology, Behaviour Modification, Deviations in Child Development, Aging or Psycholinguistics; and 3 credits from Social Psychology; Sociolinguistics, or Medical Anthropology. For those wishing to specialize in Audiology, 6 Psychology credits may be replaced by credits in Mathematics, Physics, Electronics, or Computer Science.

University of Ottawa
Admission Committee
Audiology and Speech-Language
Pathology Program
Faculty of Health Sciences
451 Smyth Road, Room 3071
Ottawa, ON   K1H 8M5
Tel: 613-562-5800 ext. 8386
Fax: 613-562-5428
E-mail: gsecr@uottawa.ca
Internet: www.sante.uottawa.ca/esr

General Information:
Degree Offered: M.Sc.S. (Audiology);
M.Sc.S. (Speech-Language Pathology)
Length: 6 semesters
Years: 2
Language: French

Admission Requirements:
Previous Education: Four-year
Baccalaureate degree (Hons.)
Prerequisite Courses: Speech-Language Pathology: 9 credits in Linguistics, 12 credits in Psychology, 3 credits in Statistics (intermediate level), 3 credits in Physiology or Anatomy and 3 credits Physics of Sound. Audiology: 3 credits in Statistics (intermediate level), 3 credits in Physiology or Human Anatomy, 3 credits in Physics of Sound, 3 credits in Linguistics (phonetics or phonetics-phonology), 3 credits psychology (perception, child development, aging, etc.)
Average GPA: 70% minimum
Range: n/a
Admission Test: n/a
Average Score: n/a
Score Report Deadline: n/a
Other Admission Criteria: English & French language competency tests and Interview

Application Information:
Deadline: February 5
Application Fee: $75
Applicant/Acceptance Ratio: n/a
Size of Incoming Class: n/a
Tuition: $5,954/year
Books/Materials: n/a

University of Toronto

Dr. L. Girolametto, Ph.D.
Department of Speech Language
Pathology
Rehabilitation Sciences Building 160-500
University Avenue
Toronto, ON   M5G 1V7
Tel: 416-978-2770
Fax: 416-978-1596
E-mail: speech.path@utoronto.ca
Internet: www.slp.utoronto.ca

General Information:
Degree Offered: M.H.Sc.
Length: Semesters
Years: 2 (full-time); 4-6 (part-time)
Language: English

Admission Requirements:
Previous Education: Four-year
baccalaureate degree or equivalent
Prerequisite Courses: Completion of
full courses in Statistics and Physiology
(preferably human), and a half course in
Developmental Psychology, Linguistics and
Phonetics
Average GPA: The departmental requires
a minimum of 3.3 GPA in the last 10 full
courses (or 20 half courses)
Range: School of Graduate Studies
requires a mid-B minimum in final year of
undergraduate degree
Admission Test: Not required
Average Score: n/a
Score Report Deadline: n/a
Other Admission Criteria: Effective
communication (personal meeting may
be requested); volunteer experience in
a speech-language pathology clinic (14
hours minimum)

Application Information:
Deadline: January 15 (M.H.Sc. full-time
and part-time)
Application Fee: $245
Applicant/Acceptance Ratio: 20:1
Size of Incoming Class: 45

Tuition: $7,557 (2008-2009) plus ancillary
fees
Books/Materials: $1,000 approx.

Comments: A two-year M.Sc. and a
four-year Ph.D. is also offered. Please see
departmental website for details.

TEACHER EDUCATION

The following fact sheets outline general information including academic requirements and application procedures for Teacher Education Schools in Canada. The data have been compiled in a concise format to assist students interested in these professional schools. Information was obtained from updates completed by each school, or in some cases from the school's Internet website.

Teacher Education Schools in Canada

Acadia University*
University of Alberta
Brandon University
University of British Columbia*
Brock University*
University of Calgary*
Concordia University
Lakehead University
Laurentian University*
University of Lethbridge
University of Manitoba
McGill University*
Memorial University of Newfoundland*
Université de Moncton*
Université de Montréal*
Mount Saint Vincent University*
University of New Brunswick*

Nipissing University*
University of Ottawa*
University of Prince Edward Island*
Queen's University
University of Regina
Université Sainte Anne
University of Saskatchewan*
Simon Fraser University
St. Francis Xavier University
St. Thomas University*
University of Toronto*
Trent with Queen's University
University of Victoria
University of Waterloo
University of Western Ontario
University of Windsor
University of Winnipeg*
York University*

Comments

1. These fact sheets act as a guide only. Students are advised to refer to the individual calendars or to write to the schools for more detailed information.

2. Application deadlines vary. Dates indicated refer to fall admission unless otherwise noted.

3. Tuition fees represent annual costs unless otherwise noted.

4. All of the schools listed above may not be represented.

This university has not updated its information. Please contact the university directly.

Acadia University

Manager of Admissions
Wolfville, NS   B4P 2R6
Tel: 902-585-1222
Fax: 902-585-1081
Internet: www.acadiau.ca

General Information:
Degree Offered: B.Ed.
Length: 4 semesters
Years: 2
Language: English

Admission Requirements:
Previous Education: Undergraduate degree
Prerequisite Courses: n/a
Average GPA: n/a
Range: 2.6/4.0 or B- minimum
Admission Test: Not required
Average Score: n/a
Score Report Deadline: n/a
Other Admission Criteria: Experience with children and interview

Application Information:
Deadline: February 1
Application Fee: $35
Applicant/Acceptance Ratio: 5:1
Size of Incoming Class: 120
Tuition: $7,242
Books/Materials: $700

Comments: As a reflection of the University's liberal education mission, emphasis in the B.Ed. program is placed on critical inquiry and the dynamic relationship among science, technology and the creative arts. The School works collaboratively with discipline-based departments on campus and with the school systems through the provision of extensive field experiences and a small number of exemplary school practitioners and instructors. MEd programs are also available in a variety of areas of specialization.

University of Alberta

Faculty of Education
Undergraduate Student Services
1-107 Education North
Edmonton, AB   T6G 2G5
Tel: 403-492-3659
Fax: 403-492-7533
E-mail: educ.info@ualberta.ca
Internet: www.education.ualberta.ca

General Information:
Degree Offered: B.Ed.*, B.Ed.(After Degree)**, B.Sc./B.Ed., B.A. (Native Studies)/B.Ed., BMUS/B.Ed., BPE/B.Ed., BSc.(Human Ecology)/B.Ed.
Length: Semesters
Years: See "Comments"
Language: English

Admission Requirements:
Previous Education: Successful completion of 24 units (8 half-courses) of course weight at the postsecondary level
Prerequisite Courses: None, but must be applicable to the degree program (no admission directly from high school)
Average GPA: C- to B+
Range: C- to B+
Admission Test: Not required
Average Score: n/a
Score Report Deadline: n/a
Other Admission Criteria: None

Application Information:
Deadline: March 1
Application Fee: $100
Applicant/Acceptance Ratio: 3:2
Size of Incoming Class: Varies from year to year. Enrolment is controlled and competitive for all points of entry
Tuition: $5,033.42
Books/Materials: $850-1,000

Comments: *Bachelor of Education (4 years/8 semesters): This is a 1+3 model where the first year is done at another institution or in another faculty outside the Faculty of Education; there is no direct entry from high school. A similar 4-year B.Ed. degree is offered in French by Faculte Saint-Jean.

** Bachelor of Education/After Degree (2 years/4 semesters): This program is designed for students who already hold an accredited 3- or 4-year degree.

*** Bachelor of Education/Bachelor of Science and Bachelor of Physical Education/ Bachelor of Education (5 years/10 semesters): These are Combined Degree programs where students receive two parchments upon graduation; one from the Faculty of Education and one from the other Faculty.

Brandon University
Admissions Office
270 - 18th Street
Brandon, MB   R7A 6A9
Tel: 204-727-9784
Fax: 204-728-3221
E-mail: admissions@brandonu.ca
Internet: www.brandonu.ca

General Information:
Degree Offered: B.Ed. (A.D.)
Length: Semesters
Years: 2
Language: English

Admission Requirements:
Previous Education: Bachelor degree in Arts, Science, Physical Education, etc.
Prerequisite Courses: n/a
Average GPA: 3.0 plus
Range: n/a
Admission Test: Not required
Average Score: n/a
Score Report Deadline: n/a
Other Admission Criteria: n/a

Application Information:
Deadline: February 15
Application Fee: $25
Applicant/Acceptance Ratio: n/a
Size of Incoming Class: 90

Tuition: $350 per half-course (3 credits hours)
Books/Materials: $500 - $700

Comments: The two-year program certifies graduates to teach at the Early and Middle or Senior years levels.

University of British Columbia
Teacher Education Office
2125 Main Mall
Vancouver, BC   V6T 1Z4
Tel: 604-822-5242

General Information:
Degree Offered: B.Ed. (Elementary); 2-year Elementary Teaching
Length: 4 semesters
Years: 2
Language: English

Admission Requirements:
Previous Education: At least 3 years (90 semester hours) of Arts, Fine Arts, Science, Music, or Human Kinetics
Prerequisite Courses: A full course in English (Composition and Literature); a half course in each of (a) Mathematics (not Statistics), (b) a Laboratory Science, (c) Canadian History or Geography; 3 full courses (18 semester hours) at third- or fourth-year level related to one Elementary School teaching subject; a half course with Canadian content in addition to above.
Average GPA: 73% and above is normally competitive
Range: 65% minimum*
Admission Test: Not required
Average Score: n/a
Score Report Deadline: n/a
Other Admission Criteria: Report of relevant experience, statement indicating what applicants have learned from their previous experience working with children and youth that will help them in their teaching careers, 2 letters of reference

Application Information:
Deadline: March 15
Application Fee: $60 (Canadian documents); $90 (Non-Canadian documents)
Applicant/Acceptance Ratio: 1.3:1
Size of Incoming Class: 144
Tuition: $76.50 per semester hour**
Books/Materials: $900 per year

Comments: Graduates normally qualify for the B.C. Professional Teaching Certificate.
* Minimum 65% on the prerequisite courses specified above, excluding a full course with Canadian content.
** Program consists of approximately 18 semester hours of courses and practica in each of 4 terms.
Program 1 of 5

University of British Columbia
Teacher Education Office
2125 Main Mall
Vancouver, BC   V6T 1Z4
Tel: 604-822-5242
General Information:
Degree Offered: B.Ed. (Elementary); 12-month Elementary Teaching (French Language)
Length: 3 semesters (September - August)
Years: 1
Language: English and French

Admission Requirements:
Previous Education: Recognized 4-year degree, including 90 semester hours of Arts, Fine Arts, Science, Music, or Human Kinetics
Prerequisite Courses: A full course in English (Composition and Literature); a half course in each of (a) Mathematics (not Statistics), (b) a Laboratory Science, (c) Canadian History or Geography; 3 full courses (18 semester hours) at third- or fourth-year level related to one Elementary School teaching subject; a half course with Canadian content in addition to above.

Average GPA: 65% and above is normally competitive
Range: 65% minimum*
Admission Test: Must pass oral and written French tests
Average Score: n/a
Score Report Deadline: n/a
Other Admission Criteria: Report of relevant experience, statement indicating what applicants have learned from their previous experience working with children and youth that will help them in their teaching careers, 2 letters of reference

Application Information:
Deadline: March 15
Application Fee: $60 (Canadian documents); $90 (Non-Canadian documents)
Applicant/Acceptance Ratio: 1.5:1
Size of Incoming Class: 36
Tuition: $148.90 per semester hour**
Books/Materials: $1,400

Comments: *Minimum 65% on the prerequisite courses specified above, excluding a full course with Canadian content.
**Program consists of a total of 67 semester hours of courses and practica over the 3 semesters.
1.Graduates normally qualify for the B.C. Professional Teaching Certificate.
2.This program prepares teachers for French Immersion and other French language Elementary Schools.
3.Applicants with some French (but not quite Native fluency) can select a program to prepare to teach French as a Second Language.
4.Candidates in French language programs take some courses in French and some in English; they do some practice teaching in French classrooms (French Immersion or French-as-a-Second-Language) and they do some practice teaching in English language classrooms where they teach the full range of Elementary School subjects.
Program 2 of 5.

University of British Columbia
Teacher Education Office
2125 Main Mall
Vancouver, BC   V6T 1Z4
Tel: 604-822-5242

General Information:
Degree Offered: B.Ed. (Elementary); 12-month Elementary Teaching
Length: 3 semesters (September - August)
Years: 1
Language: English

Admission Requirements:
Previous Education: Recognized 4-year degree, including a minimum of 90 semester hours of Arts, Fine Arts, Science, Music, or Human Kinetics
Prerequisite Courses: A full course in English (Composition and Literature); a half course in each of (a) Mathematics (not Statistics), (b) a Laboratory Science, (c) Canadian History or Geography; 3 full courses (18 semester hours) at third- or fourth-year level related to one Elementary School teaching subject; a half course with Canadian content in addition to above.
Average GPA: 75% and above is normally competitive
Range: 65% minimum*
Admission Test: Not required
Average Score: n/a
Score Report Deadline: n/a
Other Admission Criteria: Report of relevant experience, statement indicating what applicants have learned from their previous experience working with children and youth that will help them in their teaching careers, 2 letters of reference

Application Information:
Deadline: March 15
Application Fee: $60 (Canadian documents); $90 (Non-Canadian documents)
Applicant/Acceptance Ratio: 1.3:1
Size of Incoming Class: 260

Tuition: $148.90 per semester hour**
Books/Materials: $1,400

Comments: Graduates normally qualify for the B.C. Professional Teaching Certificate.
*Minimum 65% on the prerequisite courses specified above, excluding a full course with Canadian content.
**Program consists of approximately 61 semester hours of courses and practica over 3 terms.
Program 3 of 5.

University of British Columbia
Teacher Education Office
2125 Main Mall
Vancouver, BC   V6T 1Z4
Tel: 604-822-5242

General Information:
Degree Offered: B.Ed. (Middle Years); Middle Years Program
Length: 3 semesters (September - August)
Years: 1
Language: English

Admission Requirements:
Previous Education: Recognized 4-year degree, including a minimum of 90 semester hours of Arts, Fine Arts, Science, Music or Human Kinetics
Prerequisite Courses: A full course in English (Composition and Literature); a half course in each of (a) Mathematics (not Statistics), (b) a Laboratory Science, (c) History or Geography; 3 full courses (18 semester hours) at third or fourth-year level related to one middle school teaching subject; a full course with Canadian content.
Average GPA: 75% and above is normally competitive
Range: 65% minimum*
Admission Test: Not required
Average Score: n/a
Score Report Deadline: n/a
Other Admission Criteria: Report of

relevant experience, statement indicating what applicants have learned from their previous experience working with children and youth that will help them in their teaching careers, 2 letters of reference.

Application Information:
Deadline: March 15
Application Fee: $60 (Canadian documents); $90 (Non-Canadian documents)
Applicant/Acceptance Ratio: 1.4:1
Size of Incoming Class: 72
Tuition: $148.90 per semester hour**
Books/Materials: $1,400

Comments: Graduates normally qualify for the B.C. Professional Teaching Certificate.
*Minimum 65% on the prerequisite courses specified above, excluding a full course with Canadian content.
**Program consists of approximately 60 semester hours of courses and practica over 3 terms
Potential applicants must pay careful attention to middle years teaching subject requirements in their undergraduate course selection. See website.
Program 4 of 5.

University of British Columbia
Teacher Education Office
2125 Main Mall
Vancouver, BC   V6T 1Z4
Tel: 604-822-5242

General Information:
Degree Offered: B.Ed. (Secondary); Secondary Teaching
Length: 3 semesters (September - August)
Years: 1
Language: English

Admission Requirements:
Previous Education: Recognized 4-year degree

Prerequisite Courses: A full course in English (Composition and Literature); courses for selected Secondary teaching subjects (for details, consult UBC Calendar or request Admission Information at above address)
Average GPA: Mid-70s and higher is competitive for popular subject areas
Range: 65% minimum on third and fourth year courses in teaching subject(s)
Admission Test: Not required
Average Score: n/a
Score Report Deadline: n/a
Other Admission Criteria: Report of relevant experience, statement indicating what applicants have learned from their previous experience working with children and youth that will help them in their teaching careers, 2 letters of reference

Application Information:
Deadline: March 15
Application Fee: $60 (Canadian documents); $90 (Non-Canadian documents)
Applicant/Acceptance Ratio: 1.5:1
Size of Incoming Class: 300
Tuition: $148.90 per semester hour*
Books/Materials: $1,400

Comments: *Program consists of a total of 18 - 21 semester hours of courses and practica each term.
1.Graduates normally qualify for the B.C. Professional Teaching Certificate.
2.Those with native French fluency may select a program for teaching in French-language schools.
3.Potential applicants must pay careful attention to secondary teaching subjects requirements in their undergraduate course selection.
Visit their website.
Program 5 of 5.

Brock University

Office of Admissions
500 Glenridge Avenue
St. Catharines, ON   L2S 3A1
Tel: 905-688-5550, ext. 3562
E-mail: edubrock@brocku.ca
Internet: www.brocku.ca/registrar/
admissions

General Information:
Degree Offered: B.A./B.Ed.*; B.Sc./B.Ed.*;
B.Ph.Ed./B.Ed.; B.Ed. Pre-service**
Length: n/a
Years: *4; **1
Language: English

Admission Requirements:
Previous Education: See "Comments"
Prerequisite Courses: See "Comments"
Average GPA: See "Comments"
Range:
Admission Test: Not required
Average Score: n/a
Score Report Deadline: n/a
Other Admission Criteria: See
"Comments"

Application Information:
Deadline: December 1
Application Fee: $105 plus $60 service fee
Applicant/Acceptance Ratio: 10:1
Size of Incoming Class: 450
Tuition: $4,480
Books/Materials: $500 - $700

Comments: Requirements for B.Ed.
Pre-Service one-year program: 1. Primary/
Junior – must have completed grade
12 advanced or OAC (or equivalent)
courses in each of the following four
areas: mathematics, science, English,
or Canadian geography or Canadian
history. Should have some experience
working with children and/or youth;
2. Junior/Intermediate - must have 3
full undergraduate credits averaging
75% in one of the teachable subject
areas. At a minimum, 2/3 of teachable
subject courses must be completed by
January 1. Should have some experience
working with children and/or youth;
3. Intermediate/Senior – must have
at least five full undergraduate credits
averaging 75% in one teachable subject
area and three full undergraduate credits
averaging 70% in a second teachable
subject as listed. At a minimum, 3/5 of
first teachable subject and 2/3 of second
teachable subject courses to be completed
by January 1. A work experience profile
must be completed; 4. B.Ed. Pre-service
(all) - recognized university degree and
experience profile; 5. B.Ed. Pre-service
- B.Ed. in Technological Education.
Requirements for B.A./B.Ed.: Applicants
who complete Year 1 of the B.A. Child
Studies program at Brock may apply on a
competitive basis to enter B.A./B.Ed. which
begins at the Year 2 level. Enrolment is
limited.
Requirements for B.Sc./B.Ed. (Calculus):
Six OACs are required with an overall
average of 80% in 2 sciences, one math,
and English OAC or 80% in 2 maths
(including Calculus), one science, and
English OACI. Enrolment is limited.
Requirements for B.Ph.Ed./B.Ed.:
Applicants who complete Year 1 of the
Physical Education program at Brock may
apply on a competitive basis to enter B.Ph.
Ed./B.Ed. which begins at the Year 2 level.
Enrolment is limited.
M.Ed. program also offered (see Graduate
Studies Calendar).

University of Calgary

Student Programs Office
Faculty of Education
Calgary, AB   T2N 1N4
Tel: 403-220-5675
Fax: 403-282-3005
E-mail: gder@ucalgary.ca
Internet: www.educ.ucalgary.ca/gder

General Information:
Degree Offered: M.A., M.Sc., MEd, PhD, EdD
Length: semesters
Years: 2 - 4 years
Language: English

Admission Requirements:
Previous Education: B.Ed. plus minimum two years of teaching experience
Prerequisite Courses: n/a
Average GPA: Approx. 2.9 on 10 most recent half courses; 3.0/4.0 Masters; 3.5/4.0 Ph.D.
Range: n/a
Admission Test: n/a
Average Score: n/a
Score Report Deadline: n/a
Other Admission Criteria: n/a

Application Information:
Deadline: February 1 for July or September; August 15 for January
Application Fee: $60
Applicant/Acceptance Ratio: Varies
Size of Incoming Class: 191
Tuition: $609 per course for course based; $1,080 per course for distance education
Books/Materials: Varies

Concordia University
Education Department - LB 579
1455 des Maisonneuve Blvd. West
Montreal, QC   H3G 1M8
Tel: 514-848-2424 ext. 2030
Fax: 514-848-4520
E-mail: anne@education.concordia.ca
Internet: www.doe.concordia.ca

General Information:
Degree Offered: Diploma Instructional Technology
Length: 30 credits
Years: 1 (full-time), part-time is also available
Language: English

Admission Requirements:
Previous Education: Bachelor's degree
Prerequisite Courses: None
Average GPA: n/a
Range: 2.7 minimum
Admission Test: Not required
Average Score: n/a
Score Report Deadline: n/a
Other Admission Criteria: 3 good references and statement of purpose, TOEFL test for international students - minimum score 90+ (IBT version)

Application Information:
Deadline: February 1 for September admission;
September 1 for January admission
Application Fee: $75 (CDN)
Applicant/Acceptance Ratio: n/a
Size of Incoming Class: 15-20
Tuition: See Concordia University calendar
Books/Materials: See Concordia University calendar

Comments: M.A. Educational Technology program is also offered.

Lakehead University
Admissions and Recruitment
955 Oliver Road
Thunder Bay, ON   P7B 5E1
Tel: 807-343-8500 or 1-800-465-3959
E-mail: admissions@lakeheadu.ca
Internet: www.lakeheadu.ca

General Information:
Degree Offered: B.Ed.
Length: n/a
Years: 1
Language: English

Admission Requirements:
Previous Education: B.A., B.Sc. or equivalent
Prerequisite Courses: Varies with program choice
Average GPA: Admission Requirement - 70%

Range: n/a
Admission Test: n/a
Average Score: n/a
Score Report Deadline: n/a
Other Admission Criteria: Submission of Experience Profile Form

Application Information:
Deadline: Early December
Application Fee: $110 plus $40 supplementary fee
Applicant/Acceptance Ratio: n/a
Size of Incoming Class: n/a
Tuition: $4,675
Books/Materials: $750 - $2,400

Comments: Program Offered: Primary/Junior, Junior/Intermediate, Intermediate/Senior.

Lakehead University

Admissions and Recruitment
955 Oliver Road
Thunder Bay, ON   P7B 5E1
Tel: 807-343-8500 or 1-800-465-3959
E-mail: admissions@lakeheadu.ca
Internet: www.lakeheadu.ca

General Information:
Degree Offered: BA/B.Sc./B.Ed.
Length: n/a
Years: 4-5
Language: English

Admission Requirements:
Previous Education: OSSD; 6 Grade 12U or M courses
Prerequisite Courses: Varies with program choice
Average GPA: Admission Requirement - 70%
Range: n/a
Admission Test: n/a
Average Score: n/a
Score Report Deadline: n/a
Other Admission Criteria: None

Application Information:
Deadline: Early December preferred
Application Fee: $105-$150
Applicant/Acceptance Ratio: n/a
Size of Incoming Class: n/a
Tuition: $4,650
Books/Materials: n/a

Comments: Program Offered: Primary/Junior, Junior/Intermediate, Intermediate/Senior. A Native Teacher Education Program (4-year concurrent B.A./B.Ed.) is offered. For admission, Native ancestry, OSSD including 6 OACs or admission as an adult student, and recommendation from a Native organization is required. M.Ed. is also offered.

Laurentian University

Att: The Director
École des sciences de l'éducation
Sudbury, ON   P3E 2C6
Tel: 705-673-6592 or
705-675-1151 poste 5001
Fax: 705-675-4816
E-mail: clarocque@laurentienne.ca
Internet: http://laurentienne.ca/educ

General Information:
Degree Offered: B.A.Educ. (et B.Ed. en ligne à temps partie)
Length: n/a
Years: 3 (et 1)
Language: français

Admission Requirements:
Previous Education: n/a
Prerequisite Courses: B.A.
Average GPA: 65%
Range: n/a
Admission Test: Compétence linguistique et oral ècrit
Average Score: 65
Score Report Deadline: n/a
Other Admission Criteria: n/a

Application Information:
Deadline: As per Calendar criteria

Application Fee: As per Calendar criteria - full-time or part-time
Applicant/Acceptance Ratio: n/a
Size of Incoming Class: n/a
Tuition: $2,935 - $3,475.50
Books/Materials: $300 - $450

Comments: Three programs are offered, 1 concurrent, as mentioned above, a consecutive program and 1 online, part-time program.

University of Lethbridge
Student Program Services
Faculty of Education
4401 University Drive
Lethbridge, AB   T1K 3M4
Tel: 403-329-2254
Fax: 403-329-2412
E-mail: edu.sps@uleth.ca
Internet: www.uleth.ca

General Information:
Degree Offered: B.Ed. Post-degree & Combined Degrees (5 year program)
Length: 4 semesters
Years: 2
Language: English

Admission Requirements:
Previous Education: Approved degree in a teaching major
Prerequisite Courses: 20 semester courses plus major requirements, ED 2500, Writing Comp.
Average GPA: Depends on major
Range: 2.5 - 4.0
Admission Test: Writing competency
Average Score: Marginally satisfactory
Score Report Deadline: June 1
Other Admission Criteria: Depends on major

Application Information:
Deadline: May 1
Application Fee: $60
Applicant/Acceptance Ratio: 3:1
Size of Incoming Class: 222

Tuition: $2,950 (5 courses) + $325 practicum travel fee
Books/Materials: $140 per course

Comments: Teaching majors are Art, CTS: Business, Drama, English, Math, Modern Lang., Music, Native Education, P.E., Science, and Social Studies. Highly competitive in Social Studies, English, (Biology) Science Ed., Physical Education, Drama and Art.

University of Manitoba
Faculty of Education
Winnipeg, MB   R3T 2N2
Tel: 204-474-9004 or 1-800-432-1960, ext. 9004
Fax: 204-474-7551
E-mail: bachofed@umanitoba.ca
Internet: www.umanitoba.ca/education

General Information:
Degree Offered: B.Ed. (includes integrated Bachelor of Education/Bachelor of Music)
Length: Semesters
Years: 2
Language: English

Admission Requirements:
Previous Education: Undergraduate Degree
Prerequisite Courses: See Undergraduate calendar at http://webapps.cc.umanitoba.ca/calendar08
Average GPA: 3.0
Range: B
Admission Test: Not required
Average Score: n/a
Score Report Deadline: n/a
Other Admission Criteria: Experience profile, proof of writing skills, references

Application Information:
Deadline: February 1
Application Fee: $90
Applicant/Acceptance Ratio: 2:1
Size of Incoming Class: 300

Tuition: $3,400
Books/Materials: $2,750

Comments: University of Manitoba offers Two Year After Degree B.Ed. programs in Early Years (Kindergarten - Grade 4), Middle Years (Grades 5-8), and Senior Years (Grades 9-12). All programs offer small class sizes within 24 weeks of practicum.

McGill University
Teacher Education
3700 McTavish Street
Montreal, QC   H3A 1V2
Tel: 514-398-7042
Fax: 514-398-4679
E-mail: sao.education@mcgill.ca
Internet: www.mcgill.ca/education

General Information:
Degree Offered: B.Ed.
Length: 90 - 156 credits
Years: n/a
Language: English

Admission Requirements:
Previous Education: OSSD with a minimum of six OAC, 4U and/or 4M courses
Prerequisite Courses: OAC or 4U English or French
Average GPA: n/a
Range: n/a
Admission Test: English proficiency test
Average Score: n/a
Score Report Deadline: n/a
Other Admission Criteria: Fluency in French is required for certification in the Province of Quebec (admission to the Faculty of Education is limited; fulfillment of the minimum requirement does not guarantee admission)

Application Information:
Deadline: March 1st for Fall admission (Quebec students);
February 1 for Fall admission (rest of Canada)

Application Fee: $60 non-refundable
Applicant/Acceptance Ratio: n/a
Size of Incoming Class: n/a
Tuition: $1,668.30 for residents of Quebec; $4,012.50 for residents in all other provinces
Books/Materials: $1,000 - $1,500 per year

Memorial University of Newfoundland
Office of Undergraduate Student Services
Faculty of Education
St. John's, NL   A1B 3X8
Tel: 709-737-3403
Fax: 709-737-2001
E-mail: muneduc@mun.ca
Internet: www.mun.ca/educ

General Information:
Degree Offered: B.Ed. (Primary & Elementary)
Length: Semesters
Years: 5
Language: English (French Immersion Option)

Admission Requirements:
Previous Education: 20 university courses
Prerequisite Courses: * See Comments
Average GPA: n/a
Range: 65% cumulative average or 65% in last 30 credit hours which have been successfully completed
Admission Test: Not required
Average Score: n/a
Score Report Deadline: n/a
Other Admission Criteria: Resume; References; Personal Statement; Applicant must have basic computer keyboarding skills

Application Information:
Deadline: February 15
Application Fee: $40 Memorial University of Newfoundland students; $80 all others
Applicant/Acceptance Ratio: n/a

Size of Incoming Class: 60 Primary/60 Elementary
Tuition: $1,650 per semester
Books/Materials: $350 per semester (approx.)

Comments: * Prerequisite courses for admission are specific. Please visit our website at www.mun.ca/educ for details.

Memorial University of Newfoundland
Office of Undergraduate Student Services
Faculty of Education
St. John's, NL   A1B 3X8
Tel: 709-737-3403

General Information:
Degree Offered: B.Ed. Post-degree (Intermediate/Secondary)
Length: 3 Semesters
Years: 1 (12 months)
Language: English

Admission Requirements:
Previous Education: University degree
Prerequisite Courses: 12 courses and 8 courses in "reachable" subjects
Average GPA: n/a
Range: 65% minimum in Teachable Subjects and last 20 courses
Admission Test: Not required
Average Score: n/a
Score Report Deadline: n/a
Other Admission Criteria: Resume, Personal Statement

Application Information:
Deadline: February 1 for September admission
Application Fee: $40 M.U. of N. students; $80 all others
Applicant/Acceptance Ratio: 3:1
Size of Incoming Class: 120
Tuition: $1,980
Books/Materials: $350

Comments: This full-time program extends over three consecutive semesters

(September - August) enabling students to qualify for a teaching certificate within one year. For specific information, please see the MUN Calendar 1999-2000 or visit our Website at www.mun.ca/educ. For general enquiries, please e-mail to muneduc@ morgan.ucs.mun.ca

Université de Moncton
Faculté des sciences de l'éducation
Moncton, NB   E1A 3E9
Tel: 506-858-4359

General Information:
Degree Offered: B.Ed. Programme A
Length: 4 sessions - automne, hiver, automne, hiver
Years: 2 ans
Language: français

Admission Requirements:
Previous Education: Baccalauréat
Prerequisite Courses: 2 concentrations 1 - 42 crédits et 2 - 24 crédits dans des matières enseignées dans les écoles publiques
Average GPA: Statistique descriptive et une moyenne minimale de 2.6 sur l'ensemble des trois cours FR1885, FR1886, et FR2501 ou se soumettre à un examen de compétence linguistique en français et obtenir au moins la note B
Range: 2.5 sur 4.0
Admission Test: n/a
Average Score: n/a
Score Report Deadline: n/a
Other Admission Criteria: Programme à temps complet maîtrise de la langue française obligatoire

Application Information:
Deadline: 1er juin
Application Fee: $30
Applicant/Acceptance Ratio: 3:1
Size of Incoming Class: 20
Tuition: $2,810
Books/Materials: $750

Université de Montréal

Faculté des sciences de l'éducation
C.P. 6128, Succursale Centre-ville
Montréal, QC   H3C 3J7
Tel: 514-343-7822

General Information:
Degree Offered: B.Ed.
Length: Semesters
Years: 4
Language: français

Admission Requirements:
Previous Education: DEC
Prerequisite Courses: None
Average GPA: n/a
Range: n/a
Admission Test: n/a
Average Score: n/a
Score Report Deadline: n/a
Other Admission Criteria: n/a

Application Information:
Deadline: March 1
Application Fee: $30
Applicant/Acceptance Ratio: n/a
Size of Incoming Class: 40 - 80
Tuition: 61,31$/credit for Quebec residents
101,31$/credit for other Canadians
275,61$/credit for non-Canadians
Books/Materials: n/a

Comments: Other programs (full-time and part-time) are offered for those who want to expand their vocational training - short programs (15 credits), Graduate diploma (30 credits), M.Ed. (45 credits) in one of these options: educational administration, educational technology, evaluation, studies in education, didactic, psychopedagogy, adult education or orthopedagogy. An M.A. and a Ph.D. in Education in one of these options is also offered for those who want to become researchers.

Mount Saint Vincent University

The Admissions Office
166 Bedford Highway
Halifax, NS   B3M 2J6
Tel: 902-457-6117
Fax: 905-457-6498
E-mail: admissions@msvu.ca
Internet: www.msvu.ca

General Information:
Degree Offered: B.Ed.
Length: Full year terms
Years: 2
Language: English

Admission Requirements:
Previous Education: Bachelor's degree from a recognized university
Prerequisite Courses: See calendar or website
Average GPA: min 3.0
Range: n/a
Admission Test: n/a
Average Score: n/a
Score Report Deadline: n/a
Other Admission Criteria: See calendar or website

Application Information:
Deadline: February 15
Application Fee: $40-50
Applicant/Acceptance Ratio: n/a
Size of Incoming Class: n/a
Tuition: $1,127.44-1,453.00
Books/Materials: $800-1,000

University of New Brunswick

Faculty of Education
P.O. Box 4400
Fredericton, NB   E3B 5A3
Tel: 506-453-3508
Fax: 506-453-3569
E-mail: bed-prog@unb.ca
Internet: www.unb.ca

General Information:
Degree Offered: B.Ed. (Consecutive & Concurrent)

Length: 4 semesters or 60 credit hours
Years: 1 ½ - 2
Language: English

Admission Requirements:
Previous Education: *B.A., B.Sc., B.P.E., B.Kin., B.Mus., B.F.A. etc. (for Consecutive program)
Prerequisite Courses: See course calendar
Average GPA: B average & to be competitive
Range: Depends on other criteria listed below
Admission Test: Not required
Average Score: n/a
Score Report Deadline: Two letters of application; letters of intent; experience profile; interview (for selected applicants)
Other Admission Criteria: n/a

Application Information:
Deadline: January 31
Application Fee: $35
Applicant/Acceptance Ratio: 5:1
Size of Incoming Class: 240
Tuition: $5,000 (approx.)
Books/Materials: $1,000 (approx.)

Comments: A concurrent degree is done in combination with and parallel to another undergraduate degree (e.g. B.A./B.Ed.). Candidates join the Faculty of Education after the first or second year of study at U.N.B. or as transfer students from another university. The double degree program is normally completed in 5 years. Please contact the Faculty of Education for further information.

Nipissing University
Office of the Registrar
100 College Drive, Box 5002
North Bay, ON   P1B 8L7
Tel: 705-474-3450, ext. 4521
Fax: 705-474-1947
E-mail: liaison@nipissingu.ca
Internet: www.nipissingu.ca/
documents.cfm?itemid=6305

General Information:
Degree Offered: B.Ed.
Length: 2 semesters
Years: 1 (12 months)
Language: English

Admission Requirements:
Previous Education: Approved undergraduate degree from an accredited university
Prerequisite Courses: Teachers in the elementary schools are generally required to teach all subjects in the curriculum. It is most prudent for students who plan to teach at this level to take a wide range of undergraduate courses. Particularly important, but not required for admission to the B.Ed. degree program - particularly the primary/junior and junior/intermediate divisions, are courses in English, Mathematics, Science, History, Geography, Art, and Music. In addition to these traditional disciplines, courses in Educational Psychology and Introductory Sociology are important foundations for a teacher education program.
Average GPA: n/a
Range: 65% - 85% (depending on division applied to and teaching subject(s) selected)
Admission Test: Not required
Average Score: n/a
Score Report Deadline: n/a
Other Admission Criteria: Experience Profile

Application Information:
Deadline: December 1 of the year prior
Application Fee: $85 to Ontario University Application Centre; $40 Nipissing Fee
Applicant/Acceptance Ratio: 3:1
Size of Incoming Class: 700
Tuition: $5,412.50
Books/Materials: $1,400 compulsory laptop fee

Comments: Those interested in the Second Language Teaching: French option should take several courses in French as well as providing for themselves a wide variety of experiences in the language in order to prepare for teaching this specialty. Oral and Written French proficiency will be tested. Students interested in the Intermediate Division (Grades 7-10) must complete at least eighteen undergraduate credits in one particular subject area to meet the prerequisites for the teaching subject. The teaching subject disciplines offered at Nipissing are outlined in the B.Ed.-junior/intermediate division section of the Academic Calendar. Students interested in teaching in the Senior Division (Grades 11-12) must be qualified to teach in two secondary school subject areas. A minimum of thirty undergraduate credits must be completed in the first teaching subject and at least eighteen undergraduate credits are required in the second teaching subject. Refer to the B.Ed.-intermediate/senior division section of the Academic Calendar for a listing of teaching subject disciplines offered at Nipissing.

University of Ottawa

Office of the Registrar, Admissions
550 Cumberland Street
Ottawa, ON   K1N 6N5
Tel: 613-562-5700
Fax: 613-562-5290
E-mail: liaison@uottawa.ca
Internet: www.education.uottawa.ca

General Information:
Degree Offered: B.Ed.
Length: 2 semesters
Years: 1
Language: French and English

Admission Requirements:
Previous Education: Recognized university degree (or equivalent) with at least 15 full courses
Prerequisite Courses: Courses necessary to meet the requirements of chosen teaching subjects and teaching options
Average GPA: 70% minimum
Range: n/a
Admission Test: Applicants selecting French as a teaching subject must write a French Competency Test; all candidates applying to the French program must pass French Competency.
Average Score: Pass mark
Score Report Deadline: n/a
Other Admission Criteria: Applicants must submit proof of related practical experience and a letter of reference

Application Information:
Deadline: December 1
Application Fee: $85 + $35 evaluation
Applicant/Acceptance Ratio: (4:1 English, 2:1 French) Total: 6:1
Size of Incoming Class: 620 English; 420 French
Tuition: $4,549
Books/Materials: $500 - $900

Comments: The Faculty of Arts, in co-operation with the Faculty of Education, offers a B.A. program in second-language teaching (S.L.T.) designed for those who would like to teach others to perfect their second-language teaching skills (French, English, or other). The program guarantees graduates who have met all the admission requirements a place in the Faculty of Education's B.Ed. program leading to a teaching certificate. In French, the education program may also be combined with Science, lettres françaises or technical studies, and may also be completed on a part-time basis.

University of Prince Edward Island

The Registrar
550 University Avenue
Charlottetown, PE   C1A 4P3
Tel: 902-566-0439
Fax: 902-566-0795
E-mail: registrar@upei.ca
Internet: www.upei.ca

General Information:
Degree Offered: B.Ed. Post-degree; B.Ed.
Length: 4 semesters
Years: 2
Language: English

Admission Requirements:
Previous Education: See course calendar
Prerequisite Courses: See course calendar
Average GPA: n/a
Range: 70% minimum
Admission Test: Not required
Average Score: n/a
Score Report Deadline: n/a
Other Admission Criteria: Interview*, referees' forms, personal statement, resume, supplementary application

Application Information:
Deadline: January 15
Application Fee: $35
Applicant/Acceptance Ratio: 4:1
Size of Incoming Class: 75
Tuition: $4,900
Books/Materials: $1,000 per year

Comments: * Applicants may be interviewed at the discretion of the admission committee.

Queen's University

Admission Services
Richardson Hall
Kingston, ON   K7L 3N6
Tel: 613-533-6205
E-mail: admissn@post.queensu.ca
Internet: www.queensu.ca/admission

General Information:
Degree Offered: B.Ed.
Length: 2 semesters
Years: 1
Language: English

Admission Requirements:
Previous Education: For Primary/
Junior: acceptable bachelor's degree;
Intermediate/Senior: acceptable bachelor's

degree and university courses in 2 teaching subjects
Prerequisite Courses: See calendar for more detailed information
Average GPA: n/a
Range: B minimum on all university courses
Admission Test: Not required
Average Score: n/a
Score Report Deadline: n/a
Other Admission Criteria: Personal statement of experience
Application Information:
Deadline: February 20
Application Fee: $85 plus $40
Applicant/Acceptance Ratio: 3:1
Size of Incoming Class: 400 - 420
Tuition: $4,937.44
Books/Materials: $300 - $500

Comments: Technological Education program also offered. Combination of related work and post-secondary education totalling 5 years with minimum 24 months' paid work experience plus minimum Ontario Grade 12 or equivalent required. Queen's also offers B.A./B.Ed. and B.Sc./B.Ed. programs.

University of Regina

Dr. Nick Forsberg, Associate Dean
Faculty of Education, Student Program Centre
Regina, SK   S4S 0A2
Tel: 306-585-4537
Fax: 306-585-4006
E-mail: nick.forsberg@uregina.ca
Internet: www.education.uregina.ca

General Information:
Degree Offered: Bachelor of Education - 4 year degree program (Elementary Education K - 5, Middle Years 5 - 9, Secondary Education and BAC French-Elementary and Secondary Education, Arts Education K-12); and Bachelor of Education After Degree programs - 2 years

Length: Semesters
Years: BEd (4 years); BEd in Arts Education (5 years); BEAD (2 years)
Language: English

Admission Requirements:
Previous Education: Saskatchewan Secondary level standing or equivalent
Prerequisite Courses: English A30, English B30, one 30-level math or science, one 30 level language, social science or fine art, one additional 30 level course. (See web for list or approved courses). *Students applying to Elementary Education or Secondary Business Education need Math A30. Students applying to secondary education programs with a major in Chemistry, Mathematics or Physics need Math B30 and Math C30.
Average GPA: 65%
Range: n/a
Admission Test: n/a
Average Score: n/a
Score Report Deadline: n/a
Other Admission Criteria: International students must submit evidence of English proficiency

Application Information:
Deadline: Fall: Canadian and U.S. applicants - March 1; Applicants from other countries - March 1; Winter: Canadian and U.S. applicants - n/a; Applicants from other countries - n/a; BEADS/Transfers – December 1; transcripts due February 1; Early Conditional High school – March 15
Application Fee: $85
Applicant/Acceptance Ratio: Only qualified applicants accepted
Size of Incoming Class: 90+(Elementary); 90+(Secondary); 30 (Arts Educ.); 30 BACC (Elementary) and 30 BACC (Secondary)
Tuition: $3,890 (subject to change) plus compulsory fees per year (VISA student tuition differs)
Books/Materials: $1,200 - $1,500

Comments: Applicants must also submit a Teacher Education Application and Profile. Programs: Elementary Education, Secondary Education, French, Human Resource Development, Indian Education, Arts Education, Vocational/Technical Education. For more details on all programs visit www.education.uregina.ca.

Université Sainte Anne
Pointe-de-l'Église, Nouvelle Écosse
B0W 1M0
Tel: 902-769-2114

General Information:
Degree Offered: B.Ed
Length: 4 semestres
Years: 2
Language: français

Admission Requirements:
Previous Education: B.A. ou B.Sc.
Prerequisite Courses: Les préalables dépendent de l'option choisie
Average GPA: 2.30
Range: 65% minimum
Admission Test: Test de placement en français
Average Score: n/a
Score Report Deadline: n/a
Other Admission Criteria: 3 lettres de références et 1 lettre d'intention

Application Information:
Deadline: 31 juillet
Application Fee: $30
Applicant/Acceptance Ratio: n/a
Size of Incoming Class: jusqu'à 80 places
Tuition: $3,468 par semestre*
Books/Materials: $800

Comments: Les candidats dont la langue maternelle n'est pas le français ou dont la compétence en français est inférieure à celle exigée par l'Université, doivent obligatoirement suivre une session d'immersion française ou des cours de rattrapage.

*estimation: les frais de scolarité sont calculés selon le nombre de crédits.

University of Saskatchewan
College of Education
3350 28 Campus Drive
Saskatoon, SK   S7N 0X1
Tel: 306-966-7654
Fax: 306-966-7644
Internet: www.usask.ca/education

General Information:
Degree Offered: B.Ed. & B.Mus.(Mus. Ed.)***, B.Ed. Post-Academic**
Length: Semesters
Years: *4 (B.Ed.); **5 (combined B.Ed. and B.Mus.), ***2
Language: English

Admission Requirements:
Previous Education: *Grade 12
Prerequisite Courses: See "Comments" and check website for more information
Average GPA: n/a
Range: 65%
Admission Test: n/a
Average Score: n/a
Score Report Deadline: n/a
Other Admission Criteria: See "Comments"

Application Information:
Deadline: May 15
Application Fee: $75
Applicant/Acceptance Ratio: 2:1
Size of Incoming Class: n/a
Tuition: Check website for information (fees are per credit) + #388.91 student fees
Books/Materials: $500-$2,000

Comments: *Direct entry students enrol in a four-year B.Ed. 126 credit-unit program in which academic and professional courses and field experiences are taken concurrently - available only to students entering Home Economics, Industrial Arts, or Vocational Education programs.
**Applicants wishing to pursue a B.Mus. or the 5-year combined B.Ed.B.Mus. (Mus. Ed.) degree must successfully complete an audition, an interview and a placement examination with the Department of Music.
***Post-Academic students, who will have completed the academic portion of the B.Ed. degree, will be admitted to a two-year program of professional course work and field experience.
Post-Academic Two Year Program: There is one non-direct entry admission category to the Post-Academic Programs. Applicants applying to the program must have completed at least 60 credit units of academic course work which can be transferred to one of the program options (Elementary, Middle, or Secondary).

Simon Fraser University
Judith Bicknell
Undergraduate Advisor
Faculty of Education
Burnaby, BC   V5A 1S6
Tel: 778-782-3436
Fax: 778-782-3829
E-mail: educadv@sfu.ca
Internet: www.educ.sfu.ca/pdp/admissions

General Information:
Degree Offered: B.Ed.
Length: 10 semesters
Years: 5
Language: English

Admission Requirements:
Previous Education: Senior matriculation
Prerequisite Courses: Same as for admission to university
Average GPA: n/a
Range: Varying competitive GPA each semester
Admission Test: Not required
Average Score: n/a
Score Report Deadline: n/a
Other Admission Criteria: None

Application Information:
Deadline: September 30 for January; January 31 for May; April 30 for September Application Information for Professional Development Program (P.D.P.): January 15 for September admission; May 15 - January admission
Application Fee: SFU $45 or $100 evaluation fee if post-secondary is out of B.C. (subject to change) Application Fee for P.D.P.: SFU $55 application fee (paid separately) (subject to change)
Applicant/Acceptance Ratio: 4:1
Size of Incoming Class: n/a
Tuition: $151.10 per credit hour (usual course load for full-time student is 15 credit hours per semester). These fees may increase.
Books/Materials: Depends on course

Comments: A teacher training year program. The Professional Development Program (P.D.P.) may be completed as part of a degree or post-degree. Recommend related instructional experience and GPA of 2.5 minimum. Contact Diane Kelso, Assistant to Associate Dean, for further information and current admission requirements at 778-782-3620.

St. Francis Xavier University
Education Department
Antigonish, NS   B2G 1C0
Tel: 902-867-2247
Fax: 902-867-3887
E-mail: education@stfx.ca
Internet: www.stfx.ca/academic/education

General Information:
Degree Offered: B.Ed
Length: Semesters
Years: 2
Language: English

Admission Requirements:
Previous Education: Undergraduate degree in Arts & Science

Prerequisite Courses: You must have a university degree with a minimum of 90 credit hours of course work. See "Comments" section for teachable subjects. Credits in psychology and philosophy are recommended although these are not teachable subjects
Average GPA: n/a; admission is very competitive
Range: 70% minimum
Admission Test: Not required
Average Score: n/a
Score Report Deadline: n/a
Other Admission Criteria: Relevant qualitative data, interview, reference letters, essay

Application Information:
Deadline: January 31
Application Fee: $40
Applicant/Acceptance Ratio: 4:1
Size of Incoming Class: 100
Tuition: Revised annually
Books/Materials: n/a

Comments: St. Francis Xavier offers both Elementary and Secondary Education Programs. There are certain subject fields deemed teachable in elementary schools: English, French, Music, Physical Education, Art, Social Studies (History, Geography, Economics, Political Science, Sociology, Anthropology, Mi'Kmaq Studies), Mathematics, and Science (Biology, Chemistry, Physics, Astronomy, Ecology, Geology). All candidates for elementary are required to have at least English course to be considered for admission, as well as a 6-credit course in each of mathematics and science, and a course in developmental psychology. Secondary Education students must be prepared to teach two subject fields. A minimum of 5 (6-credit) courses must be in the first teachable (i.e. English, Social Studies, Science, Mathematics, Diverse Cultures, or Physical Education). For the second teachable students must have 3 (6-credit) courses in English, Social Studies, Science, Mathematics, or Diverse Cultures, or 5 (6-credit) courses in Physical Education, French, or Music. Please see calendar for details.

They are not accepting music as a teachable subject for the 2008-2009 school year.

St. Thomas University

Admissions Office
51 Dineen Drive
Fredericton, NB   E3B 5G3
Tel: 506-452-0532
Fax: 506-452-0617
Internet: www.stthomasu.ca/prospective/programmes/ed.htm

General Information:
Degree Offered: B.Ed. Post-degree
Length: n/a
Years: 1
Language: English

Admission Requirements:
Previous Education: Four year (120 credit hours) Bachelor's degree from a recognized university
Prerequisite Courses: 60 credit hours in subjects which satisfy the teachable requirement of the Department of Education, Province of New Brunswick
Average GPA: 2.7/4.3
Range: 70% or B- minimum
Admission Test: Not required
Average Score: n/a
Score Report Deadline: n/a
Other Admission Criteria: Academic records, letters of intent and reference letters will be reviewed for evidence of academic strength, teaching-related experience and those qualities likely to contribute to teaching success. Prior to final acceptance, candidates may be interviewed either in person or by telephone.

Application Information:
Deadline: January 15
Application Fee: $25
Applicant/Acceptance Ratio: 4:1
Size of Incoming Class: 60
Tuition: $5,900
Books/Materials: $600 - $800

Comments: Three areas of concentration are: Elementary, Secondary, and Second Language (French). Practical component provides 15 weeks of educational internship.

University of Toronto

Att: Ian MacLeod, Assistant Registrar
Ontario Institute for Studies in Education
252 Bloor Street West
Room 4-455
Toronto, ON   M5S 1V6
Tel: 416-926-4701
E-mail: admissions@oise.utoronto.ca
Internet: www.oise.utoronto.ca/admissions

General Information:
Degree Offered: B.Ed.
Length: Semesters
Years: 1
Language: English

Admission Requirements:
Previous Education: Acceptable university degree (4-year preferred) for Primary/Junior, Junior/Intermediate, and Intermediate/Senior options
Prerequisite Courses: See calendar
Average GPA: n/a
Range: B minimum required in 15 full course degree equivalents
Admission Test: Not required
Average Score: n/a
Score Report Deadline: n/a
Other Admission Criteria: Applicant Profile; English language requirement

Application Information:
Deadline: December 1 for following September

Application Fee: $70
Applicant/Acceptance Ratio: 4:1
Size of Incoming Class: 1233
Tuition: $5,520.10 including incidentals (Winter 2004/05)
Books/Materials: $700

Comments: Technological Studies Program also offered. Grade 12 minimum with combination of related work and post-secondary education totalling 5 years with minimum of 24 months paid work experience with no less than 16 months continuous. For more detailed information, see calendar.

Trent with Queen's University

Sharon Carew, Coordinator
Queen's-Trent Concurrent Teacher Education Program
N124, Lady Eaton College
600 West Bank Drive
Peterborough, ON   K9J 7B8
Tel: 705-748-1011, ext. 7464
Fax: 705-748-1008
E-mail: concurrented@trentu.ca
Internet: www.trentu.ca/education/concurrent

General Information:
Degree Offered: Hons. B.A./B.Ed.; Hons. B.Sc./B.Ed.
Length: n/a
Years: 5
Language: English

Admission Requirements:
Previous Education: O.S.S.D. including six Grade 12 U or M courses (including English 4U plus minimum of two additional 4U courses
Prerequisite Courses: None
Average GPA: n/a
Range: minimum 80%
Admission Test: n/a
Average Score: n/a
Score Report Deadline: n/a
Other Admission Criteria: Personal statement of experience

Application Information:
Deadline: OUAC due January; personal statement of experience due February
Application Fee: n/a
Applicant/Acceptance Ratio: 10:1
Size of Incoming Class: 125
Tuition: Regular Trent tuition fee; Queen's per course tuition fee
Books/Materials: Range from $25 to $100

Comments: This is a co-operative program whereby students pursue the Honours Arts/Science degree from Trent University concurrently with the B.Ed. degree from Queen's University.

University of Waterloo

Office of the Registrar
Admissions
200 University Avenue West
Waterloo, ON   N2L 3G1
Tel: 519-888-4567, ext. 32259
Internet: http://arts.uwaterloo.ca

General Information:
Degree Offered: B.A.; B.Ed.
Length: Trimesters
Years: 4-2/3 years
Language: English

Admission Requirements:
Previous Education: Secondary School Diploma, including six Grade 12 U or M courses
Prerequisite Courses: Grade 12 English
Average GPA: n/a
Range: 75%
Admission Test: Not required
Average Score: n/a
Score Report Deadline: n/a
Other Admission Criteria: Admission information form

Application Information:
Deadline: Application deadline is June 30. Supporting documents are due July 28.
Application Fee: $110 plus an $80 document assessment fee

Applicant/Acceptance Ratio: 2:1
Size of Incoming Class: 670 (all Honours Arts Regular students)
Tuition: $2,600 per term first year; upper year $2,700 per term
Books/Materials: $900 books and supplies

University of Waterloo
Office of the Registrar
Mathematics Admissions
200 University Avenue West
Waterloo, ON   N2L 3G1
Tel: 519-888-4567, ext. 36284
Internet: www.math.uwaterloo.ca

General Information:
Degree Offered: B.Math, B.Ed.
Length: Trimesters
Years: 4-2/3 years
Language: English

Admission Requirements:
Previous Education: Secondary School Diploma, including six Grade 12 U or M courses
Prerequisite Courses: Advanced Functions; Calculus and Vectors; English; Grade 12 M Computer and Information Science or one other Grade 12 U course
Average GPA: n/a
Range: Low to mid 80's
Admission Test: Not required
Average Score: n/a
Score Report Deadline: n/a
Other Admission Criteria: Admission Information Form which includes a teacher reference; it is also is encouraged to write the Euclid Mathematics Contest the year of application

Application Information:
Deadline: Application deadline is March 31. Supporting documents are due April 15.
Application Fee: $110 plus an $80 document assessment fee
Applicant/Acceptance Ratio: 2:1

Size of Incoming Class: 637 (entire Mathematics Faculty)
Tuition: $2,600 per term
Books/Materials: $900 per term

University of Waterloo
Office of the Registrar
Science Admissions
200 University Avenue West
Waterloo, ON   N2L 3G1
Tel: 519-888-4567, ext. 36243
Internet: www.sci.uwaterloo.ca

General Information:
Degree Offered: B.Sc.; B.Ed.
Length: Trimesters
Years: 4-2/3 years
Language: English

Admission Requirements:
Previous Education: Secondary School Diploma, including six Grade 12 U or M courses
Prerequisite Courses: See website for details
Average GPA: n/a
Range: mid 70's
Admission Test: Not required
Average Score: n/a
Score Report Deadline: n/a
Other Admission Criteria: Admission Information Form

Application Information:
Deadline: Application deadline is March 31. Supporting documents are due April 15.
Application Fee: $110 plus an $80 document assessment fee
Applicant/Acceptance Ratio: 2:1
Size of Incoming Class: 750 (all students of Biochemistry, Biology, Chemistry, and Physics)
Tuition: $2,600 per term first year
Books/Materials: $900 books and supplies

University of Western Ontario

Perservice Education Office
Faculty of Education
1137 Western Road
London, ON   N6G 1G7
Tel: 519-661-2093
Fax: 519-661-2095
E-mail: eduwo@uwo.ca
Internet: www.edu.uwo.ca

General Information:
Degree Offered: B.Ed.; Diploma in Education (Technological Studies)
Length: September – April, full time
Years: 1
Language: English

Admission Requirements:
Previous Education: Primary/Junior: minimum 3-year undergraduate degree or equivalent; Junior/Intermediate: minimum 4 full university courses or equivalent in teaching subject (French and Phys. Ed require 5 full courses); Intermediate/Senior: minimum 5 full courses in first teaching subject, minimum 3 full courses in second teaching subject (French and Spanish - require 5 full-year courses and Drama as a second requires 2)
Prerequisite Courses: See Faculty Calendar for more detailed information: www.edu.uwo.ca
Average GPA: n/a
Range: 70% overall minimum on undergraduate degree, 70% in teaching subject(s)
Admission Test: Not required
Average Score: n/a
Score Report Deadline: n/a
Other Admission Criteria: All necessary/ required documentation must be received by specified deadline

Application Information:
Deadline: November 28
Application Fee: $110 application fee, plus $55 non-refundable supplementary fee (subject to increase)

Applicant/Acceptance Ratio: n/a
Size of Incoming Class: 800
Tuition: $6,206.09 (subject to increase in summer of 2008)
Books/Materials: $1,000 plus practice teaching expenses

Comments: Students completing 4 years of undergraduate study are given preference in the selection process. Technological Studies Program - Applicants are required to present documented training, experience, and qualifications related to one of the 7 following broad-based Technological Studies areas: Communications, Construction, Hospitality Services, Manufacturing, Personal Services, Technological Design, and Transportation. In accordance with Ontario Regulation 184/97, applicants must hold an Ontario Secondary School diploma or equivalent, proof of completency in the chosen Technological Studies area, and one of the following: five years of full-time related wage-earning, business or industrial experience; a combination of education related to the chosen area or areas of technological studies and related wage-earning experience that totals at least five years, including at least two years of full-time, wage-earning experience, no less than 16 months of which is continuous employment; or at least 3,700 hours of related wage-earning experience and graduation from a post-secondary education program of at least 24 months related to the chosen Technological Studies area. Preference will be given to candidates with formal apprenticeship, technician, or technologist training who can demonstrate expertise in more than one occupation housed within their broad-based Technological Studies teaching subject. Admission is conditional upon an applicant successfully passing a pre-admission examination once his or her formal training and experience have been deemed acceptable.

University of Windsor

Office of the Registrar
401 Sunset Avenue
Windsor, ON   N9B 3P4
Tel: 519-253-4232

General Information:
Degree Offered: B.Ed. Pre-Service,
Junior/Intermediate
Length: Sept-April (two semesters)
Years: 1
Language: English

Admission Requirements:
Previous Education: Undergraduate
degree
Prerequisite Courses: Six semester
courses in the teaching subject
Average GPA: n/a
Range: 70 - 85%
Admission Test: English Proficiency test
for applicants who's first language is not
English
Average Score: All applicants whose
first langue is not English and who
have not lived in an English-speaking
country for five years or more must take
the test of English as a Foreign Language
(TOEFL), with a minimum IBT score of 92
(with a minimum speaking and writing
component of 25) or a computer-based
total score of 237 or a paper-based score
of 580 (5.5 on the essay writing is required
for both the computer and paper-based),
and a Test of spoken English (TSE) score
of 55 (TSE is required for computer and
paper-based tests only). All official test
scores must be submitted no later than
November 30.
Score Report Deadline: December 1
Other Admission Criteria: None

Application Information:
Deadline: December 1
Application Fee: $110 Ontario University
Application Centre
(OUAC) fee plus $33 for each choice after
three, and $40 evaluation fee

Applicant/Acceptance Ratio: 6:1
Size of Incoming Class: 210
Tuition: approx. $5,500 (Canadian citizens
and Permanent Residents)
Books/Materials: approx. $500 - $700

Comments: Program 1 of 3

University of Windsor

Office of the Registrar
401 Sunset Avenue
Windsor, ON   N9B 3P4
Tel: 519-253-4232

General Information:
Degree Offered: B.Ed. Pre-Service,
Intermediate/Senior
Length: Sept-April (two semesters)
Years: 1
Language: English
Admission Requirements:
Previous Education: Undergraduate
degree
Prerequisite Courses: Ten semester
courses in first teaching subject, 6
semester courses in second teaching
subject
Average GPA: n/a
Range: 70 - 94%
Admission Test: English Proficiency test
for applicants who's first language is not
English
Average Score: All applicants whose
first langue is not English and who
have not lived in an English-speaking
country for five years or more must take
the test of English as a Foreign Language
(TOEFL), with a minimum IBT score of 92
(with a minimum speaking and writing
component of 25) or a computer-based
total score of 237 or a paper-based score
of 580 (5.5 on the essay writing is required
for both the computer and paper-based),
and a Test of spoken English (TSE) score
of 55 (TSE is required for computer and
paper-based tests only). All official test
scores must be submitted no later than
November 30.

Score Report Deadline: December 1
Other Admission Criteria: None

Application Information:
Deadline: December 1
Application Fee: $110 Ontario University Application Centre
(OUAC) fee plus $33 for each choice after three, and $40 evaluation fee
Applicant/Acceptance Ratio: 6:1
Size of Incoming Class: 140
Tuition: approx. $5,500 (Canadian citizens and Permanent Residents)
Books/Materials: approx. $500 - $700

Comments: Program 2 of 3

University of Windsor
Office of the Registrar
401 Sunset Avenue
Windsor, ON   N9B 3P4
Tel: 519-253-4232

General Information:
Degree Offered: B.Ed. Pre-Service, Primary/Junior
Length: Sept-April (two semesters)
Years: 1
Language: English

Admission Requirements:
Previous Education: Undergraduate degree
Prerequisite Courses: None
Average GPA: 76.23%
Range: n/a
Admission Test: English Proficiency test for applicants who's first language is not English
Average Score: All applicants whose first langue is not English and who have not lived in an English-speaking country for five years or more must take the test of English as a Foreign Language (TOEFL), with a minimum IBT score of 92 (with a minimum speaking and writing component of 25) or a computer-based total score of 237 or a paper-based score of 580 (5.5 on the essay writing is required for both the computer and paper-based), and a Test of spoken English (TSE) score of 55 (TSE is required for computer and paper-based tests only). All official test scores must be submitted no later than November 30.
Score Report Deadline: December 1
Other Admission Criteria: None

Application Information:
Deadline: December 1
Application Fee: $110 Ontario University Application Centre
(OUAC) fee plus $33 for each choice after three, and $40 evaluation fee
Applicant/Acceptance Ratio: 6:1
Size of Incoming Class: 396
Tuition: approx. $5,500 (Canadian citizens and Permanent Residents)
Books/Materials: approx. $500 - $700

Comments: Program 3 of 3

University of Winnipeg
Admissions Office
515 Portage Avenue
Winnipeg, MB   R3B 2E9
Tel: 204-786-9159
Internet: www.uwinnipeg.ca

General Information:
Degree Offered: B.Ed. After-Degree
Length: 60 credit hours
Years: 2
Language: English

Admission Requirements:
Previous Education: Undergraduate degree
Prerequisite Courses: Coursework complete in 2 teachable subject areas
Average GPA: n/a
Range: 2.5 or C+ minimum
Admission Test: Not required
Average Score: n/a
Score Report Deadline: n/a

Other Admission Criteria: Relevant experience with appropriate age groups

Application Information:
Deadline: March 1
Application Fee: $35
Applicant/Acceptance Ratio: 2:1
Size of Incoming Class: 55
Tuition: $3,109.33
Books/Materials: $1,395.00

Comments: Program 1 of 2

University of Winnipeg
Admissions Office
515 Portage Avenue
Winnipeg, MB   R3B 2E9
Tel: 204-786-9159
Internet: www.uwinnipeg.ca

General Information:
Degree Offered: Integrated B.Ed./B.A. or B.Sc.
Length: 150 credit hours
Years: 5
Language: English

Admission Requirements:
Previous Education: See website for details
Prerequisite Courses: See website for details
Average GPA: 2.5
Range: 70%
Admission Test: Not required
Average Score: n/a
Score Report Deadline: n/a
Other Admission Criteria: Relevant experience with appropriate age groups

Application Information:
Deadline: March 1
Application Fee: $35
Applicant/Acceptance Ratio: 2:1
Size of Incoming Class: 200
Tuition: $3,109.33
Books/Materials: $1,395.00

Comments: Program 1 of 2

York University
Director of Student Programs
Faculty of Education
S835 - Ross Building
Toronto, ON   M3J 1P3
Tel: 416-736-5001
Fax: 416-736-5409
E-mail: osp@edu.yorku.ca
Internet: www.edu.yorku.ca

General Information:
Degree Offered: B.Ed. Post-degree
Length: n/a
Years: 10 months
Language: English

Admission Requirements:
Previous Education: Undergraduate degree
Prerequisite Courses: n/a
Average GPA: B
Range: n/a
Admission Test: Not required
Average Score: n/a
Score Report Deadline: n/a
Other Admission Criteria: Interview, experience profile, and 2 references (from previous professor and supervising teacher) required
Application Information:
Deadline: December 1
Application Fee: $85 OUAC plus $40 to York
Applicant/Acceptance Ratio: 10:1
Size of Incoming Class: 750
Tuition: $5,200
Books/Materials: $500

Comments: Programs for elementary, junior high and high school are offered.

VETERINARY MEDICINE

The following fact sheets outline general information including academic requirements and application procedures for Veterinary Medicine Schools in Canada. The data have been compiled in a concise format to assist students interested in these professional schools. Information was obtained from updates completed by each school, or in some cases from the school's Internet website.

Veterinary Medicine Schools in Canada

University of Guelph*
Université de Montréal*

University of Prince Edward Island
University of Saskatchewan*

Comments

1. These fact sheets act as a guide only. Students are advised to refer to the individual calendars or to write to the schools for more detailed information.

2. Application deadlines vary. Dates indicated refer to fall admission unless otherwise noted.

3. Tuition fees represent annual costs unless otherwise noted.

4. All of the schools listed above may not be represented.

This university has not updated its information. Please contact the university directly.

University of Guelph

Admissions
Guelph, ON   N1G 2W1
Tel: 519-824-4120
E-mail: vetmed@uoguelph.ca
Internet: www.ovc.uoguelph.
ca/Undergrad/
potential/index.shtm

General Information:
Degree Offered: D.V.M.
Length: 8 Semesters
Years: 4
Language: English

Admission Requirements:
Previous Education: Two years science at the university level prior to admission to the Doctor of Veterinary Medicine Program
Prerequisite Courses: Admission requirements for Doctor of Veterinary Medicine Program: biological sciences - 3 semester courses (one must be a cell biology); genetics - 1 semester course; biochemistry - 1 semester course; statistics - 1 semester course (with a calculus prerequisite; humanities or social sciences - 2 semester courses
Average GPA: n/a
Range: Mid 80's
Admission Test: MCAT required
Average Score: n/a
Score Report Deadline: June 15
Other Admission Criteria: Relevant experience and knowledge of animals; background information sheet including confidential referee assessments and, where appropriate, an interview

Application Information:
Deadline: February 1
Application Fee: $85
Applicant/Acceptance Ratio: 6:1
Size of Incoming Class: 110
Tuition: $4,544.00
Books/Materials: $500 - $1,000 per semester

Université de Montréal

Secrétariat aux affaires étudiantes
Faculté de médecine vétérinaire
C.P. 5000, 3200 rue Sicotte
Saint-Hyacinthe, QC   J2S 7C6
Tel: 450-773-8521, ext. 8271
Fax: 450-778-8114
E-mail: saefmv@meduet.umontreal.ca
Internet: www.medvet.umontreal.ca

General Information:
Degree Offered: D.V.M.
Length: 10 semesters
Years: 5
Language: French

Admission Requirements:
Previous Education: D.E.C. (Junior College Diploma), obtained in Quebec, in Nature Sciences (two years post-high school) or the equivalent (Students from other provinces must have completed 1 or 2 years of biology at university level.
Prerequisite Courses: Chemistry, mathematics (including calculus), physics, biology
Average GPA: Preselection of about the best 100 university students and 100 CEGEP (Junior College) students
Range:
Admission Test:
Average Score:
Score Report Deadline:
Other Admission Criteria: Only Canadian citizens or Permanent residents in Canada are considered

Application Information:
Deadline: March 1 (for Junior College diplome), January 15 (cthor)
Application Fee: $30 (by e-mail), $50 (by mail)
Applicant/Acceptance Ratio: 6:1
Size of Incoming Class: 84
Tuition: $2,500 (the program consists of 198 credits), tuition is $55.67 by credit (when students come from province of Quebec); $139.12 by credit (when

students come from another province of Canada)
Books/Materials: $1,200 - $1,400

Comments: 1. Standardized interview for preselected candidates (preselection based on academic marks)
2. Only Canadian citizens or Permanent residents in Canada are considered.
3. All lectures given in French. All examinations written in French.
4. French test: Success in passing this language test is not a prerequisite for admission in the first year of the veterinary program, but each student must pass the test successfully to earn a diploma.

University of Prince Edward Island
Registrar
Atlantic Veterinary College
550 University Avenue
Charlottetown, PE C1A 4P3
Tel: 902-566-0608 or 902-566-0781
Fax: 902-566-0795
E-mail: registrar@upei.ca
Internet: www.upei.ca

General Information:
Degree Offered: D.V.M. (Atlantic Canadian Applicant)
Length: 8 semesters
Years: 4
Language: English

Admission Requirements:
Previous Education: Minimum 2 years university
Prerequisite Courses: See Course Calendar – www.upei. ca/registrar/3_prof_degree_dvm
Average GPA: n/a
Range: n/a
Admission Test: Not required
Average Score: n/a
Score Report Deadline: n/a
Other Admission Criteria: Veterinary work experience, interview, GRE

Application Information: Please see www.upei.ca/registrar/3_prof_degree_dvm
Deadline: November 1
Application Fee: $50
Applicant/Acceptance Ratio: 4:1
Size of Incoming Class: **60
Tuition: $8,642 (CDN) per year
Books/Materials: $3,000 per year

Comments: *All pre-requisite courses must be identified by a numerical or letter grade and all must have a passing grade. Science courses would normally have a lab component. **The college accepts 36 students from Atlantic Canada and 24 International students.

University of Saskatchewan
Western College of Veterinary Medicine
52 Campus Drive
Saskatoon, SK S7N 5B4
Tel: 306-966-7447
Fax: 306-966-8747
Internet: www.usask.ca/wcvm

General Information:
Degree Offered: D.V.M.
Length: n/a
Years: 4
Language: English

Admission Requirements:
Previous Education: Two years pre-veterinary coursework (60 credit units) at an accredited college or university
Prerequisite Courses: English or Literature (6 credit units), Chemistry (6 credit units), Organic Chemistry (3 credit units), Biochemistry (6 credit units), Physics (6 credit units), Mathematics or Statistics (6 credit units), Biology (6 credit units), Genetics (3 credit units), Introductory Microbiology (3 credit units), Electives (15 credit units)
Average GPA: n/a
Range: 70%
Admission Test: Not required

Average Score: n/a
Score Report Deadline: n/a
Other Admission Criteria: References
and personal interview, related work
experience is highly recommended

Application Information:
Deadline: January 3
Application Fee: $75
Applicant/Acceptance Ratio: 5:1
Size of Incoming Class: 70
Tuition: $6,553.00 + $388.91 student fees
Books/Materials: $500 - $2,000

Tired of searching for a job?

Find all the career information you need in one convenient place.

career**BOOKSTORE**.ca
great books, better prices.

**With hundreds of books at your fingertips,
your job search just got easier.**

we have what you are looking for at CareerBookstore.ca

Part III

Professional Schools

Index

Books by Sentor Media

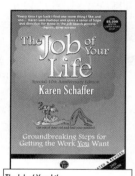